The Next Crisis?

David Woodward is an economist who was educated at the University of Oxford. After several years working in the British Foreign and Commonwealth Office, including a two year secondment to the UK Executive Director's Office at the IMF and World Bank in 1986-88, he resigned to work for the voluntary sector. He spent two years (1990–92) with Save the Children Fund (UK) as a researcher. Since that time he has been an independent economic/development consultant, in which capacity he has done research and writing for UNCTAD, UNDP and the Institute of Child Health, as well as a variety of development NGOs including (amongst others) Oxfam, One World Action, the European Network on Debt and Development (Eurodad), the Catholic Institute for International Relations, Jubilee 2000 and International Alert. In 1998 he joined the staff of the CIIR as Asia policy officer and in 2000 took up an appointment in the Health and Sustainable Development Department of the World Health Organization (WHO).

He is the author of numerous reports and working papers, as well as the following books:

Debt, Adjustment and Poverty in Developing Countries (two volumes)
(London: SCF/UK and Pinter Publishers, 1992)

Human Face or Human Facade? Adjustment and the Health of Mothers and Children
(coauthored with Anthony Costello and Fiona Watson)
(London: Institute of Child Health, 1994)

The Next Crisis?
Direct and Equity Investment in Developing Countries

DAVID WOODWARD

Zed Books

LONDON AND NEW YORK

The Next Crisis was first published in 2001
by Zed Books Ltd, 7 Cynthia Street, London N1 9JF,
UK and Room 400, 175 Fifth Avenue, New York, NY 10010, USA

in association with

Eurodad, Rue Dejoncker 46, 1060 Brussels, Belgium

Distributed exclusively in the USA by Palgrave,
a division of St Martin's Press, LLC,
175 Fifth Avenue, New York 10010, USA.

Cover design by Andrew Corbett
Designed and set in 10/12 pt Bembo
by Long House, Cumbria, UK
Printed and bound in Malaysia

A catalogue record for this book
is available from the British Library

US CIP has been applied for

ISBN Hb 1 85649 669 4
      Pb 1 85649 670 8

Contents

••••

List of Boxes

List of Tables

List of Figures

◤ Preface

The Next Crisis? started its life as a chance remark to Ted van Hees, coordinator of the European Network on Debt and Development (EURODAD), on the long-term financial implications of foreign direct investment in developing countries, some time in 1994. It then became a short article in EURODAD's World Credit Tables, 1994–5 – a sort of NGO counterblast to the World Bank's annual World Debt Tables (which, coincidentally or otherwise, they renamed the following year). Following the interest this article generated, Ted asked me to make a presentation on the subject at a EURODAD conference. The ideas became better formed, and numerous graphs appeared illustrating the ideas with country data.

There it might have stayed, but for a chance meeting with Robert Molteno, who suggested turning the ideas into a book. I agreed, and I suspect that Robert, like myself, has been questioning the wisdom of this decision from the perspective of our respective sanities ever since. Ideas developed during other freelance consultancies, primarily for the Bretton Woods Project (on the new paradigm of development finance), UNCTAD (on globalisation and poverty) and UNDP (on globalisation and unequal development) were drawn in along the way. And eventually, after a long and often painful gestation, *The Next Crisis?* was born.

This long gestation is evident in some of the graphs, which use data sources which were current while I was working on the relevant part of the book, rather than more recent ones. This is largely because, had I updated them every time a new data source came out (or twice a year for the last three years), the book would at best have been delayed substantially longer, and would probably never have been published at all. As discussed in chapters 5 and 6, successive publications of data not only provide an extra year, and modify the previous year's latest figures, but often completely rewrite the historical data too.

Thanks are due to Ted van Hees of EURODAD for his initiation of the process which culminated in this book; to Angela Wood of the Bretton

Woods Project, for commissioning and collaborating in the preparation of 'Drowning by Numbers', which forms much of the basis for chapters 4 and 11; to Tony Woodfield, formerly of UNCTAD, and Terry McKinley of UNDP, who engaged me for consultancies which also fed into various parts of the book; and to all my friends and family, who somehow managed to stop me having a nervous breakdown along the way.

Above all, however, I would like to thank Robert Molteno, without whose quite exceptional kindness and quite extraordinary patience this book would undoubtedly never have been completed.

◥ Abbreviations

BIT	Bilateral investment treaty
CAL	Capital account liberalisation
CEPR	Centre for Economic Policy Research
FDI	Foreign direct investment
FDI(C)	Foreign direct investment through construction
FDI(P)	Foreign direct investment through purchase
GATT	General Agreement on Tariffs and Trade
GFCF	Gross fixed capital formation
HIPC	Highly indebted poor countries (Initiative)
ICOR	Incremental capital–output ratio
IFC	International Finance Corporation
IFC/FIAS	International Finance Corporation/Foreign Investment Advisory Service
IMF	International Monetary Fund
MIGA	Multilateral Investment Guarantee Agency
NAFTA	North American Free Trade Agreement
ODI	Overseas Development Institute
OPEC	Organisation of Petroleum Exporting Countries
pa	per annum
TNC	Transnational companies
UNCTAD	United Nations Conference on Trade and Development
WTO	World Trade Organisation

One of the difficulties of economics is that it is too easy to explain after a particular event has happened, why it should have happened; and too easy to explain before it happens, why it should not happen.

M.G. Kendall, quoted in *The Montreal Star*, 19 December 1960

Ever since the birth of capitalism, there have been periodic financial crises, often with devastating consequences. To prevent recurrence, both banks and financial markets have been subjected to regulations, but the regulations usually addressed the last crisis and not the next one.

George Soros, *The Crisis of Global Capitalism: Open Society Endangered*, London: Little, Brown and Co., 1998, p. 118

▶ 1
Introduction

Over the last decade, there has been a change little short of revolution in the flow of capital from developed to developing countries. The dramatic decline in capital flows following the debt crisis of the 1980s gave way to a resurgence in the 1990s, but these new flows were radically different in nature from those of the 1970s. North–South capital flows are now dominated by direct investment in productive capacity by transnational companies (TNCs), purchases of shares by institutional (and some individual) investors, and investment in various other kinds of financial instruments.

Apart from some second thoughts on portfolio investment in shares since the East Asian financial crisis of 1997–8, the reaction of economists to these flows has been overwhelmingly positive, especially in the case of direct investment. A recent briefing paper produced by the Overseas Development Institute, for example, noted that

> Foreign direct investment is viewed as a major stimulus to economic growth in developing countries. Its ability to deal with two major obstacles, namely, shortages of financial resources and technology and skills, has made it the centre of attention for policy-makers in low-income countries in particular. (ODI 1997: 1)

The prevalence of this positive view is striking. The *Economist* recently made the sweeping, and only slightly overstated, assertion that 'virtually all economists agree [that liberalising foreign direct investment] is good for growth'.[1] László Halpern (1998) refers to 'an embarrassingly wide consensus in the economics profession on the positive impact of foreign direct investment (FDI) on long-run current account deficits'. Hopefully, this book will help to spare his blushes.

A broad consensus about the ultimate *objectives* of society is, in some respects, highly beneficial; but too great a consensus about the *means* of

1

achieving such objectives may be altogether more dangerous, if it encourages uncritical acceptance and complacency. Such optimistic consensus has become characteristic of the mainstream of the economics profession. A discipline of which George Bernard Shaw could once say that 'if all the economists in the world were laid end to end, they still wouldn't reach a conclusion', and which Thomas Carlyle could refer to as 'the Dismal Science', has very largely united behind a determinedly optimistic world view, wherein all our problems can be resolved simply by letting market forces do their work, subject to no more than minor adjustments by governments (to support basic education and health services, for example).

The current positive view of direct investment is but one manifestation of this phenomenon, though a particularly striking one. For anyone who, like the author, has worked on developing country debt problems since the early 1980s, there are surely too many echoes of the past in the present state of thinking on direct investment to feel wholly comfortable with the present unalloyed enthusiasm.

We have, in some respects, been here before – and not only in the 1970s and 1980s. Balance of payments crises related to external liabilities have recurred roughly every fifty years through the nineteenth and twentieth centuries, and they have generally been preceded by an optimism, at least among creditors, that the financial flows which created those liabilities would not generate crises. Otherwise, they would not have put their money at risk, the liabilities would not have been created, and the crises would not have occurred. Optimistic consensus has contributed directly to the creation of financial crises in developing countries repeatedly in the course of the nineteenth and twentieth centuries; if the current optimistic consensus is mistaken, there is a real risk that this will occur again early in the twenty-first century.

Attitudes to direct investment have not always been so positive or so consensual. Until the early 1980s its net foreign exchange effects were widely regarded as a matter of some concern and several investigations (e.g. Lall and Streeten 1977; UNCTC 1981) came to less than reassuring conclusions. However, interest in direct investment waned with the reduction in flows following the 1982 debt crisis; during its subsequent recovery, interest in its balance of payments effects has not resurfaced. This may be due in part to relief at the re-emergence of North–South capital flows in whatever form after the financial drought of the 1980s, and to the development of the 'Washington consensus' in favour of market mechanisms. The United Nations Conference on Trade and Development (UNCTAD) has, belatedly, renewed the discussion of this issue (UNCTAD 1997b); but there remains some way to go before the consensus is seriously challenged.

This book does not argue that all direct and equity investment in developing countries is always and necessarily harmful. It does, however, argue that this will be the case much more often than the current consensus would seem to imply; and that there is a need for a more complex, critical and selective view of these forms of investment than is implied by the current consensus in favour of blanket liberalisation.

The next three chapters present the general view of direct and equity investment.

- Chapter 2 outlines the role of capital flows in the development process and in the generation of balance of payments crises, and draws some parallels between the present situation and the lead-up to the 1980s crisis.

- Chapter 3 outlines the nature of direct and equity investment and the prevalent positive view of its financial and developmental benefits.

- Chapter 4 describes the recent evolution of financial flows to developing countries, and the increasing importance of direct and equity investment.

The second part of the book presents a more critical view of the subject.

- Chapter 5 assesses how much we really know about the stocks of direct and equity investment in developing countries, and the reliability of what we think we know.

- Chapter 6 takes a similarly sceptical view of statistics on flows of direct and equity investment and the profits on them, and considers the implications for estimates of investment stocks.

- Chapter 7 presents a general framework for considering the foreign exchange effects of direct and equity investment.

- Chapter 8 applies this framework to equity investment and direct investment in different sectors, to consider their effects on the balance of payments.

- Chapter 9 discusses other effects of direct investment flows on the host country, for example on overall investment, employment and the transfer of technology to developing countries.

- Chapter 10 considers the global dimensions of direct investment, particularly the implications of competition between developing countries for investment flows; the effects on this competition of the efforts of developed country governments and international institutions to promote such flows; and the potential effects on world markets and prices for developing country exports.

- Chapter 11 discusses the potential for outward net resource transfers as a result of direct investment, and the build-up of stocks of inward investment needed to avoid such outflows.

- Chapter 12 considers the pattern of direct and equity investment flows over time, and the dangers of inter-country 'contagion' posed by financial crises.

Finally,

- Chapters 13 and 14 (supplemented by a more detailed analysis in Appendix I) consider the roles of direct and equity investment in the East Asian financial crisis; and

- Chapter 15 summarises the argument, draws together the conclusions, and considers the policy implications.

2

Capital Flows, Development and Debt Crises

North–South Capital Flows and Development

Generally speaking, economists see free markets as helping to correct inequalities in the geographical distribution of assets such as capital. If an asset is scarce in one area, and plentiful in another, then its greater scarcity in the former area will push its price up above the price in the latter area. In the absence of natural (such as geographical or practical) or artificial (such as policy) barriers, the owners of the asset concerned in the area where it is plentiful will respond to the higher rate of return in the area of scarcity, and move their assets there. This will reduce supply where the asset is plentiful, increasing its price; and increase supply where it is scarce, reducing its price. In principle, this process will continue until the difference in rates of return between the two areas is no greater than the cost of transferring the asset. In other words, economic theory predicts that geographical inequalities in the distribution of assets can only persist to the extent that there are obstacles to their transfer between areas.

A particularly important case in point is the distribution of capital between countries. Traditionally this has been seen as a key element – if not the defining characteristic – of the difference between developed and developing countries.[2] Developed countries are developed largely because they have (relatively) plentiful capital; developing countries are not yet developed because they have relatively scarce capital; and the transition from developing to developed status (as achieved in recent years by the first-generation 'newly industrialised' economies of Hong Kong, Singapore, Taiwan and Korea) is largely characterised by an increase in capital.

Thus a major part of the development process is seen as being the flow of capital from developed, capital-rich countries to developing, capital-poor countries. This is the rationale for developed countries' aid programmes and

the operations of agencies such as the World Bank and the regional development banks: they are largely intended to transfer capital from developed to
developing countries.

However, these official financial flows are by no means the only source of
capital movements from North to South. Various mechanisms for commercial capital flows are also available. These include:

* lending by commercial banks in the North, either to governments or to
companies in the South;

* export credits provided by suppliers in the North to importers of their
products in the South;

* bond issues by governments or companies in the South, bought by institutional or individual investors in the North;

* foreign direct investment (FDI), whereby TNCs construct or buy productive capacity in the South;

* the purchase of shares in companies in the South by Northern institutional or individual investors (portfolio equity investment);

* the purchase of various other kinds of financial instruments (such as
derivatives) issued in the South; and

* deposits (by banks, institutional investors or individuals) in banks in
developing countries.

All of these types of financial flows can effect a movement of capital from
developed to developing countries; but their relative importance has varied
considerably, both between countries and regions and over time. Until the
Second World War, bond issues were generally the preferred means of capital
movement, together with some element of direct investment (particularly,
but by no means only, from the colonising powers to their respective
colonies). After 1945, the importance of official flows and direct investment
increased; bond issues gave way to syndicated bank lending following the oil
price crisis of the 1970s. In the 1980s, commercial financial flows to many
developing countries largely dried up following the debt crisis, while their
recovery in the 1990s has seen a major shift to direct investment and, for
some countries, equity and other portfolio investment, as well as a resurgence of bond issues (see Chapter 4).

Capital flows and risk

International financial flows have never been without their problems. If investors are to transfer their capital to another country, they need to be confident that it will be possible both to get the original capital back and to receive the income it generates. This process is subject to various risks which tend to be more acute in developing than in developed countries.

Political risks

There may be a danger, especially in potentially unstable political systems, that assets will be seized or expropriated by governments (as in nationalisation without compensation); or that a government will refuse to honour the debts it (or its predecessor) has incurred. For a variety of reasons, political instability tends to be more widespread in developing countries: their greater and more widespread poverty, lower levels of education and under-resourced public institutions provide a weaker base for democracy and political stability; and these factors are often compounded (especially in sub-Saharan Africa) by historical factors such as colonial experiences, poorly managed transitions to independence or artificially imposed colonial borders retained thereafter.

Commercial risks

Where money is lent to or invested in a company, there is a risk that the company will fail, so that the money is lost. The rate of business failure is likely to be higher in developing than in developed countries, because of the greater volatility and vulnerability of developing country economies.

Foreign exchange risks

Generally, international capital movements take place in convertible currencies; debt-service payments, capital repatriation, profit remittances and dividend payments therefore need to be made in such currencies – otherwise, the proceeds could only be used in the recipient country, so that the capital (and income on it) would effectively be trapped. Most developing countries' currencies are not convertible, so that lenders and investors are dependent on the supply of foreign exchange available in the recipient country to retrieve their capital and income. In the event of a balance of payments crisis, repatriation may be delayed, or the money may be lost in part or in full. Even if the currency is convertible, there is a risk that the value of capital and the income on it will be reduced by devaluation of the exchange rate. Again, this is more likely in developing than developed countries, as their economies are generally much less diversified and thus more vulnerable to external shocks such as falls in export prices or rises in international interest rates.

All of these types of risk are interrelated.

• If there is a balance of payments crisis, the exchange rate is ultimately likely to be devalued, and there may well be other adjustment measures such as reductions in government spending and increases in interest rates. This in turn may affect the profitability of enterprises dependent on the local market, as well as increasing the cost of servicing both local and foreign debts, and this adds to commercial risks. Balance of payments crises and the associated adjustment may also provoke political instability or a change of government, giving rise to political risk.

• Similarly, widespread company failures due to commercial risk considerations may provoke a loss of confidence among international lenders and investors, both directly and through their effect on the banking system; this in turn is likely to reduce the availability of foreign exchange and may thus provoke a balance of payments crisis.

• Developments which constitute political risks (such as the outbreak of conflict, debt repudiation or the seizure of assets) may also provoke a loss of international confidence and a balance of payments crisis, as well as widespread problems for companies (commercial risk). Government actions in the regulation of productive sectors may also affect the viability of domestic producers and thus add to commercial risk.

Different types of investment are affected differently by these three categories of risk. Loans to and bond issues by governments are relatively unaffected by commercial risk and the risk of asset seizure; but they are more directly affected by conflict and may be more prone to repudiation. For loans to companies (and still more for investments in companies), this is reversed: the primary risks are commercial, while the effects of political risks (other than expropriation) are only indirect. Bank deposits are subject primarily to the risk of failure of the bank concerned and of devaluation; but the former may be provoked by widespread company failures, generating large banking losses, or by a balance of payments crisis.

The one universal vulnerability of international capital flows is to foreign exchange risk. Whether capital is transferred to the public or the private sector, and whatever form it takes, the repatriation of the capital and the receipt of the income due on it is dependent on the availability of foreign exchange.

Moreover, whereas political and commercial risks tend to be mainly country-specific, shortage of foreign exchange is related in large measure to developments in the international economy, and may spread quickly between developing countries through 'contagion' effects, so that it tends to affect large groups of developing countries – often whole regions – simultaneously. This is demonstrated by numerous recent examples: the Latin American debt crisis of the 1980s, the ongoing African debt crisis, the 'Tequila' shock following the Mexican crisis of 1994 and the aftermath of the East Asian and Russian crises in 1997–8.

Consequently, it is balance of payments crises which constitute the greatest risk of a general loss of capital and income to international lenders and investors. While such crises in individual countries may themselves be provoked by the effects of political or commercial risk, it is generally the balance of payments crisis which follows that does the greatest damage, both to the interests of lenders and investors and to economic development and living conditions in the country concerned.[3]

This is not a one-way process, however, whereby balance of payments crises caused by international economic developments cause problems in the servicing of foreign obligations. On the contrary, the accumulation of foreign exchange liabilities arising from financial flows is generally a major element of the weakening of countries' balance of payments positions which culminates in a financial crisis.

- In Latin America, it was largely the rise in interest rates on commercial bank debts, coupled with the sudden drying up of commercial flows, which precipitated the debt crisis of the 1980s.

- In Mexico, it was the abrupt reversal of flows into the banking sector and the bunching of maturities on short-term government debt which caused the crisis at the end of 1994.

- In East Asia, too, it was the reversal of commercial capital flows which precipitated the 1997 crisis.[4]

In all these cases, the effects on the confidence of lenders and investors, and thus on flows to countries they saw as similar, was the main factor spreading the crisis to other developing countries.

A Historical Perspective

While balance of payments crises have come thick and fast in the last twenty years, they are far from being a new phenomenon. Since the 1830s there have been several major international financial crises primarily affecting (at the time) developing countries, resulting from their failure to meet the obligations arising from international capital flows. These have occurred fairly regularly, at intervals of approximately 50 years. This interval seems to reflect the time it takes lenders to forget the lessons of the last crisis, and/or to find new instruments which they believe will avoid the past problems, and then to transfer an unsustainable amount of capital through those instruments.

The debt crisis which began in the early 1980s was merely the latest manifestation of this cycle. The crisis of the 1930s discouraged providers of capital from venturing into lending to developing countries for forty years, and North–South capital transfers were largely left to official sources (together with some direct investment). Then, in the 1970s, the change in the world economy associated with the first oil price crisis gave rise to new, and apparently safe and profitable, opportunities for capital transfers. At the same time, a new instrument for such transfers – the syndicated bank loan – was applied to this purpose.

The development of syndicated bank lending to developing countries was at least tacitly encouraged, both by the major developed country governments and by international financial institutions such as the IMF and the World Bank. The major oil-exporting countries were generating massive balance of payments surpluses, which they deposited with Western commercial banks, while the oil-importing developing countries had large deficits which they wanted to finance. Completing the circle by 'recycling' the oil surpluses to the deficit countries through bank lending seemed to resolve the problem, avoiding a financial crisis and sustaining development. However, the tacit support for this process reinforced the banks' perception that this was a profitable enterprise subject to limited risk.

In the event, this view proved to be gravely mistaken, and within ten years the accumulated debt had become unsustainable. This occurred partly because of the scale of lending, but very largely as a result of further changes in the world economy following the second oil price crisis in 1979, together with the failure of creditors to appreciate their significance and of debtors to adjust quickly enough to them. The general cessation of lending once the potential problems became apparent spread the problems quickly to countries which might not otherwise have been affected.

Widespread balance of payments crises ensued, and many developing countries ceased to service their debts in full. Commercial capital flows to developing countries (and particularly syndicated loans) became unfashionable, and governments and international agencies were left as almost the only source of financing for most developing countries. Virtually the only commercial lending to developing countries that took place was in the form of 'concerted' lending packages put together for the major debtor countries with the active support of the IMF, to cover part of the interest payments due to the banks themselves.

Commercial capital flows were much quicker to recover from the 1980s crisis than after previous debt crises; but they resumed in a very different form, dominated by direct and equity investment (see Chapter 4). These newly important forms of financing have come to be seen in a much more favourable light than debt-related commercial flows such as bond issues and syndicated loans.

Once again, commercial providers of capital believe that they have found a profitable and relatively safe way of transferring capital to developing countries; and once again they have been encouraged in this view – this time more actively and explicitly – by developed country governments and international institutions. The question is whether we have at last seen the development of instruments which really can provide a stable and mutually beneficial means of financing development, or whether history is in the process of repeating itself. Is today's direct and equity investment promoting sustainable development, or is it merely setting the scene for the next financial crisis for the developing world?

How Did the 1980s Debt Crisis Happen?

There are some interesting parallels between current developments in North–South financial flows and the evolution of the 1980s debt crisis – not so much in the immediate causes of the crisis, but rather in the circumstances which allowed it to happen. These parallels do not, in themselves, necessarily mean that the process will culminate in a new crisis; but they do suggest that this may be a possibility, and that there is a need to learn the lessons of the past and to take a more cautious and critical approach.

First, there was a remarkable level of ignorance about the scale of the liabilities which were accrued, and therefore of their potential cost in the future. Until well into the 1980s, the amount of debt which major borrowing governments had accrued was in some cases unknown even to the government concerned. Statistical systems were relatively weak, reporting requirements limited, and the data available were therefore seriously unreliable. In some cases, government creditors themselves had little idea even how much they themselves were owed by a country when it approached the Paris Club (the informal organisation through which government creditors renegotiate their loans to other governments) for rescheduling, and a lengthy reconciliation process was necessary.

A second critically important element in the genesis of the 1980s debt crisis was the existence of a pervasive myth among creditors that lending to governments was relatively risk-free. This was embodied in the oft-repeated idea that (in the words of Walter Wriston, then chairman of Citibank) 'countries don't go bankrupt'. In effect, it was assumed that, because the country would always be there, it would always be possible to secure repayment; and that there would always be new lenders on hand to provide the foreign exchange necessary.

When the Mexican government announced in 1982 that it could not borrow enough to meet its debt-service obligations, this myth was exposed: the lenders' unquestioning confidence was punctured; they realised the risks; and they stopped lending, not only to Mexico but also, over the following months, to most other developing countries. The resulting lack of foreign exchange prevented other countries from servicing their debts; and the debt crisis spread through much of the developing world. It quickly became apparent that the notion of sovereign lending as risk-free was indeed a myth.

In effect, the whole system had come to depend critically on belief in the myth: debtor countries could go on servicing their debts only because they could borrow enough new money to do so; and lenders were willing to provide this money only because they believed in the myth. The moment their faith faltered, the whole system collapsed.

It is not clear why the myth lasted for so long. Apart from the previous repeated debt crises (which also generally involved non-payment of sovereign debts), there were numerous more recent cases of default. The Paris Club of government creditors was established as early as 1956, in response to debt-servicing problems in Argentina, and by the late 1970s numerous smaller debtors were seeking rescheduling. However, the creditors somehow managed to ignore these cases as insignificant aberrations. It was only when they were joined by Poland, a much larger debtor, that serious doubts became apparent; and only when Mexico – one of the two largest developing country debtors at the time – failed to meet its debt-service obligations did creditors seriously lose faith in the myth.

The international financial institutions and the governments of the major developed countries may have helped to extend the life of the myth, while the IMF had some misgivings about the scale of recycling after 1973 (James 1996: 321–2),

> The recycling that took place after the second [1979] oil crisis had initially seemed less problematic than that following the earlier shock of 1973-4. Partly the new confidence arose from inappropriate lessons drawn from the earlier experience. It appeared in the late 1970s, with the benefit of a rather short-sighted hindsight, that the uncertainty and nervousness that had arisen in the immediate wake of the oil price increases had been misplaced, that the world financial system could handle the flows easily, unproblematically and profitably, and that the outcome had allowed the pace of world development to proceed substantially unchecked. The result was a widespread feeling that global surveillance was not really very

much needed. It became difficult in consequence for any institution to provide it. (James 1996: 349)

Another important factor underlying the over-borrowing and over-lending of the 1970s was a determined optimism about trends in the global economy which proved, in the event, to be wholly unjustified. Once again, there is a risk that this may be repeated in the present resurgence of financial flows.

Following the 1973 oil price shock, the major developed country governments gave priority to maintaining their economic growth rather than controlling the inflationary impact of higher oil prices, and therefore ran relatively relaxed monetary policies. The result was low or negative real interest rates on the major currencies, and continued growth of demand for developing countries' commodity exports, whose prices therefore increased in real terms. This implied that a country could borrow internationally to meet its foreign exchange needs, and then borrow more to cover the interest payments as they fell due; but its export earnings, and thus its debt-servicing capacity, would always rise faster than the debt accumulated. Implicitly, debtors and creditors expected these conditions to persist for the lifetime of the loans that were negotiated.

However, the policy response of the developed countries to the second oil price shock of 1979 was radically different. Rather than putting growth first, they prioritised controlling the inflationary impact of the crisis, and therefore tightened their monetary policies drastically. As a result, demand contracted, developing countries' export prices collapsed, and real interest rates increased dramatically to historically high levels.

The developing countries were therefore faced with a triple shock: not only did the price of their oil imports double overnight, but the interest rates on their foreign debts to commercial creditors doubled over the following three years, while the prices they received for their major exports dropped sharply. Unable to adjust quickly to a shock of this scale, they made use of the established mechanisms for syndicated lending – and the creditors' continued enthusiasm for sovereign lending – to borrow still more to fill the growing gap in their balance of payments; but this added further to their debts, and thus interest payments, widening the gap still further.

It seems that both creditors and debtors saw the new circumstances as a temporary aberration, which would quickly be reversed. Had they been right, there probably would not have been a debt crisis. In the event, however, they were spectacularly wrong, and with the benefit of hindsight it seems difficult to justify their optimistic expectations.

Above all, syndicated lending simply became fashionable in the 1970s. Virtually every bank of a significant size felt the need to take the opportunity

Syndicated loan spread

– and to be seen as taking the opportunity – for high and apparently risk-free returns which it offered. The form of the syndicated loan facilitated this: it was possible for a bank to take a small stake in a syndicated loan at little cost, and with little or no knowledge of the country to which it was lending. The myth and the near-universal belief in it created a herd instinct among investors, who crowded into lending to fashionable countries, most notably (but by no means exclusively) in Latin America. Once the myth was punctured, the process was reversed: the herd rushing into these countries suddenly changed direction and moved out.

In both cases, the actions of each individual creditor were entirely rational. As long as others were willing to lend, the risk was indeed limited. Once others ceased to lend, there was little alternative but to withdraw as quickly as possible. In other words, the rational strategy for each individual creditor had nothing to do with the economic fundamentals of an individual borrower – it was simply to follow the herd (or, in the case of withdrawal, to get out just before the herd). This type of behaviour inevitably created a very considerable potential for instability. It also enabled debts to continue piling up for some time after they had reached unsustainable levels.

Conclusion

Direct investment (and, to a lesser extent, equity investment) are widely seen as the answer to the development problem: they are seen as allowing the transfer of both capital and technology from developed to developing countries, and as allowing the risks of investment to be shared between investors and the recipient countries. However, similarly optimistic views have been held about different forms of capital flows in the past, and have subsequently proven to be mistaken: ultimately they have created financial liabilities so much greater than their developmental benefits that they have culminated in financial crises.

The question is whether the current favourable attitude to direct investment will ultimately be seen as exhibiting the same naïve optimism as earlier attitudes, for example to syndicated bank lending in the 1970s. The parallels between current trends in direct and equity investment and the factors described above, which helped to create the circumstances in which the 1980s debt crisis could occur, are the subject matter of the remainder of this book.

▶ 3

The Nature of Direct and Equity Investment and the Positive View

What Are Direct and Equity Investment?

There are two key distinguishing features of direct and equity investment, as compared with other forms of international financial flows:

1 they confer on the investor ownership of assets – generally productive assets – in the recipient country; and

2 unlike loans and bond issues, which produce a stream of payment obligations according to a fixed schedule, the return on direct and equity investments is determined by the financial performance of the investment.

The distinction between direct and portfolio equity investment is, in some respects, somewhat blurred. Essentially,

- *direct investment* entails the purchase or construction of productive capacity in a country by a company or individual based outside the country; and

- *portfolio equity investment* entails the purchase of shares in a company or productive enterprise, usually through a stock exchange.

The blurring of the distinction arises because the purchase of shares amounting to more than 10 per cent of the total capital of a company is classified as direct rather than portfolio investment. The intention is that investments which allow the investor a significant level of control over the investment should be classified as FDI. While the 10 per cent threshold is essentially arbitrary, and some countries use a different figure (Germany and Japan use 20 per cent), most direct investment entails majority ownership by the foreign investor (IMF 1993: para. 364); this pattern is likely to be particularly marked in most developing countries unless majority ownership is impeded by ownership restrictions.

In considering the economic effects of direct investment, a subdivision is helpful, to distinguish between:

- *direct investment through construction (FDI(C))*, which entails the creation of new productive capacity; and

- *direct investment through purchase (FDI(P))*, which entails a foreign investor purchasing productive capacity (including complete companies or shares in a company) which already exists.

In some respects, these two types of direct investment have very different implications. This will be a recurring theme in later chapters.

Motivations for Direct and Equity Investment

The motivations for portfolio equity investment are relatively simple. They relate primarily to profit (seeking the optimal combination of rates of return to capital and risk), and portfolio diversification (spreading risks and returns across a wider range of markets). In some cases, portfolio equity investment may be a first step towards direct investment – that is, the purchase of a sufficient stake in a quoted company to confer a degree of control over its operations.

While the key motivation for direct investment is also profit, it differs from portfolio equity investment in two important respects. First, the main consideration is the overall profitability of the company as a whole, rather than that of each individual investment; second, the time horizon over which rates of return are considered is generally much longer. This brings a number of other considerations, beyond short-term profitability, into investment decisions.

This gives rise to a much broader range of motivations for FDI than for portfolio equity investment. The main categories may be summarised as follows (based on Dunning 1993: Chapter 3):

1 *access to resources*, particularly minerals, agricultural products, locational advantages (as for tourism) and low-cost labour, which are unavailable or more expensive in the home market;

2 *access to markets*, so as to avoid import restrictions or tariffs, to reduce transport and other transaction costs, to increase the responsiveness of production to local demand conditions, or because a presence is necessary as a means of supply (as in most service sectors);

3 *increased efficiency*, through the location of specific operations in the

lowest-cost locations (possibly, but not necessarily, as part of a globalisation of production processes);

4 *strategic objectives*, such as the establishment of alliances with other corporations, market domination, access to distribution networks or public sector procurement, and product diversification;

5 *to escape restrictions* in or affecting the investor's home country, such as environmental regulations or international sanctions;

6 to provide *support services* to existing FDI operations, such as distribution and marketing; and

7 *passive investment* – essentially, portfolio equity investment on a scale large enough to be classified as FDI.

Clearly, there is some overlap between these objectives. In particular, access to low-cost labour and materials (category 1) will be an important factor determining lowest-cost locations for production (category 3).

The relative importance of these objectives will vary considerably between countries.

- Access to physical resources will be a motivation primarily in countries which have mineral resources, low-cost production of (especially tropical) agricultural products, or favourable conditions and/or reputations for tourism (as in the case of the Caribbean).

- Low-cost labour is much more widely available in developing countries, and generally needs to be accompanied by other favourable conditions – good infrastructure, political stability, low taxation – if it is to attract FDI.

- Access to markets is of significance primarily for large, relatively prosperous countries with rapidly growing markets (such as Brazil and China), although regional trade arrangements may help to enable smaller countries to benefit. For example, the Central American Common Market encouraged direct investment in member countries in the 1970s; and the prospect of the North American Free Trade Agreement (NAFTA), providing access to the US market, was a major factor attracting FDI to Mexico in the early 1990s.

- Passive investment is likely to be most important in countries where equity markets are most developed and open.

Factors Influencing the Location of Direct Investment

In many cases, the above considerations will suggest a number of alternative locations for a particular investment, between which potential investors will need to choose. While such decisions are inevitably too complex (and probably too variable) to analyse in detail, at least within the limited scope of this book, there is a growing body of evidence on the considerations which are most often taken into account, and their relative importance.

Historically, it tended to be assumed that low labour costs were a critical factor attracting investment from developed to developing countries, and that restrictive policies towards FDI were a major obstacle. However, this view is now changing. Low labour costs may be one consideration in location decisions, but other conditions also need to be conducive to direct investment, and these are increasingly regarded as being of greater importance (Bergsman and Shen 1995). (This also suggests that their historical importance is largely a matter of conjecture.) Equally, there are increasing signs that the liberalisation of policies towards FDI are only a necessary and not a sufficient condition for increased flows, that 'the existence of a liberal FDI regimen acts as a minimum enabling element but is not in and of itself a strong inducer of FDI' (Agosin 1995: 17).

For a relatively low-wage economy to be successful in attracting FDI flows, even with liberal policies towards foreign investors, it must also benefit from various other advantages. These include, in particular (Bergsman and Shen 1995):

• a stable political and macroeconomic environment;

• strong and sustained growth of demand;

• relatively free trade policies and a liberalised domestic economy;

• effective legal systems providing adequate protection for investors;

• a skilled and educated workforce;

• reliable access to supplies of inputs, including infrastructure and business services, of appropriate quality.

These factors tend to skew the distribution of FDI flows to developing countries away from the poorest and least developed countries, and towards the middle-income countries. While one should not generalise unduly, the resource constraints facing the poorest developing countries tend to limit domestic demand and the effectiveness of legal systems; macroeconomic stability is often impaired by debt problems and over-dependence on a narrow range of commodity exports; poor economic performance and low living standards (often combined with historical factors) often undermine political stability; the chronic weakness of the economy limits the supply of infrastructural and business services; the supply of educated labour is typically limited by weak education systems and outward migration of educated workers; and these factors combine to undermine effective economic policy making (and arguably the appropriateness of liberalisation policies).

In short, the circumstances which are conducive to FDI are the polar opposite of the archetype of the low-income economy. This limits the supply of FDI to most low-income countries, which in turn limits the overall flow of capital to these countries in an international capital market increasingly dependent on FDI flows (Chapter 4). It also increases the rate of return required to attract such investment to low-income countries, with serious implications for long-term financial sustainability (Chapter 8); and it conditions the competition for FDI flows between developing countries, reducing its benefits and increasing its costs to developing countries as a whole (Chapter 10).

Financing of Direct Investment

Direct investment can be financed in various ways. The essential element is equity finance by a foreign investor, which confers ownership of a company or productive facility. Without an element of equity finance sufficient to provide the investor with some degree of control, a transaction is not defined as direct investment. Equity finance may entail the purchase of shares on a stock exchange; the purchase of a company or productive facility (or of a share in its ownership); or the creation of productive capacity within the ownership of the investor.

Normally, equity finance in direct investment represents a transfer of capital into the host economy. In some cases, however, the investment may be in kind – for example the provision of a licence to use technology or other patented or copyright materials (such as trademarks) owned by the parent company, together with management or other services, in exchange for an equity stake in the recipient company. This option may be preferred, for example, when an investment is seen as particularly risky due to the political or economic circumstances of the host country. This is generally only feasible for direct investment by purchase.

In most cases, all of the equity finance is provided by one (or occasionally more than one) foreign investor, so that the enterprise is wholly foreign-owned. In some cases, however, some equity finance is provided by local sources, or a previously existing enterprise is left partly in local ownership.

However, equity finance (in cash or in kind) is by no means the only way in which direct investment may be financed. Other elements may include:

- *inter-company loans* from the parent company or another of its foreign affiliates to the direct investment enterprise, generally in foreign currency, and subject to a specified repayment period and interest rate, which is used to finance part of the investment and serviced from the profits generated;

- loans from other foreign creditors, again normally in foreign currency; and

- loans from financial institutions in the host country, normally in local currency.

The provision of additional finance in any of these forms increases the capital value of the investment. However, only intra-company loans are categorised as part of direct investment. Other foreign loans are classified as part of the foreign borrowing of the private sector, while domestic borrowing is excluded from the balance of payments entirely, as it entails no foreign exchange transaction.

Interest payments on loans come out of the profits generated by the investment. However, if the money borrowed is invested wisely, the rate of return on the investment should exceed the interest rate on the loans. This will increase the overall profit, and thus the rate of return on equity financing.

Production, Income and Expenditure

Any productive enterprise purchases inputs which it uses to produce outputs (in each case of goods and/or services), which it sells. The difference between the cost of purchased inputs (excluding labour and capital) and the amount received for outputs is the *value added*. In the context of FDI, the value added by a particular direct investment enterprise is generally referred to as the *local value added*, as it excludes the value which is added by operations of the same company in other countries. The value added is divided between the returns to labour (wage costs) and the returns to capital; and the latter is subdivided between interest payments (on borrowed capital) and profits (on equity capital). This is illustrated in Figure 3.1.

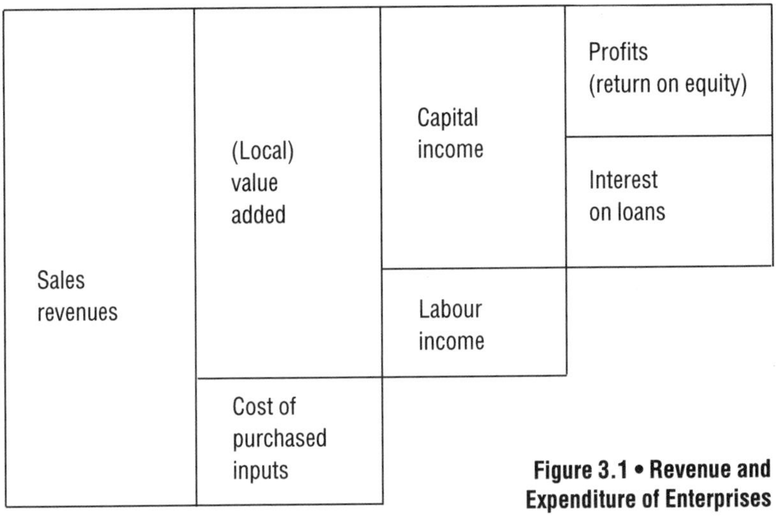

Figure 3.1 • Revenue and Expenditure of Enterprises

Profits, Capital Gains, Reinvestment and Remittances

Profits are a critical consideration in the context of direct and portfolio equity investment, as they accrue to the (foreign) owners, who can ultimately transfer the proceeds out of the country, together with the capital they originally invested.

The returns on portfolio investment (and FDI through the purchase of shares in a quoted company) are made up of two elements:

• the capital gain arising from increases in the market value of the shares; and

• dividend (or other) payments to shareholders.

Typically, dividends are transferred out of the economy when paid, unless the investor makes a deliberate decision to reinvest them. Capital gains, however, are realised only when the investment is sold. Most of the profit on share ownership is normally in the form of capital gains rather than dividends.

The returns on other forms of direct investment are also made up of two components:

• the operating profits made by the investment (or the foreign investor's share of the profits where the enterprise is only partly owned), net of depreciation, taxation and interest payments; and

- capital gains arising from increases in the value of assets such as land and property.

It is important to note that the expected depreciation of other assets (as, for example, in the case of the normal deterioration or obsolescence of equipment) is considered as a production cost and so does not off-set profits and capital gains. Only an unanticipated loss of value – caused, for example, by damage to uninsured assets – represents a capital loss. Capital gains, however, are not generally included in revenue, so they are effectively excluded from profits. This is of some importance in assessing the value of the stock of direct investment, as discussed in Chapter 5. As in the case of portfolio equity investment, capital gains are realised only when the assets concerned are sold, but they increase the value of the FDI stock in the interim.

These profits can also be divided into three parts according to their uses.

- Part of the profits may be paid to the owners. The profits paid to foreign owners are referred to as profit remittances.[5]

- Part may be reinvested in the purchase or construction of additional productive capacity.

- Part may be retained by the enterprise concerned, in the form of cash, bank balances, stocks of inputs or outputs.

Statistically, no distinction is made between the last two categories: any part of (the foreign equity-holders' share of) profits which is not remitted is simply classified as reinvestment. Even though the money does not leave the country, it is treated as if it had been transferred to the owner and then returned, and it is added to the stock of investment.

Other payments from the direct investment enterprise to the parent company (or to another of its foreign affiliates) may also have the characteristics of profit. In particular, royalties or licence fees may be paid for the use of intellectual property (such as patented technologies or designs, copyright material and trademarks), the rights to which are owned by the parent company or another of its foreign affiliates. If these payments were not made, the result would be an equivalent increase in profits. In the case of a wholly-owned enterprise, the outcome (in terms of the transfer of resources to the parent company) would be identical.

This suggests that, though classified as a production cost (and as an import of services in the balance of payments), royalties are in effect a part of profits.[6] This means that measured rates of return based only on profits will tend to understate the true figure if royalty charges are made. Equally, this suggests that, in the absence of royalty payments at market valuation, part of measured profits are in fact attributable to the incomes associated with intellectual property rights rather than with capital as such.

Other payments may also be made to the parent company for purchased inputs of goods and non-financial services. This is particularly important where a direct investment enterprise represents part of a globalised production process (in which different stages in the production of a particular good are located in different countries, so as to maximise the cost advantages to the company as a whole). In principle, these transactions represent genuine production costs rather than transfers: while there will be benefits to the parent company from having a captive market, it makes little difference whether inputs are purchased from the parent company or an alternative source, so long as the price paid is the same.

However, there is a critically important caveat to this general principle: the parent company may use its control over both sides of the transaction (as buyer and seller) to engage in *transfer price manipulation* – that is, to set the price at a non-market level. If the parent company (or another foreign affiliate) uses this mechanism to over-price sales to, or to under-price purchases from, a direct investment enterprise, this will represent a further unrecorded component of profit. If the reverse is the case, recorded profits will over-report the true value. Transfer price manipulation is discussed in greater detail in Chapter 6.

Interest payments on intra-company loans essentially come into the same category. However, while transfer pricing could in principle be used (interest rates could be set at artificially high levels to reduce recorded profits for tax reasons, for example), this is likely to be more difficult to conceal; and it would not affect the balance of payments (as interest on intra-company loans is classified as part of FDI income). It should be noted, however, that repayments of intra-company debt are recorded as a negative flow of FDI – that is, in effect, as disinvestment. This has potentially important implications for the estimation of the stock of direct investment, as discussed in Chapter 5.

Thus dividend payments and profit remittances represent a continuing outflow of foreign exchange on direct and equity investment. In addition, part of the investment (or of a company's assets) may be sold, and the capital transferred back to the investor. In this event, the reinvested profits and capital gains on FDI, and the capital gains on share purchases, will be realised.

To make an analogy with debt instruments, the overall profits and capital gains on FDI, and the capital gains plus payments to shareholders on equity investment, are equivalent to interest due on debt (except that they are determined by the financial performance of the investment rather than at a fixed rate or a fixed margin above a specified market interest rate). However, capital gains and that part of FDI profits which is retained by the direct investment enterprise are effectively refinanced. When investments are sold, a part of the payment received by the investor equal to the original cost of the investment is equivalent to the repayment of the original debt; the remainder is equivalent to the repayment of the accumulated refinancing of interest payments. However, the timing of this transaction is at the discretion of the investor rather than being predetermined.

Capital Flows and the Stock of Investment

The stock of direct and equity investment in a particular country is essentially the value of shares and productive capacity located in the country which is owned by non-residents. FDI and equity investment flows add directly to the value of this stock, as do reinvested profits on FDI. The stock of investment is also increased by capital gains – the increase in the value of assets such as land and property owned by direct investment enterprises, and the increase in share values.

Financing of direct investment enterprises from other sources (apart from domestic equity financing) also add to the stock of investment. If a direct investment enterprise borrows money, either abroad or from domestic lenders, to finance the construction or purchase of a factory, the factory is owned by the foreign investor, and thus forms part of the stock of inward direct investment.

The stock of investment forms the base for profits. If the average rate of return on capital is, say, 10 per cent per annum, then profits on FDI in a particular year will be 10 per cent of the FDI stock. Similarly, the value of foreign-owned equities (including capital gains) will be the basis of dividends, so that dividends will increase roughly in proportion to the stock of investment.

This means that all the profits and capital gains on FDI and equity investment either are transferred out of the country or add to the stock of direct and equity investment. In the latter case, they will add to future profits, and thus either to profit remittances or to the growth of the stock of investment in subsequent years.

Some (mainly higher-income) developing countries have increasing stocks of direct investment abroad as well as inward investment. However, there is an important asymmetry between inward and outward direct investment. For the host country, the profits on direct investment necessarily entail either an outward transfer of foreign exchange or an increase in the stock of foreign-owned assets. For the home country, by contrast, there is no assurance that profits will return to the parent company: they may equally be reinvested elsewhere, transferred to other foreign affiliates, placed in off-shore bank accounts or distributed to shareholders in third countries. This is all the more likely during the current phase in the evolution of the world economy, while companies are becoming increasingly globalised.

This asymmetry between inward and outward FDI may become institutionalised if, as some observers predict, transnational companies become effectively stateless. Thus, while stocks of outward FDI tend to off-set the balance of payments effects of inward investment from an accounting perspective, it is primarily the gross inward investment stock which matters rather than the net investment position in terms of the actual economic effects.

The Positive View of Direct and Equity Investment

As demonstrated by the quotes in Chapter 1, direct investment has been strongly welcomed by most neoliberal economists, who see it as having a number of major advantages as compared with debt financing. First, it provides financing to the private sector for productive investment, whereas most lending has tended to go to the public sector, often for general balance of payments and budget support (effectively, for consumption rather than investment). Moreover, because the returns to the investors are determined by the success or failure of the investment, they have a strong incentive to invest in the most profitable sectors, increasing the overall efficiency of capital use. By contrast, lenders have no interest in the use of the funds they provide, but only in the repayment capacity of the borrower.

Equally, direct investment is seen as a useful means of transferring risk from the host country to the investor. Since profit remittances have to be made from profits, it is argued, direct investments will always generate the funds necessary to meet their costs to the host country. This is in contrast with debt financing, which requires a stream of payments irrespective of the success or failure of the investment which is financed.

This view is summarised by Ishrat Husain of the World Bank.

> In debt financing, service charges are fixed. Irrespective of whether the enterprise or the project for which debt has been incurred makes profits or losses, debt service has to be paid. In the case of equity financing [including FDI], foreign partners or shareholders will enjoy dividends and profits only if the enterprise or the project is able to generate positive returns and cash flows. Even in that best-case scenario, the reinvestment of dividends, tax payments and dividends to local

partners reduces the amounts that are remitted abroad and require foreign exchange transfers. (Husain 1996: 133)

However, the benefits attributed to direct investment go far beyond the purely financial. In particular, direct investment by transnational companies is also seen as offering the potential for a transfer of technology from the parent company to the host country, as the investor (who generally has greater access to technology) will seek to use it to maximise the profitability of the investment. Transnational companies also generally have better established contacts with the world economy, which are seen as giving FDI an advantage over locally owned investments in developing export markets. These benefits are seen as essential to development, and FDI is often presented as the key to – and sometimes, at least implicitly, as the only means of – attaining them. Thus the World Bank argues that

> FDI is a large and growing source of equity investment that brings with it considerable concomitant benefits: technology transfer, management know-how, and export marketing access. Many developing countries will need to be more effective in attracting FDI flows if they are to close the technology gap with high-income countries, upgrade managerial skills, and develop their export markets. (World Bank 1993: 27)

The benefits of portfolio investment in equities (beyond the foreign exchange they provide) are more indirect. The main benefit is from the development of stock exchanges, which make it easier for shares to be bought and sold, and provide a ready source of information on companies and markets. This facilitates stock market flotations, which allow companies to raise equity capital, and allows equity capital to be transferred more readily between companies and sectors. By opening the market to foreign investors, the scale of the market can be increased, increasing both the capital available and the stability of the market (as the effects of single large transactions are diluted).

As discussed in Chapter 10, this very positive view of direct investment has been embodied in strenuous efforts to promote it, led by the international financial institutions and the major developed country governments, but followed avidly by the developing countries themselves.

▶ 4

Recent Trends in Development Finance

The Changing Composition of Financial Flows

There has been a fundamental shift in the pattern of capital flows to developing countries over the last 20 years (Figure 4.1a). In 1980, most financial flows to developing countries were in the form of loans to governments from commercial banks, developed country governments and international institutions such as the World Bank. Together with aid grants and a small amount of public sector bond issues, these sources of finance represented around 85 per cent of total net financial flows to developing countries as a whole, the remainder being made up of loans to (and international bond issues by) private companies and foreign direct investment, at about 10 and 5 per cent respectively.

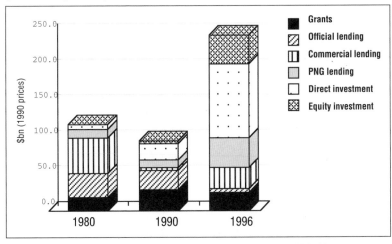

Figure 4.1a • Net Financial Flows to Developing Countries, 1980–96

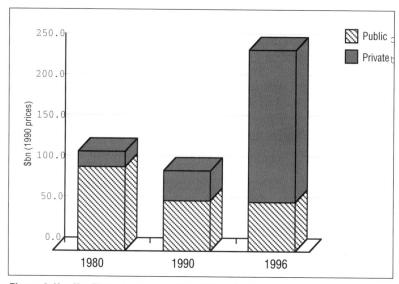

Figure 4.1b • Net Financial Flows, 1980–96, by Destination

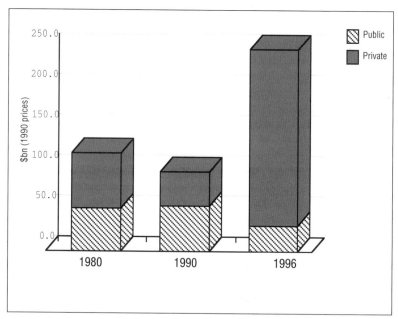

Figure 4.1c • Net Financial Flows, 1980–96, by Source

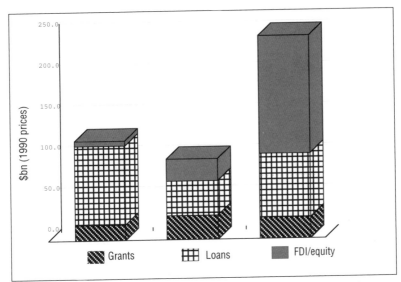

Figure 4.1d • Net Financial Flows to Developing Countries, 1980–96, by Nature of Liability

Following the debt crisis of the early 1980s, commercial bank lending to governments virtually dried up; and, despite major increases in lending from international institutions and in FDI flows, total net financial flows fell by 24 per cent in real terms between 1980 and 1990. By the mid-1990s, however, there had been a remarkable turnaround. Net financial flows increased by more than 150 per cent between 1990 and 1996, to nearly double their 1980 level in real terms.

Not only have financial flows increased in real terms, they have also increased relative to exports. Excluding grants, net financial flows fell from 11.3 per cent of exports in 1980 to 7.7 per cent in 1990; but by 1996 the figure had risen to 16.6 per cent. In other words, developing countries were taking on foreign exchange liabilities twice as fast relative to their foreign exchange earnings in 1993-6 as they were in 1980 – near the height of the borrowing that led to the debt crisis of the 1980s.

However, the new surge of financial flows was fundamentally different from that of the 1970s. The increase was entirely due to increased financing from commercial sources, especially in the form of direct and equity investment. Taken together, inflows of FDI and equity investment increased by 440 per cent between 1990 and 1996, to a level more than twenty times that in 1980 in real terms; and loans to private companies increased by 325 per cent. Net commercial lending to governments recovered somewhat from its very low level in 1990, but remained 40 per cent below the 1980 level, while net official lending fell by more than 80 per cent and grants by 12 per cent.

Implications of the New Paradigm

This radical change in the nature of financial flows has three important aspects.

1 It represents a massive shift in the *destination* of financial flows, from the public sector to the private sector (Figure 4.1b). Total net financial flows to the public sector fell by 45 per cent in real terms between 1980 and 1996, while net flows to the private sector increased by 520 per cent.

2 There has been a similar change in the relative importance of the public and private sectors as *sources* of financial flows since 1990 (Figure 4.1c). The proportion of total flows from official sources fell from 43 per cent in 1990 (only marginally below the figure for 1980) to less than 13 per cent in 1996.

3 There has also been a dramatic change in the *types* of financial flows, from grants and loans to FDI and equity investment (Figure 4.1d). The latter increased from less than 5 per cent of net financial flows in 1980 to nearly 60 per cent in 1996.

The first of these shifts implies a major change in the purposes for which financial flows can be used. Loans and grants to the public sector can be used to support political and administrative systems as well as social services such as health and education, while private sector financing is essentially limited to commercial productive activities. The scope of the private sector has expanded at the expense of the public sector in recent times, through the retrenchment of the state from commercial activities and the privatisation of infrastructure and other enterprises; but government finances remain a critical constraint on economic development in many (especially low-income) developing countries.

Government revenues are constrained by narrow tax bases, low incomes and reductions in tax rates imposed under economic reform programmes (on trade taxes and corporate taxation, for example), as well as by factors such as weak administrative and tax collection capacity; and a large proportion of the revenues which are raised are often diverted to meet external and domestic debt-servicing obligations. The result is that constraints on recurrent expenditure seriously limit the availability and the quality of basic health services and education, while weakening the capacity for effective decision making, policy implementation and administration. As well as having direct adverse effects on economic and human development, these factors may also undermine democratisation and political development.

The switch from loans and grants to direct and equity investment has two critically important implications, which form much of the basis of this book. First, together with the shift from official to commercial sources of financing, it implies a major increase in the cost of capital flows, especially for low-income countries. Second, it implies a transfer of ownership of the capital base and productive potential of developing countries to entities outside their borders.

Grants, by definition, impose no direct financial cost on the recipient. Loans from official sources generally bear interest at about commercial rates for middle-income countries (around 6 per cent on average in 1991-6), but at far below commercial rates for most low-income countries (around 3.5–4 per cent on average over the same period, but less for sub-Saharan Africa, falling from 3.5 per cent to 1.5 per cent). Private loans to the public sector are more consistently at commercial rates, and therefore somewhat more expensive for poorer developing countries (an average of 6.5 per cent both for low-income countries as a whole and for sub-Saharan Africa in 1991–6). Loans to private sector borrowers are more expensive again, as lenders require a risk premium to compensate them for the commercial risks involved (of the borrower's bankruptcy, for example). While data are not generally available, this might add about another 2 per cent to the interest rate.[7]

However, the rates of return on direct and equity investment are of an altogether higher order of magnitude. For developing countries as a whole, the World Bank estimates that the rate of return on FDI was around 16–18 per cent per annum in 1990–4 – more than twice the cost of commercial borrowing (World Bank 1997b: 34). Moreover, the rate of return is generally much higher for poorer countries, reflecting investors' perceptions of higher risks and less favourable conditions such as weak markets or inadequate infrastructure. For sub-Saharan Africa, the Bank estimates the average rate of return on FDI at 24–30 per cent per annum – about four times the cost of commercial lending to the public sector, and 16–20 times the average cost of official loans to the region in 1996. The rate of return on equity investment in developing countries averaged 29 per cent per annum between 1976 and 1992 (Woodward 1996: 46).

As regards ownership, if a company in a developing country borrows money from abroad to build or buy a factory, it is the company which owns the factory, so that its ownership, and the profits it generates, remain in the country where it is located. If, instead, the factory is bought or built by a transnational corporation through FDI, it is the TNC which owns the factory and the future profits. In effect, therefore, the shift of financing from loans and grants towards direct and equity investment implies an accelerating transfer of ownership of the assets which make up the economies of developing countries from the people of those countries to transnational companies.

The Geographical Distribution of Direct and Equity Investment

It is often observed that the geographical distribution of equity investment has been conspicuously skewed. Just seven countries accounted for more than 60 per cent of the total in 1995 (Figure 4.2a). However, this way of looking at the figure is potentially misleading, as the dominance of some of these countries, in varying degrees, reflects their size. This applies in particular to India and China, whose shares in total equity flows to developing countries are respectively less than half and less than one-third of their shares in the total population of developing countries. As a result, the seven largest recipients of equity flows, taken as a whole, actually represent a slightly larger share of the population of the developing world than of the equity flows to them (Figure 4.2b).

A more enlightening way of looking at the issue is to divide developing countries according to their per capita receipts of portfolio equity finance. This is done in Figures 4.3a and 4.3b, countries being categorised as having very high (more than $30), high ($15–30), moderate ($5–15), low ($1–5) or minimal (less than $1) per capita equity flows in 1996. (The average figure for developing countries as a whole is just under $10 per capita.) All but the last group contain around ten countries. The eleven countries in the 'very high' group receive nearly half of all equity flows, but account for just 8.1 per cent of the population of the developing world. Adding in the ten countries in the 'high' group takes the total to 75 per cent of equity and 21.8 per cent of population. At the other end of the scale, the 71 countries in the 'minimal' group, with 22.3 per cent of population, received just 0.1 per cent of the flows; and the 'minimal' and 'low' groups together (the latter including India and China) account for 70 per cent of population but only 17.7 per cent of flows.

Clearly, this pattern of flows is very uneven. It is also heavily skewed towards the better-off developing countries: no low-income country appears above the middle of the 'moderate' group; and only two of the 14 upper-middle income countries for which data are available are below this point. These two countries – Gabon and Trinidad and Tobago – are among the three smallest countries in this income category.

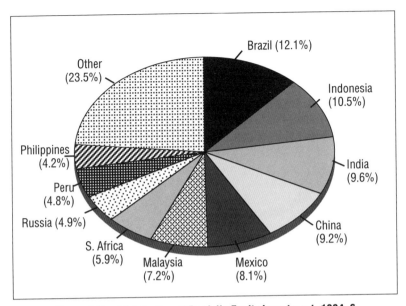

Figure 4.2a • Distribution of Portfolio Equity Investment, 1994–6

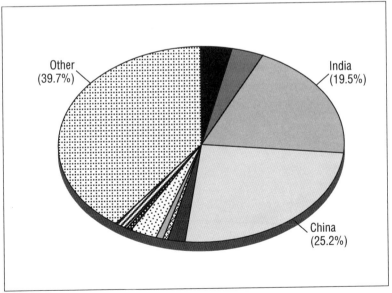

Figure 4.2b • Population Shares
of Major Equity Investment Recipients, 1995

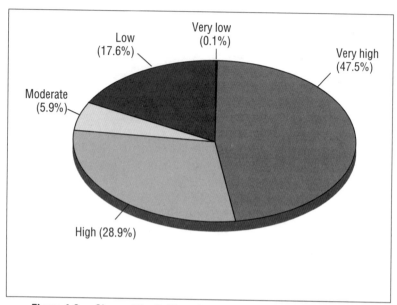

Figure 4.3a • Share of Equity Flows by Equity per Capita Category, 1996

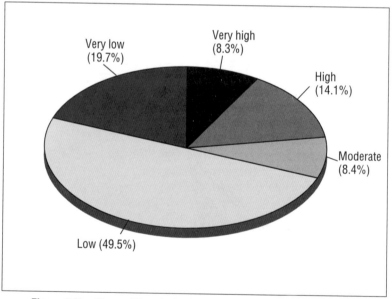

Figure 4.3b • Share of Population by Equity per Capita Category, 1996

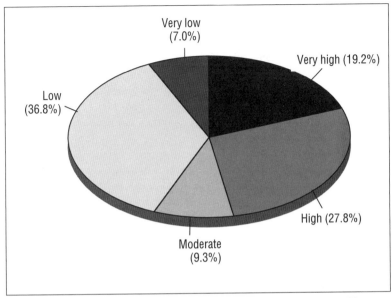

Figure 4.3c • Share of FDI Flows by Equity per Capita category, 1996

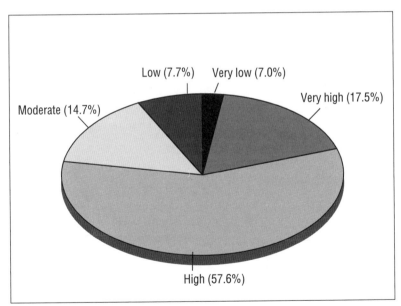

Figure 4.3d • Share of Commercial Lending by Equity per Capita Category, 1996

The 'high' and 'very high' equity recipients also receive disproportionate amounts of other forms of commercial financing (Figures 4.3c and 4.3d). Together, their share of direct investment is more than double their share of population at 47 per cent; their share of bank lending and trade financing is more than three times their population share at 66 per cent; and their share of bond financing nearly four times their population share at 83 per cent. Overall, the 21 countries in these categories account for 61.7 per cent of all commercial capital flows to developing countries, compared with their 21.8 per cent share of population.

The situation of the 'low' and 'minimal' countries in terms of other commercial flows is somewhat distorted by China, which receives considerably more FDI than equity financing. Excluding China, the 79 countries in these two groups represent 44.2 per cent of the population of the developing world; but they account for less than 10 per cent of FDI flows, 3 per cent of banking and trade financing, and 0.7 per cent of bond issues. Their overall share of commercial capital flows is just 7.2 per cent, less than one-sixth of their population share.

While the countries which receive the largest proportion of equity flows also receive larger than average amounts of FDI, the distribution of FDI is, in some respects, more complex than that of equity financing. While large middle-income countries again receive a disproportionate share of the flows, very small economies (with total GNP less than $500m) receive the largest amounts relative to the size of their economies. The weakest performers are middle-sized low-income countries: of 19 low-income countries with GNP between $4 billion and $25 billion, only one (Sri Lanka) received FDI flows in excess of 0.5 per cent of GNP in 1993 (Woodward 1996: 41).[8] Low-income countries which are successful in attracting FDI are generally those with particular advantages in terms of location and/or natural resources (Bachmann and Kwaku: 1994).

This pattern leaves many developing countries – especially smaller and poorer countries – with limited access to direct and equity investment, the predominant forms of commercial capital flows. Since other commercial flows (lending to and from the private sector) tend to vary broadly in line with direct and equity investment, those countries which receive relatively limited financing from these sources are critically dependent on official flows, and particularly aid.

Official flows even out the resulting differences in overall capital flows, but only partly, as shown in Figure 4.4. As a result, countries with direct and equity investment inflows in excess of 5 per cent of GDP received total net capital inflows of 7.4 per cent of GDP in 1996, and those with direct and equity inflows of at least half that level received overall net inflows of 5.7 per

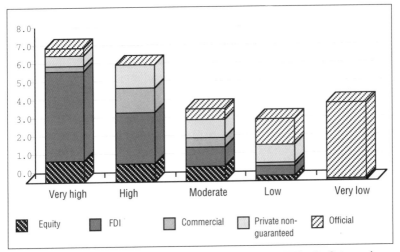

Figure 4.4 • **Net Financial Flows, 1996 (% of GDP, by FDI/Equity Category)**

cent. All the country groups with smaller inflows of direct and equity investment received overall capital inflows of around 4 per cent of GDP – although they are in general poorer countries, whose domestic savings are generally smaller, and whose need for capital flows is commensurately larger. In other words, *the pattern of North–South capital flows is skewed away from those developing countries whose need is greatest.* This tendency can be expected to become progressively stronger if direct and equity investment continue to grow in importance and aid flows continue to decline.

Figure 4.4 also illustrates a second pattern: the dominance of direct and equity investment as sources of capital flows to the largest recipients. Four-fifths of total net flows to the largest recipient group were from these sources in 1996, and two-thirds for the second group, compared with half for the third, a quarter for the fourth, and just one-twentieth for the smallest recipients. In other words, *many of the larger and better-off developing countries are critically dependent on direct and equity investment flows as a source of capital.* As discussed in chapters 8 and 12, this is a matter of potential concern because of the high cost of these types of capital flow and the volatility of equity investment.

The Sectoral Distribution of Direct Investment

Published data on the sectoral composition of FDI flows and stocks, as on many other aspects of FDI, appear to be very limited. According to IFC/FIAS

(1997:16), 'Information on sectoral distribution of FDI is available for only 16 developing countries' – and even these data are for 1990.

Nonetheless, it seems clear, and is generally recognised, that there has been an important shift in recent years. Historically, FDI was concentrated primarily in extractive industries such as oil and mineral production, while manufacturing industry played a secondary role. FDI in the manufacturing sector was largely directed towards domestic markets: it was viewed by transnational companies primarily as a means of selling products into markets protected by import barriers.

During the 1980s, the relative importance of manufacturing increased; and the composition of FDI within manufacturing shifted markedly from import substitution to export industries. The shift from extractive industries to manufacturing may in part have reflected the weakness of the international markets for many primary commodities. Of greater importance, however, was the movement towards the globalisation of production processes – that is, the location of different stages of the production of each product in different countries, according to where costs are lowest. This often entails the sale of components or part-finished products between different parts of the same company in different countries ('intra-firm trade').

Various factors have contributed to the process of globalisation, including

- the liberalisation of trade and FDI régimes (particularly, but not only, under structural adjustment programmes), allowing the necessary investments to take place and reducing the cost of intra-firm trade;

- changing corporate strategies and management attitudes, favouring the international integration of production processes;

- improvements in transport and communications, reducing costs and making global management more practicable; and

- devaluation and falling real wage costs in many developing countries, increasing the cost savings available from relocating production.

Since the late 1980s, in particular, there has been a second, and in some respects more important, shift in the sectoral composition of FDI – away from industry and towards services. Historically, most services have been regarded as not being internationally tradeable: by their nature, services such as retailing, hairdressing or transport can only be consumed in the same place that they are produced. Consequently, they can be traded internationally only if the providers move to the country in which the services are to be consumed (as in consultancy), or if the purchasers move to the country in which they are produced (as in tourism).

Over the last decade, this view has changed. An increasing range of services such as data processing can now be traded internationally in a similar way to goods, due to improvements in communications and information technology. At the same time, financial services such as banking and insurance are becoming more internationalised. More important in the present context, FDI is increasingly being seen as a means of international trade in otherwise non-tradeable services – not only on a conceptual level, but also in regulatory terms, for example in the General Agreement on Trade in Services negotiated in the Uruguay Round of multilateral trade negotiations. Thus a fast-food chain establishing an outlet in another country is regarded, not merely as making an investment, but also as exporting its services to the host country.

Various factors may have contributed to the shift towards services in FDI. One is the increasing importance of services in the developed countries, which has spawned a growing number of major service companies, and increased their relative size. In order to expand beyond the confines of their national markets, these companies have had to export their services, which in turn requires them to undertake FDI. Privatisation has also played a crucial role: the privatisation of public utilities such as transport systems in the developed countries has given rise to whole new sectors of large service companies, and provided an opportunity for rapid expansion of existing companies. The same process in developing countries has encouraged them to expand internationally by acquiring other privatised enterprises.

The scale of the change in the sectoral composition of FDI is difficult to quantify, particularly with regard to developing countries. According to UNCTAD, 'There has been a steady shift towards FDI in services, which now accounts for well over half of the total stock of FDI' (UNCTAD 1997a: 71). This is a global figure, and that for developing countries is likely to be somewhat smaller. IFC/FIAS (1997: Figure 2.5) shows the share of the services sector in FDI in sixteen major recipient countries[9] increasing from less than 22 to more than 28 per cent between 1980 and 1990. The stock of FDI in the primary sector (extractive industries, agriculture and fisheries) declined only after 1985, from 24 to 21 per cent of the total in 1990 – still marginally above the 1975 level – while the share of the manufacturing sector fell progressively from 54 per cent in 1975 to 48 per cent in 1990.

However, while the countries included in these data account for two-thirds of all FDI in developing countries, two important caveats should be noted. First, these major recipients of FDI are likely to exhibit a markedly different pattern from the great majority of developing countries. The primary sector is generally of much more limited importance in the former (both generally and in terms of FDI inflows), and they have been much more important as destinations for FDI in manufacturing.

Second, since the data extend only to 1990, they exclude much of the effect of privatisation, which occurred largely after this date. The total proceeds of privatisations with foreign participation in East Asia and the Pacific and Latin America and the Caribbean averaged about $1 billion per annum in 1988–90 (almost all of this occurring in Latin America in 1990), but more than $6 billion per annum in 1991–3 (Sader 1995: Table A-1). This is likely to have given rise to a marked acceleration in the increase in the share of services in FDI in the 1990s.

Stocks of Direct and Equity Investment

Figure 4.5 shows the evolution of the stock of direct investment for three regions (South and East Asia, Latin America and the Caribbean and sub-Saharan Africa)[10] between 1980 and 1996. The geographical pattern is little short of astonishing. Latin America and East Asia are generally seen as having been highly successful, and Africa as having been conspicuously unsuccessful, in attracting FDI flows. However, sub-Saharan Africa's stock of inward FDI has increased much more quickly relative to GDP than the other regions both in absolute terms (by 33 percentage points, compared with 15 for South and East Asia and 18.5 for Latin America and the

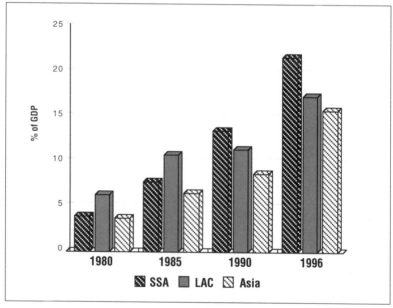

Figure 4.5 • FDI Stocks by Region, 1980–96

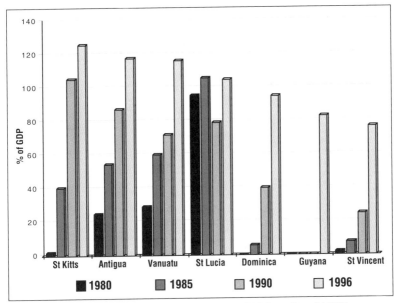

Figure 4.6a • Inward FDI Stocks, 1980–96: GDP Less than $1 Billion

Caribbean), and still more strikingly in relative terms (by a factor of 11 compared with five and two).

It is interesting to compare these figures with the averages for the developed countries over the same period. The ratio of inward FDI stock to GDP in the developed countries in 1996 was only 7.6 per cent – half that of South and East Asia, and a quarter of that of sub-Saharan Africa. It also increased much more slowly in absolute terms in 1980–96, by less than four percentage points compared with 15–33 points for the three developing regions. In relative terms, its growth was in line with that for South and East Asia, but far below that for Latin America and the Caribbean and sub-Saharan Africa.

While these levels of regional FDI stocks appear moderate, at least for South and East Asia and Latin America and the Caribbean, they conceal very considerable differences between individual countries. In a number of smaller developing countries, in particular, FDI stocks were between 70 and 125 per cent of GDP in 1996 (Figure 4.6a). In many cases, these figures have grown rapidly in recent years: in three of the seven countries with FDI stocks greater than 70 per cent of GDP in 1996, where 1980 data are available, they were 2 per cent or below in 1980; in three other cases, they were between 25 and 30 per cent. Only in St Lucia has the ratio remained broadly unchanged over this period.

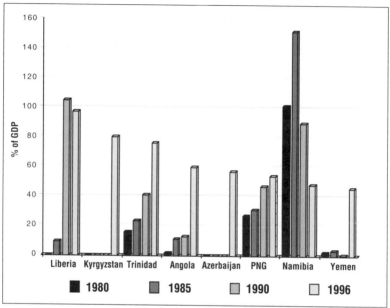

Figure 4.6b • Inward FDI Stocks, 1980–96: GDP $1–20 Billion

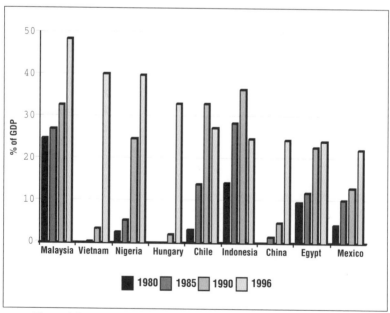

Figure 4.6c • Inward FDI stocks, 1980–96: GDP more than $20 Billion

In moderately sized economies, stocks are smaller, but nonetheless very substantial in some cases (Figure 4.6b) – nearly 100 per cent for Liberia, 80 per cent for Kyrgyzstan, 55–60 per cent for Angola, Azerbaijan and Papua New Guinea, and between 30 and 50 per cent in several other countries. Again, these have generally increased considerably since 1980, though less than for the smaller economies. Only in Namibia has the figure fallen over this period; and only in Fiji has it less than doubled.

Even some large developing economies have very substantial inward FDI stocks relative to GDP (Figure 4.6c) – 49 per cent in Malaysia, 40 per cent in Nigeria and Vietnam, 33 per cent in Hungary, and between 22 and 27 per cent in Mexico, China, Indonesia, Chile and Egypt. This last group includes three of the seven largest developing economies in terms of GDP. Again, the ratios have increased rapidly in recent years, starting from 4 per cent or less in 1980 in all but three cases.

While accurate data for the stock of portfolio equity investment are not readily available, some rough estimates can be made on the basis of cumulative flows, assuming a plausible rate of capital gain on outstanding investments. Based on a rate of return of 20 per cent per annum – somewhat below the historical level – four or five countries might have had outstanding stocks of inward equity investment in the order of 20 per cent of GDP at the end of 1996 (Bulgaria, Ghana, Malaysia, Mexico and possibly South Africa),[11] with figures of around 10–15 per cent for five more (Indonesia, Papua New Guinea, Peru, the Philippines and Thailand). Another nine countries may have had stocks in a range of about 4–8 per cent on the same basis (Argentina, Brazil, Chile, Hungary, India, Pakistan, Panama, Venezuela and Vietnam).

Two points should be noted with regard to these figures. First, some of the countries with the highest stocks of inward equity investment have accumulated them over a very short period, notably Ghana and Bulgaria (around 20 per cent of GDP over three years) and Papua New Guinea and Peru (around 15 per cent of GDP, over two years and four years respectively). If the stock of equity investment in these countries continues to accumulate at anything approaching these rates over the next few years, it could rapidly assume alarming proportions, given the possibility of investors withdrawing their capital if economic circumstances deteriorate (see Chapter 12).

Second, many of the countries with very large stocks of inward equity investment are also among those with the largest inward FDI stocks. Malaysia and Mexico, for example, each have equity investment of around 20 per cent of GDP in addition to inward FDI stocks of 49 and 22 per cent respectively; Papua New Guinea has equity investment around 15 per cent in addition to inward FDI of 54 per cent; and Indonesia has equity investment of 10 per cent and inward FDI of 25 per cent. This means that the overall stock of equity-type investments in these countries is considerably greater than is shown in Figure 4.6.

Finally, it is instructive to note, in the present context, that these figures for stocks of inward direct and equity investment are in many cases as high as, or higher than, the stock of external debt of the major Latin American countries immediately before the 1982 debt crisis. The total external debts of Brazil, Mexico and Argentina were between 30 and 35 per cent of GNP at the end of 1980 (World Bank 1998a), and their stocks of inward FDI were just 4–7 per cent (UNCTAD 1997b).

This comparison is a matter of still greater concern for two reasons.

• First, the current large stocks of inward FDI and equity investment are additional to external debts which are themselves greater relative to national income than those of the major Latin American debtors in 1980. Among the larger economies with large stocks of inward direct and equity investment, Chile and Malaysia had external debt/GNP ratios around 40 per cent in 1996, Egypt and Mexico 45–50 per cent, Indonesia and Hungary around 60 per cent, and Vietnam and Nigeria in excess of 100 per cent. Only China (16 per cent) was below the 30–35 per cent range.

• Second, as discussed in chapters 6 and 7, there are a number of compelling reasons to believe that the published estimates of the stock of inward direct investment understate the true figures in many cases – possibly by a considerable amount.

The Importance of Direct Investment in Overall Investment, Production and Exports

FDI represents a very large proportion of total investment in many (especially smaller) developing countries (Figure 4.7a). In at least eight countries – Hungary, Nigeria, Bolivia, Angola, Papua New Guinea, Trinidad and Tobago, Vanuatu and St Vincent and the Grenadines – foreign direct investment constitutes between 40 per cent and 60 per cent of all investment in the economy. (Several other Caribbean and Pacific island economies may also come into this category, but there are numerous gaps in the data.) At least four, mostly smaller, countries (Fiji, the Seychelles, Dominica and Guyana) have FDI inflows between 30 per cent and 40 per cent of total investment, while a further dozen countries, including China, Peru,

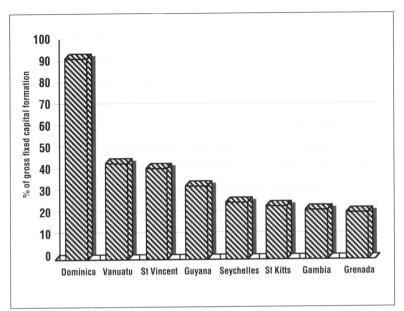

Figure 4.7a • FDI Flows as Percentage of Total Investment, 1994–6: GDP Less than $1 Billion

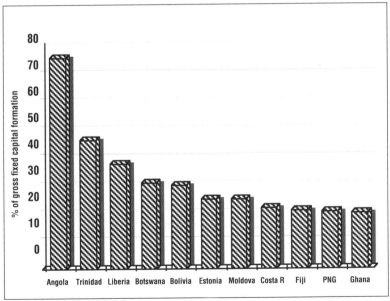

Figure 4.7b • FDI Flows as Percentage of Total Investment, 1994–6: GDP $1–20 Billion

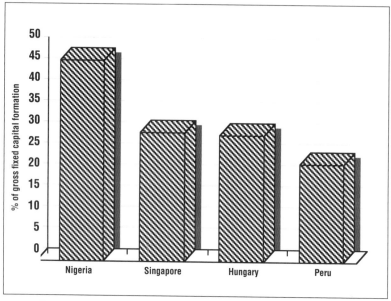

Figure 4.7c • FDI Flows as Percentage of Total Investment, 1994–6: GDP More than $20 Billion

Singapore, Ghana and Uganda, depend on FDI for 20–30 per cent of total investment.

It is equally clear that FDI plays a major (though less easily quantifiable) role in the production of many developing countries. Estimates of the share of foreign affiliates' output in GDP by regions suggest figures of around 7 per cent for the Middle East, 9–10 per cent for Latin America, Africa and Asia, and 25 per cent for the Pacific in 1994 (UNCTAD 1997b: Annex Table A.4).[12] Moreover, these figures increased for all regions except the Pacific between 1990 and 1994, by between one-tenth and two-thirds. If the same proportional change occurred between 1994 and 1998, the figure would rise to 10.5–11.5 per cent in all regions except the Pacific, where it would fall to around 18 per cent.

Again, it is worth noting that, with the exception of non-EU Western Europe, the figures for developed countries in 1994 were both generally lower than those for the developing regions (5.2 per cent for North America, 7.7 per cent for the EU, and 1.9 per cent for other developed countries in 1994) and fell between 1990 and 1994 in all cases. In non-EU Western Europe (which includes only Gibraltar, Iceland, Norway and Switzerland), the figure was 11 per cent in 1994, a marginal increase from 1990.

The contribution of FDI to exports (and imports) is likely to be still greater, because direct investment enterprises tend to be more outward-oriented and integrated into the global economy than locally owned enterprises (Caves 1996: 33). As shown in Table 4.1, US majority-owned affiliates alone accounted for more than 7 per cent of total developing country exports, and in some countries for more than 20 per cent. Since the US accounts for around 25 per cent of the worldwide stock of FDI flows, if this pattern were similar for investment from other sources, the production of foreign affiliates could account for some 25–30 per cent of total developing country exports. Once again, this figure is likely to be growing, because of the rapid growth of the stock of inward direct investment in developing countries.

Table 4.1 • Share of US Majority-Owned Affiliates in Total Host Country Exports, 1993 (%)

Latin America/Caribbean	14.1
Brazil	13.1
Mexico	20.9
Newly industrialising Asia	8.0
Hong Kong	9.9
Korea	0.9
Singapore	23.7
Taiwan	2.7
Other Asia	6.0
India	0.3 (1986)
Malaysia	11.2
Philippines	16.7
Thailand	5.7
All developing countries	7.1

Source: UNCTAD 1996: 110, Table IV.8.

Data for individual countries show even higher figures. The proportion of total exports produced by foreign affiliates was 31 per cent in China in 1995, and 52 per cent in Malaysia in 1994 (based on UNCTAD 1997b: Table II.9 and World Bank 1997c). The figure for Malaysia is likely to be atypically high, as the stock of FDI was particularly large at 46.2 per cent of GDP in 1994; but, while FDI in China has been very substantial in recent years, the ratio of the stock of inward FDI to GDP was only slightly above the average for developing countries, at 18.2 as compared with 15.4 per cent (UNCTAD 1996: Annex Table 6; UNCTAD 1997b: Annex Table B.6). In Malaysia, the share of foreign affiliates in imports was almost identical to their share in exports, at 52.8 per cent in 1994. In China, however, it was considerably higher, reaching no less than 78.4 per cent in 1995 ($62.9 billion out of $80.3 billion).

Conclusion: the Story So Far

Economic theory suggests that capital flows from developed (capital-rich) countries to developing (capital-poor) countries will be both profitable for those who effect them and beneficial for the recipients. This suggests that the dramatic recovery of financial flows from the post-debt-crisis lows of the 1980s should be beneficial to all participants. However, the benefits of financial flows are critically dependent on their nature: the flows of the 1970s, in retrospect, did anything but help the developing countries who borrowed, and were less profitable to the lenders than they had hoped or anticipated.

At first sight, the current resurgence of North–South financial flows looks very different to the pattern of the 1970s, in that the main mechanisms and financial instruments involved – direct and equity investment – are radically different in nature. A strong body of opinion has emerged which sees these financial flows as highly beneficial, not only because they entail a North–South transfer of capital, but also because of their specific form. This very positive view has inspired a considerable global programme of promotional efforts, led by the international financial institutions and the major developed country governments; and these efforts have been spectacularly successful in increasing the flows of direct and equity investment to developing countries over the last decade.

However, financial flows (apart from aid grants) always create liabilities, which ultimately need to be met; and previous episodes of large-scale financial flows to developing countries have regularly generated financial crises among at least some recipient countries because of their inability to meet these obligations. The scale of these liabilities in some developing countries suggests a *prima facie* case that this scenario could be repeated.

The latest occurrence of this phenomenon was the debt crisis of the 1980s. Beyond the immediate causes of the crisis, it is possible to identify certain circumstances which contributed substantially to creating the conditions in which this crisis could happen:

- a conspicuous lack of reliable information on (and even of interest in) the scale of the liabilities which were being created;

- a pattern of financing based on a faith in the mechanisms involved which ultimately proved to be unjustified;

- active encouragement of this faith, and of the flows themselves, by the major developed country governments and the international financial institutions;

- expectations about the international economic environment which proved in the event to be seriously over-optimistic; and

- herd-like behaviour, whose ultimate reversal in direction, though inevitable (with the benefit of hindsight) was not anticipated.

It will be argued in the following chapters that these factors have striking parallels in the current wave of financial flows.

5

Ignorance is Bliss (I)
Data on the Stocks of Direct and Equity Investment

The Significance of Data Problems

Chapter 4 summarised the current situation of developing countries in terms of inward direct and equity investment, on the basis of published data. It showed a moderate level of inward investment overall, though with much higher figures for some countries, and generally very rapid rates of growth over recent years. However, this is only part of the story. In practice, as will be shown in this chapter and the next, these official data almost certainly understate both the true value of inward FDI stocks and their absolute rate of increase by a substantial margin, owing to shortcomings in the data.

This is a critically important issue, especially if, as has been suggested, direct investment is more problematic than is often supposed. The dangers are illustrated by the experience of the 1980s debt crisis: as noted in Chapter 2, the ignorance among lenders, borrowers and regulatory bodies of the volumes of debt that had been accumulated was a major element in allowing this crisis to occur. Had their perception of the true levels of debt been more accurate, the crisis might have occurred sooner, but it would almost certainly have been less serious in its economic and social impact.

Moreover, their ignorance was avoidable. Data on public sector debt have been improved very considerably since the early 1980s, largely through the very creditable efforts of the World Bank's Debtor Reporting System; and generally reliable data are published regularly in the World Bank's annual *Global Development Finance*. There is no obvious reason why this could not have been done in the 1970s. It is difficult to avoid the conclusion that it was not done because it was not seen as important – that is, because of an almost universal complacency about the potential risks of sovereign lending and over-indebtedness.

As in other respects, there is a danger that history is in the process of repeating itself. While we now have a far more accurate picture of the external liabilities of governments, our knowledge about the scale of private sector liabilities – including the foreign debts of companies and inter-bank liabilities as well as direct and equity investment – is at least as limited as knowledge of public sector debts was in the 1970s.

This is clearly not because commercial capital flows are seen as insignificant. The title of *Global Development Finance* was changed from *World Debt Tables* in 1996, specifically to reflect the increasing importance of 'non-debt-creating flows' such as direct and equity investment. Even before the change of name, data were included for private sector debts not guaranteed by the government, and for inflows of FDI and (more recently) equity investment.

However, serious data problems remain. In particular, the World Bank provides no figures for the stocks of inward direct and equity investment, or for the outflow of profits on equity investments. This would seem to reflect, at least partly, a lack of concern about (or an unwillingness to draw attention to) the potential significance of these variables. Some data are available for these variables elsewhere; but estimates of the stock of inward FDI are of questionable reliability; and even approximate figures for stocks of equity investment and profits on them are available for only a handful of developing countries. Even where apparently reliable data are available – for example on private non-guaranteed debt and flows of direct investment – they may be subject to serious shortcomings.

While not strictly a part of the subject matter of this book, the problems which have recently been exposed in the data on private non-guaranteed debts as a result of the East Asian financial crisis illustrate the potential for serious failures in data, and the significance of their realisation. In the wake of the crisis, the World Bank made major revisions in its estimates of the debts of two of the worst-affected countries, suggesting that, as in the 1980s, the severity of their potential problems had been seriously underestimated (World Bank 1997a; 1998a).

- The estimate of *Indonesia's* long-term private sector non-guaranteed debt at end-1995 was increased from $20.1 billion to $33.1 billion, and that for public and private short-term debt from $22.3 billion to $26 billion, in early 1998. Other informed sources put the total external debts of private Indonesian companies at $74 billion.[13]

- The estimate of *Thailand's* public and private short-term debt at end-1995 was more than doubled from $18.3 billion to $41.1 billion in early 1998, while its estimated long-term private sector non-guaranteed debt was increased from $21.2 billion to $25.1 billion. The overall effect was to increase the estimated debt/exports ratio by nearly half, from 76.6 to

112.2 per cent. Reliable reports in early 1998 that Thailand had success-fully 'rolled over' more than $60 billion of short-term private sector debt in early 1998 suggests that even the revised estimate may remain substan-tially too low.[14]

- The official estimate of *Korea's* short-term debts (public and private) was increased from $65 billion to $100 billion in late 1997,[15] having last appeared in the *World Debt Tables* as $13.9 billion at the end of 1994 (World Bank 1996).

The magnitude of these discrepancies is clearly very considerable, and the unrealised ignorance of the true situation may have contributed to (though not caused) the crisis itself. These data were collected through a supposedly reliable reporting system, and were not subject to any obvious serious distor-tions. If they have proven so inaccurate, how much more serious may be the discrepancies for data on direct and equity investment, where there is no effective reporting system and – as shown in this chapter and the next – data are subject to much more obvious, and potentially serious, uncertainties and distortions?

General Problems: Definitions, Data Collection and Coverage

In most developing countries, estimates of direct investment and the profits on it are based on survey data. Moreover, there is a continuing shift in this direction, as direct investment régimes and exchange restrictions are liber-alised. This means that the data are heavily dependent on the quality of the survey, particularly the comprehensiveness (or representativeness) of its coverage and the accuracy of the responses given by enterprises.

Some experiences of surveys are not encouraging.

- In the Gambia, 'No data on direct investment income are available because of lack of response to enterprise surveys' (IMF 1997a: Part 3, 188).

- In Samoa, 'Initial response to the questionnaire [intended to provide regular information on direct and equity investment from 1997] has been poor and fragmented' (IMF 1997a: Part 3, 275).

- In the Czech Republic, there are a 'limited number of respondents' to enterprise surveys (IMF 1997a: Part 3, 169), so that the data have to be supplemented by estimates.

- In Namibia, dividend payments are measured by tax information, which 'is compared with survey data and has proven to be more comprehensive'

(IMF 1997a: Part 3, 242). Since tax information is itself likely to be an underestimate (to the extent that tax is successfully evaded), this suggests that survey data are likely to under-report profit remittances significantly.

Banking records and returns are another widely used data source. However, these mean that direct investment transactions which do not pass through the local banking system are likely to be excluded. Among such exclusions are investment and profit remittances made in kind rather than in cash. In Nepal, for example, where direct investment estimates are based on information collected from banks and other enterprises, 'data ... are not being captured in detail' (IMF 1997a: Part 3, 244).

There is some indication that the extent of the resulting discrepancy could be substantial: when Mauritius changed its data source for direct investment income from exchange control records to commercial bank returns in July 1994, the estimate of such income fell by 40 per cent (from an average of $21.5 million per annum in 1990–3 to $12.5 million in 1995–6).

In some cases, the coverage of data collection excludes some categories of direct investment enterprises.

- In El Salvador, coverage is limited to enterprises that register their capital with the Ministry of the Economy (IMF 1997a: Part 3, 177).

- In the Dominican Republic, 'free zone' enterprises were excluded until 1994 (IMF 1997a: Part 3, 172).

- In Guinea, the coverage is limited to mining companies which are partly publicly owned – 'Direct investment in other companies ... is difficult to identify and is usually included under "other business services"' (IMF 1997a: Part 3, 194).

- In Oman, profit figures cover only the oil sector, commercial banks and investments by foreign construction companies (IMF 1997a: Part 3, 255).

- Syrian profit figures appear to be limited to the oil sector (IMF 1997a: Part 3, 298).

Where only specific sectors are covered, these are likely to be the sectors most important to direct investment, so that the effects should be relatively limited. The effect in the Dominican Republic is likely to be substantially greater, while the extent of the discrepancy in El Salvador is unclear.

The extent of foreign ownership used as a criterion for distinguishing direct investment from equity investment also often differs from the recommended 10 per cent guideline; and this almost always entails a higher threshold, and therefore an underestimation of direct investment flows and profits. The thresholds used are 20 per cent in Estonia and Korea; 25 per cent in China; 35 per cent in Myanmar; and 50 per cent in Côte d'Ivoire, Malaysia, Mali, Senegal, Sierra Leone and Togo.

In principle, this merely means that some direct investment will be mis-classified as portfolio equity investment, which is significant primarily in terms of the degree of foreign control of local productive capacity (as opposed to foreign ownership, or foreign exchange flows). However, in most of the countries which use thresholds above 10 per cent, no data are available (at least in IMF sources)[16] for portfolio equity investment – the exceptions in the above list are Estonia, Korea, Senegal and Togo.

The scale of the resulting discrepancy will depend critically on the extent of direct investment which entails equity stakes between 10 per cent and the threshold used. Where the political and/or economic environment is seen as potentially unstable (as tends to be the case in many low-income and sub-Saharan African countries) and there are no restrictions on foreign owner-ship, direct investors generally prefer to have majority stakes or even complete ownership. In such cases, the scale of the discrepancy is likely to be limited. This appears to be the case in Senegal, for example, where total recorded portfolio investment flows were 7 per cent of direct investment flows in 1990–5. In Togo, however, portfolio equity investment was 30 per cent of direct investment flows in 1990–1, suggesting the possibility of a larger discrepancy. (No later data are available in either case.)

Major Statistical Sources

One might reasonably expect the IMF and the World Bank, with their remits respectively to promote international financial stability and develop-ment, to be the main sources of information on direct investment. In practice, however, their efforts to monitor the stock of FDI in developing countries appear to be minimal. As noted above, while the World Bank's *Global Development Finance* – generally regarded as the definitive statistical source on developing countries' external liabilities – includes flow data on direct and equity investment, it provides no figures at all for the stocks of such investment.

The IMF's *Balance of Payments Statistics Yearbook* provides some data on stocks of direct and equity investment, but the coverage of developing countries is extremely limited. The 1998 edition (IMF 1998c) included such data only for ten (mostly new) countries in Eastern Europe and the former Soviet Union (the Czech Republic, Estonia, Hungary, Latvia, Lithuania, Poland, Romania, Russia, the Slovak Republic and Slovenia); four countries of the Southern African Customs Union (Botswana, Namibia, South Africa and Swaziland); and just six other developing countries (Cambodia, Chile, Colombia, Korea, Malaysia and Venezuela). Within the last group, data are provided only for direct investment in Cambodia; and only for portfolio equity investment in Chile and Korea.

The resulting picture for Eastern Europe and the former Soviet Union appears reasonably complete: the data provided for all ten countries in this region extend to 1997; and the countries covered account for 90 per cent of the region's total stock of inward FDI, based on UNCTAD (1998) data. While the IMF figure for Russia is seriously inaccurate, because it only covers the banking system, even excluding this case the coverage is around 70 per cent.

For non-European developing countries, however, the picture is considerably worse. The eight countries for which the IMF provides data represent only 9 per cent of the total stock of inward FDI, based on UNCTAD (1998) data. Of these, 1997 figures are provided for only three countries (Cambodia, Colombia and Swaziland), representing just 1.3 per cent of the stock, and 1996 data for a further three (Botswana, Namibia and South Africa), representing 1.8 per cent.

Further doubts are raised about the quality of data by comparing the estimates from the two sources – the more so because IMF data are a major source for the UNCTAD figures. As shown in Table 5.1, where UNCTAD provides valuation-based data, the figures coincide exactly in six out of 15 cases, and differ by only 0.1 per cent in one other case; in two other cases there are relatively small (3–6 per cent) differences between the two sources. However, the discrepancies for seven countries are substantially greater, ranging between 11 per cent and 34 per cent of the larger figure (12–52 per cent of the smaller figure). There is no systematic tendency for the IMF or the UNCTAD figures to be larger, and there is no *prima facie* reason to presume that either source is necessarily more accurate. Nonetheless, these inconsistencies do raise questions about the accuracy of the estimates in both sources.

Even where data are available based on valuations of the assets of foreign investors, these will often understate the true (current market) value of foreign-owned assets, as many countries use instead the principle of historic cost (the value of assets when they were purchased or constructed). The result is that any capital gains (on land or property, for example) which are made after the initial investment are excluded from the valuation of the stock of inward FDI. (Expected depreciation of assets such as buildings and equipment are included in costs, and therefore do not give rise to off-setting capital losses.)

Table 5.1 • IMF and UNCTAD Estimates of Stocks of Inward FDI

	Year	Inward FDI Stock, $m		Discrepancy (% of higher estimate)
		IMF	UNCTAD	
Developing Europe and the Former Soviet Union				
Czech Republic	1997	6,763	6,763	0.0
Estonia	1997	1,148	1,148	0.0
Hungary	1997	15,869	15,882	0.1
Latvia	1997	1,272	901	30.0
Lithuania	1997	1,041	1,041	0.0
Poland	1996	11,463	11,463	0.0
Slovak Republic	1997	1,804	1,293	28.3
Slovenia	1997	2,120	2,349	10.8
Other developing countries				
Cambodia	1996	678	849	20.1
Colombia	1996	11,079	9,305	16.0
Korea	1993	7,715	11,727	34.2
Namibia	1996	1,492	1,492	0.0
South Africa	1996	12,538	12,538	0.0
Swaziland	1996	431	407	5.6
Venezuela	1995	6,772	6,975	2.9

Notes: Data are from IMF (1998c) and UNCTAD (1998). Figures are for the latest year for which the IMF provides an estimate and the UNCTAD estimate is based on valuation. In the case of Korea, the UNCTAD (1996) figure for 1993 is derived from the stated 1994 stock (estimated by UNCTAD as the 1993 stock plus 1994 flows) and UNCTAD's figure for 1994 flows. Botswana, Malaysia, Romania and Russia are excluded from this table because the UNCTAD estimates are based wholly or partly on cumulative flows for all years of IMF data.

This problem is acknowledged by the IMF.

In principle, all external financial assets and liabilities should be measured at current market prices.... For *direct investment*, book values from the balance sheets of direct investment enterprises generally are utilized to determine the value of the stock of direct investments.... If based on historical cost or on an interim but not current valuation, such balance sheet values would not conform to the principle.... [H]istorical cost balance sheet values ... may be substantially less than current market values. (IMF 1993: paras 467 and 476)

Further doubts are raised by a comparison of the changes in the IMF's stock data with the corresponding flows of inward FDI over the same period. In principle, as discussed later, the increase in the stock of FDI should generally be greater than the total flow of FDI during the same period, again because of the exclusion of capital gains. Even if the stock is measured on a historic cost basis, the two should be approximately equal. However, as shown in Table 5.2, this is by no means always the case in the IMF data. In only five cases (all but one in Europe and the former Soviet Union) does the expected pattern of an implied capital gain apply. While the rate of capital gain appears very high in two of these cases (the Slovak Republic at 10.4 per cent per annum and Lithuania at 13.1 per cent per annum), it is not impossibly so, given the relatively short periods covered by the data (three years in each case) and the economic transformations undergone by the countries in the period concerned. In one other case, the data imply a very small (0.4 per cent per annum) annual capital loss.

In the majority of the countries, however, the data imply a more substantial rate of capital loss, mostly ranging from around 1.5 per cent per annum

Table 5.2 • Comparison of IMF Stock and Flow Data for Inward FDI ($m)

	Years	Change in stock	Cumulative flow	Difference	Implied capital gain/loss (% pa)
Czech Rep.	1994–7	+4,160	6,167	–2,007	–8.1
Estonia	1997	+323	266	+71	+6.0
Latvia	1996–7	+657	982	–325	–12.4
Lithuania	1995–7	+778	580	+198	+13.1
Poland	1997	+3,124	4,908	–1,784	–12.7
Romania	1992–7	+2,260	2,409	–149	–3.5
Slovak Rep.	1995–7	+1,008	629	+379	+10.4
Slovenia	1995–7	+789	682	+107	+2.1
Botswana	1995–6	–74	160	–234	–34.5
Cambodia	1996–7	+427	497	–70	–4.6
Colombia	1991–7	+11,483	15,282	–3,799	–6.7
Korea	1991–4	+2,884	3,307	–423	–1.6
Malaysia	1991–4	+12,598	18,529	–5,931	–8.4
Namibia	1991–6	–555	662	–1,217	–11.1
South Africa	1991–6	+3,340	2,246	+1,094	+1.8
Swaziland	1991–7	+70	336	–266	–9.0
Venezuela	1991–5	+4,630	4,715	–85	–0.4

Notes: Data are from IMF (1998c), and cover the period from the first to the last observation of inward FDI stock for each country. The implied rate of capital gain/loss is the annual rate at which the initial stock and subsequent flows would need to increase or decline regularly during this period for the stock and flow data to be consistent, on the simplifying assumption that all the inflows in a particular year are received at the mid-point of that year.

in Korea to around 12.5 per cent per annum in Latvia and Poland. In one case (Botswana) the rate is -34.5 per cent per annum.

While it is by no means impossible for capital losses to be incurred by foreign investors in a particular country during a particular period, the extent of the losses implied by the IMF data seems wholly implausible. Capital losses were incurred in more than two-thirds of the countries for which data are provided (more than three-quarters if weighted by the length of the period considered for each country).[17] Excluding Europe and the Former Soviet Union, eight out of nine countries show capital losses, representing 86 per cent of the sample weighted by length of period. The weighted average rate of capital gain/loss was -7 per cent per annum for this group, and marginally negative (-0.7 per cent per annum) for Europe and the former Soviet Union.

Similar discrepancies between stock and flow data arise in the case of equity investment. To take the most extreme case, cumulative flows to the Slovak Republic in 1993–5 amounted to $560 million, but the stock at end-1995 is valued at only $43 million. Conversely, no inflows at all are recorded for Malaysia, but the stock was valued at $3.2 billion at end-1992 (although this appears to represent a misclassification of flows rather than a mis-measurement of stocks, as *Global Development Finance* records positive inflows in several years up to 1992).

The timeliness of data has been improved to some extent by the inclusion of figures in the IMF's monthly *International Financial Statistics* since April 1997. However, the coverage has not been improved (the spread of countries for which data are provided is broadly the same as in the *Balance of Payments Statistics Yearbook*); and, while data can now be provided within a month of becoming available, only end-year figures are given, with data for some countries still seriously out of date.

In short, the data provided by the IMF and the World Bank on stocks of direct and equity investment are extremely limited; what data are provided are often too old to be useful and appear to be of questionable quality, or at least inconsistent with flow data. Neither does there seem to be any effort to improve these data comparable to the development of the World Bank's Debtor Reporting System. On the contrary, the liberalisation of direct invest-ment régimes which the Fund and the Bank have promoted in recent years has actually reduced the availability of data and the possibility of collecting it.

> Recent liberalization of FDI policy [in Argentina] has gone so far as to dissolve the FDI registration requirement, and thus there exists no complete set of official data on the sectoral distribution of recent FDI flows.... This has made it difficult to carry out statistical or economic analysis of FDI and its effects on development in Argentina. (Agosin 1995: 8, 12)

For portfolio equity investment, stock data do not appear to be available from other major statistical publications. For direct investment, however, one can turn to UNCTAD's annual *World Investment Report*, which provides figures for all but a few countries. Unfortunately, while UNCTAD is to be commended for its efforts to fill the gap left by the Bretton Woods institutions, it has neither the resources nor the remit to undertake its own data collection and must therefore rely heavily on the IMF for its primary data. As a result, most of the figures provided are inevitably estimated rather than measured, largely on the basis of flow data; and these estimates must be interpreted with some caution.

Cumulative Flow Estimates of FDI Stocks

In the 1997 edition of the *World Investment Report*, valuation-based data are provided for the stock of inward FDI in 1995 (in terms of book value or historical cost) for only ten developing countries:[18] Argentina, Bolivia, Brazil, Chile, El Salvador, Estonia, Korea, Peru, Poland and Venezuela. Reasonable approximations are made for three other developing countries (Pakistan, Singapore and South Africa) by adding net flows in 1995 to the stock at the end of 1994. For seventeen countries, the figure is estimated by adding subsequent net inflows to a measured stock figure for 1988, 1989 or 1990, which gives a much less reliable figure. For the remaining 123 developing countries for which estimates are given, the 1995 stock figures are estimates based purely on cumulative flows since reporting began. This was 1970 in 49 cases; later in the 1970s for 31 countries; in the 1980s for 18; and in the 1990s for 25 (mostly in Eastern Europe and the former Soviet Union).

Estimates based on cumulative flows of direct investment provide a starting point for assessing the value of investment stocks; but they cannot be regarded as an approximation, even where the flow data are complete and accurate (they often are not, as discussed in the next chapter), because they systematically tend to underestimate the true value of the stock.

Estimates based *only* on cumulative flow data (without any historical valuation) are particularly problematic, because they necessarily exclude any investments made before the period covered by the flow data. Even where this period begins in 1970 (the earliest point), the resulting discrepancy may be very substantial.

At first sight, investment prior to 1970 might appear to be of limited relevance to the current value of the stock of FDI, as most equipment installed by foreign investors prior to that date would by now be obsolete. However, this conclusion would be seriously misleading, for three reasons.

- Any property or land owned by foreign investors in 1970 would still be of substantial (and in most cases much greater) value.

- The same would apply, for example, to mineral rights, where these were granted over a sufficient period.

- In the case of capital equipment (and that of mineral rights), depreciation is deducted from recorded profits. This means that a company can reinvest in new equipment to an equivalent value without this being recorded as a new inflow of investment.

For these reasons cumulative flows since 1970 will underestimate the stock of inward FDI by an amount at least equivalent to the stock of investment at that date, and possibly substantially more. This is likely to be particularly important in the case of former colonies (such as those in sub-Saharan Africa) where there may have been substantial foreign-owned productive capacity prior to independence.

Even where estimates are based in part on an accurate past valuation of assets, the exclusion of subsequent capital gains will mean that the true value of the stock is likely to be underestimated, the discrepancy increasing with the length of the period since the last valuation. This problem is compounded by the fact that valuation is often made at historic cost (that is, the price paid for an asset) rather than at the current market price, so that all capital gains are effectively excluded.

The capital gains problem would seem to be particularly acute where direct investment is in the form of an equity stake in a company whose shares are traded on a stock exchange. Here, the whole value of the investment changes in accordance with its stock market valuation (which will generally increase the real value over the long term, although it is subject to strong fluctuations in the shorter term).

It is also important to bear in mind that data on direct investment flows are based the amount paid for the investment, rather than its true market value. This is particularly important where the price paid is substantially below the market value – as, for example, in the case of some privatisations, or where assets are purchased at 'fire-sale' prices due to economic problems (as recently in East Asia). This will result in the increase in the stock of investment being under-reported (although the capital flow itself will be correct), as the subsequent increase in the value of the assets will take the form of capital gains which are not recorded in the flow data.

Conversely, where a financial crisis such as that in East Asia substantially reduces the value of companies, productive facilities, property and shares, the resulting capital losses will reduce the stock of investment without being reflected in cumulative flow data. While this may be merely (as in the East Asian case) a reversal of previous increases in value, if investment took place disproportionately at the peak of market values, the result may be that cumulative flow estimates exaggerate the value of the FDI stock.

Other factors may also increase the value of investments over time, without being included either in capital flows or even in the valuation of assets. This applies particularly to 'goodwill' – a catch-all term used by accountants to cover the value to a firm of intangible assets such as relationships with customers and suppliers, local contacts or political influence. This is a very important part of the value of a company as a going concern, but does not appear to be included in the value of direct investment enterprises for balance of payments purposes. This will result in a growing discrepancy over time between the true value of the stock of direct investment and its estimated value as the value of goodwill increases.

A further discrepancy (though a less serious one) may arise from the reclassification of investments between portfolio equity investment and direct investment. As noted earlier, a purchase of up to 10 per cent of shares in a company is classified as portfolio investment, while a larger purchase is classified as direct investment. However, if an investor purchases, say, 5 per cent of the shares in one year and 10 per cent in the next, the original purchase is not reclassified as direct investment. This again suggests that the stock of direct investment will be underestimated by cumulative flow data. Still, such transactions are likely to be relatively limited in most developing countries; and the result is in principle a distortion of the balance between direct and portfolio investment liabilities rather than of the overall level of liabilities.

Another complication arises from non-equity financing of direct investment enterprises. Foreign affiliates may borrow money from one of three types of source:

- the parent company or its other affiliates (intra-company borrowing);

- other foreign sources; or

- sources within the host country (domestic borrowing).

Intra-company borrowing is treated (at least in theory) as part of the flow of direct investment; and the interest on such borrowing is treated in the same way as the profits on direct investment. The problem arises because the repayment of loans is regarded, in effect, as disinvestment – equivalent to the sale of that part of the investment financed by the loan, and the transfer of the proceeds out of the country. This means that, if the stock of investment is measured by the cumulative flow of capital on the FDI account, only the amount of the loan which has yet to be repaid is included.

This is illustrated in the first two parts of Table 5.3. For simplicity, we assume an investment of $100 million, financed equally by foreign equity and an intra-company loan. The rate of return on the investment is 20 per cent per annum, with no reinvestment, and the loan is repayable over five years at an interest rate of 10 per cent per annum. Because all of the profits are remitted, the actual value of the investment remains at $100 million throughout (assuming no capital gains or losses).

Table 5.3 • Non-Equity Financing and Cumulative Flow Estimates of the Stock of Direct Investment

		Year						
		0	1	2	3	4	5	6/later
1. Assumptions								
Value of investment		100	100	100	100	100	100	100
Gross profit	(= A)	0	20	20	20	20	20	20
Equity flow	(= B)	50	0	0	0	0	0	0
Lending	(= C)	50	0	0	0	0	0	0
Repayments	(= D)	0	10	10	10	10	10	0
Interest	(= E)	0	5	4	3	2	1	0
Net profit	(= A – D – E)	0	5	6	7	8	9	20
2. Intra-company loan (standard treatment)								
FDI flow	(= B + C – D)	100	-10	-10	-10	-10	-10	0
FDI stock (cumulative flow estimate)		100	90	80	70	60	50	50
FDI income	(= A – D)	0	10	10	10	10	10	20
Rate of return (%)		0	10	11	12.5	14	17	40
3. Intra-company loan (loan repayments as FDI income)								
FDI flow	(= B + C)	100	0	0	0	0	0	0
FDI stock (cumulative flow estimate)		100	100	100	100	100	100	100
FDI income	(= A)	0	20	20	20	20	20	20
Rate of return (%)		0	20	20	20	20	20	20
4. Other borrowing (foreign or domestic)								
FDI flow	(= B)	50	0	0	0	0	0	0
FDI stock (cumulative flow estimate)		50	50	50	50	50	50	50
FDI income	(= A – D – E)	0	5	6	7	8	9	20
Rate of return (%)		0	10	12	14	16	18	40

Notes: Assumptions are as described in the text.

However, while the full $100 million is initially included in the measured stock of investment, this declines progressively as the loan is repaid. Once the loan is fully repaid, the stock of investment is undervalued by the amount of the loan.[19] It should also be noted that the profits are underestimated until the loan is repaid, because the loan repayments are deducted. A truer picture would be obtained by counting repayments of intra-company loans as part of profit remittances, as shown in the third part of Table 5.1. Both the stock of investment and the income generated would then be accurate from the point of view of the country's foreign exchange liabilities. The underlying problem is that the measured direct investment flows in the balance of payments accounts are not designed to enable cumulative flows to be used directly to estimate the stock of investment. It is assumed that the stock position will be measured separately; but this is not done in practice.

In practice, intra-company loans are often not included in reported direct investment flows to developing countries. In most respects, this is not a serious problem – it simply means that investments financed by intra-company loans are treated in the same way as investments financed by other foreign borrowing. In the context of cumulative flow estimates of the stock of inward FDI, however, it *is* a problem. Foreign borrowing by direct investment enterprises (other than intra-company borrowing) is treated in the same way as borrowing by any other company. As a result, the debt appears as a liability until it is repaid; but the continuing liability arising from foreign ownership of the investment financed by the loan will not appear if the stock of FDI is calculated on the basis of cumulative flows. (Domestic borrowing is subject to essentially the same problem, except that the loan does not appear in the balance of payments at all.)

This is illustrated in the final part of Table 5.3. While the stock of investment, measured at $50 million throughout the period, initially corresponds with its net worth (that is, the value of the investment less its debts), this increases progressively as the debt is repaid, ultimately reaching $100 million. The result is that the stock of inward direct investment is undervalued.

As a result of all the considerations discussed above, even where accurate flow data are available it is almost inevitable that the stock of inward FDI in virtually all developing countries will be underestimated to a greater or lesser degree. The greater the reliance on flow data (the longer the period since the last actual valuation), and the shorter the period for which flow data are available where there is no past valuation, the greater this discrepancy is likely to be, and the more the true value is likely to be underestimated. In some cases, this undervaluation may be very considerable. Even in the few cases where reliable data are available, it could mean that the actual market value of the stock of direct investment is double the published figure.

6

Ignorance is Bliss II
Data on Capital Flows, Profits and FDI-Related Trade

Capital Flows

Apart from the considerations discussed in Chapter 5, cumulative flow estimates of the stock of FDI can only be as accurate as the flow data themselves; and these are also problematic in many cases. The 1997 *World Investment Report* records flow data as being estimated rather than measured for 51 countries in 1995, and for 11 of the same countries in 1994. Even where flows are 'measured', there are serious gaps in the data: apart from the shortcomings in data collection and coverage discussed in Chapter 5, the flow data for more than two-thirds of developing countries omit at least one of three financial components of direct investment (equity investment, reinvested earnings and intra-company loans) for part or all of the period. Even where they are included in the data, there is also a serious risk that reinvested earnings will be under-reported. The extent and implications of their exclusion and under-reporting are discussed in the section on profit data in this chapter.

There may also be serious problems of misreporting in the original (IMF) data on which the figures are based. According to an internal IMF paper on Uganda in 1997, 'Investigations into private transfers suggest that they incorporate a significant component of foreign direct investment (FDI), estimated at US$115 million in 1995/96' (IMF/World Bank 1997: 5, footnote 3). It was presumably the correction of this problem that led to the estimate of total FDI flows in 1993–5 being increased from $11 million to $264 million (World Bank 1997a; 1997e), and the estimated stock of investment at the end of 1995 (based on cumulative flows) from $23 million to $272 million (UNCTAD 1996; 1997b). This suggests that the total FDI inflow in this period was believed to be 2.7 per cent of annual export revenues when it was in fact 64.5 per cent.

Similarly, a footnote in a (published) IMF study notes that 'Thailand's data tend to understate substantially the share of FDI [in capital inflows], much of which appears to be recorded as inflows to the banking system' (Goldsbrough *et al.* 1996: 54, footnote 70). The historical data have not been amended since the publication of this paper. (The possible implications of this and other discrepancies in the Thai data are discussed in Appendix I.)

Even China, the largest developing country recipient of direct investment, is subject to serious data problems on FDI flows, this time in the opposite direction. According to a the Overseas Development Institute,

> The amounts [of FDI flows to China] reported are gross overestimates ... arising from the phenomenon of 'round tripping', whereby domestic money is funnelled out of the country and back in again to take advantage of tax breaks for foreign investors. A 1997 World Bank study pointed to a 37 per cent overestimation of total flows in 1994 plus a further 12 per cent as a result of the overvaluation of capital equipment contributed to joint ventures by foreign investors. (ODI 1997: 1)

At the time of writing, the official figures for FDI flows to China have not been revised in the light of the 1997 World Bank study. This suggests, not only that FDI flows to China in 1994 are overestimated by nearly half, but also that total flows to developing countries as a whole may be overestimated by as much as 15 per cent. Since the causes are not obviously specific to 1994, it seems likely that errors of a similar order of magnitude apply in other years.

On the other hand there also appears to be some degree of underreporting of FDI flows to China due to avoidance of the registration system, at least by Taiwanese investors. According to the *Economist*,[20] 'many small businessmen from Taiwan [aim] to avoid taxes by keeping their investments secret'.

It is impossible to tell how many other countries may suffer from similar data problems – but if round tripping and non-registration are possible in China, under one of the most extensively and, on the whole, effectively regulated economies, it is likely to be much easier in other countries. Only an assiduous reading of the footnotes to documents, including unpublished papers on unrelated subjects, has thrown up the Uganda and Thailand examples, neither of which is noted in any major statistical source on FDI.

If major revisions of historical data (usually unexplained) are a reliable indication, it appears that such discrepancies may be widespread. To take some extreme examples, between 1997 and 1998 the estimate of total FDI flows to Vietnam between 1991 and 1995 was increased from $331 million (2.4 per cent of GNP) to $3,279 million (24 per cent); that for flows to Guyana in 1992–5 from $6 million (1.8 per cent) to $398 million (117.1 per cent); and that for flows to Equatorial Guinea in 1995 from $1 million (0.7 per cent) to

Table 6.1 • The Global Discrepancy in Direct Investment Flow Data ($bn)												
	1985	1986	1987	1988	1989	1990	1991	1992	1993	1994	1995	1996
Recorded flows:												
Total credit	58.3	93.8	139.6	171.6	216.8	238.3	194.1	191.7	223.4	252.4	321.5	318.1
Total debit	51.0	76.1	122.2	150.4	190.5	200.8	154.8	169.2	217.3	237.0	332.6	330.8
(of which LDCs)	12.5	12.4	14.7	22.3	26.3	31.5	41.5	50.8	74.1	98.8	116.0	136.8
Discrepancy:												
$bn	7.3	17.7	17.4	21.2	26.3	37.5	39.3	22.5	6.1	15.4	−11.1	−12.7
% of total debit	14.3	23.3	14.2	14.1	13.8	18.7	25.4	13.3	2.8	6.5	−3.3	−3.8
% of LDC debit	58.4	142.7	118.4	95.1	100.0	119.0	94.7	44.3	8.2	15.6	−9.6	−9.3

Sources: IMF 1992; 1997a. LDCs = developing countries.

$127 million (84 per cent) (World Bank 1997a; 1998a). Again, such changes are neither highlighted nor explained, and their very existence is revealed only by a minute entry-by-entry comparison of successive editions of *Global Development Finance*.

A comparison with other data casts further doubt on the reliability of the published estimates of FDI flows. For example, UNCTAD (1997b: Annex Table B.7) provides figures for cross-border merger and acquisition transactions compiled by the accountancy group KPMG. In principle, the figures for mergers and acquisitions resulting in majority stakes for overseas investors should be included fully in FDI flow data;[21] and the latter should be at least as large, and generally substantially larger, as they also include elements such as smaller equity stakes (of 10–50 per cent), greenfield investment and upgrading of existing investments. Similarly, the sum of FDI flows and equity flows should be at least as large as total mergers and acquisitions.

In practice, however, this is not the case for a substantial number of developing countries; and in some cases the differences are considerable. Again to take some extreme examples, cross-border mergers and acquisitions resulting in majority stakes in Poland in 1992 are estimated at $2,545 million, compared with total recorded FDI inflows of $678 million; for Romania in 1993, the figures are $650 million and $94 million; for Pakistan in 1994, $1,730 million and $419 million; and for North Korea in 1995 $102 million and $1 million.[22]

Similar discrepancies arise between the figures for total mergers and acquisitions and the total of the official figures for direct and equity investment in the corresponding years. In principle, the former figure should always be at least as much as the latter, but this is by no means always the case – and again the discrepancy is often considerable. In Russia in 1993–5, for example, the figures were respectively $23.3 billion and $3.1 billion; for Sri Lanka in 1995, they were $2,873 million and $117 million; for Azerbaijan in 1996 they were $5,330 million and $601 million; for Kazakhstan in 1996 they were $1,551 million and $310 million; and for Myanmar in 1995 they were $632 million and $115 million. These figures also suggest that even the revised figures for Vietnam cited above remain substantially too low: total mergers and acquisitions in 1993–5 are estimated at $7,198 million, compared with revised figures for total direct and equity investment over the same period of $3,190 million.

The overall scale of the problems in FDI flow data can be gauged from the discrepancy between measured inflows and outflows of direct investment for the world as a whole. In principle, the two should be equal, because every country's outflow of FDI should be an inflow for another country. In practice, however, this is not the case. Rather, as shown in Table 6.1, total outflows exceeded total inflows in every year from at least 1985 until 1992.

It seems more likely that the outflow figure is correct, because measurement problems arise primarily in the developing countries, which were of very limited importance as a source of FDI during the relevant period. There is little obvious reason to expect 'phantom' FDI outflows from host countries – and still less to expect these to outweigh any under-recording of actual outflows (as discussed below). This would seem to suggest that the global figure for outflows is, if anything, a conservative estimate of the actual volume of direct investment flows.

On this basis, the global discrepancy would appear to suggest an undervaluation of global FDI inflows of between 13 and 25 per cent in each year from 1985 until 1992. In practice, however, it seems likely that the errors will arise disproportionately in developing countries, because of their generally much weaker data collection systems, so that this is a minimum likely error for developing countries. If we make the opposite extreme assumption – that the whole discrepancy arises in developing countries, the margin of error over this period rises to 44–143 per cent (and the upper half of this range in all but two years). This suggests that actual direct investment flows to developing countries in this period may have been in the order of 50 per cent above reported levels[23] – but with a very large margin of error on either side.

As noted above, the discrepancy has fallen markedly in the 1990s, and was roughly zero on aggregate in 1993–6. However, the negative figure in 1995–6 should be treated with some caution. First, there is no reason to expect direct investment inflows to be over-reported in aggregate. A negative discrepancy therefore seems more likely to reflect an underestimation of outflows than an overestimation of inflows. If this underestimation also occurred in earlier years, the extent of the error will be greater than that suggested above.

Second, the latest figures in each year's *Balance of Payments Statistics Yearbook* are necessarily preliminary, and subject to subsequent revision. A comparison of the 1996 and 1997 editions suggests that these revisions may reduce or reverse initial negative discrepancies: the discrepancy for 1995 was reduced from −$19.2 billion to −$11.0 billion, and that for 1994 was reversed from −$3.2 billion to +$15.4 billion. Moreover, in both years the estimates of both global inflows and global outflows were increased (by a total of $22 billion and $49 billion respectively). Similar adjustments would roughly neutralise the negative discrepancies in 1995–6.

Finally, it should also be noted that not all of the errors in the estimation of inflows will necessarily be captured in outflow estimates from source countries, and that the latter are also likely to underestimate the total amount of global FDI by a significant margin. As in the case of FDI inflows, reinvested profits are often omitted from outflow data. Countries for which this is the case include Japan (until 1995), France, Italy, Belgium–Luxembourg, Austria and Norway (until 1994),[24] as well as almost all developing countries. These countries accounted for 45–60 per cent of FDI flows excluding reinvestment in each year from 1985 to 1993, falling to 31 per cent in 1996 (partly due to the incorporation of data from Japan). If the excluded countries' share in reinvested profits were the same as their share in other FDI throughout the period, this would imply total FDI flows around 20 per cent higher than the recorded outflows on average in each year between 1985 and 1996. Since there is no reason to expect this discrepancy to be concentrated in flows to developing (or to developed) countries, this would suggest an additional 20 per cent increase in their inflows.

Other sources of error are less easy to quantify.

- Many countries do not report outward FDI at all; and, while most of these are unlikely to be the source of significant outflows, some may well be – for example, Malaysia, Mexico, Greece and (until 1993) Indonesia.

- Some major source countries (notably Germany) use ownership thresholds greater than 10 per cent.

- As on the inflow side, there is a risk that, even where reinvested profits are included in the data, they may be under-reported.

These sources of error are almost certainly smaller than the exclusion of reinvestment, but they point consistently towards further under-estimation.

Profits, Remittances and Reinvestment

There is also a serious risk that the profits of direct investment enterprises may be under-reported. Such enterprises have a clear incentive to under-report their profits as a means of avoiding taxation; and weak or under-resourced tax administrations may have a limited ability to prevent this occurring. Profit repatriation should, in principle, be relatively easy to measure, as it entails a foreign exchange transaction; but liberalisation of exchange restrictions and FDI régimes (as in the relaxation or removal of registration requirements) may impede this process.

It may be still easier to under-report reinvested or retained profits, as these remain within the direct investment enterprise, if the regulatory and tax régimes are sufficiently weak to enable enterprises to get away with this. Moreover, reinvested profits are often not included in the balance of

Table 6.2 • The Global Discrepancy in Direct Investment Income Data ($bn)												
	1985	1986	1987	1988	1989	1990	1991	1992	1993	1994	1995	1996
Recorded flows:												
Total credit	50.5	59.4	80.1	102.8	113.7	120.4	107.7	109.7	125.9	158.4	203.8	220.1
Total debit	44.8	44.8	55.2	74.3	72.9	77.8	62.4	70.9	85.5	112.4	167.0	175.6
(of which LDCs)	15.0	12.9	13.8	14.9	19.1	22.3	22.9	25.4	27.9	31.8	44.1	49.2
Discrepancy:												
$bn	5.7	14.6	24.9	28.5	40.8	42.6	45.3	38.8	40.4	46.0	36.8	44.5
% of total debit	12.7	32.6	45.1	38.4	56.0	54.8	72.6	54.7	47.3	40.9	22.0	25.3
% of LDC debit	38.0	113.2	180.4	191.3	213.6	191.0	197.8	152.8	144.8	144.7	83.4	90.4

Sources: IMF 1992; 1997a LDCs = developing countries.

payments accounts either as income or as investment. This means that both the flow of FDI and the profits on it will be underestimated, as, in consequence, will the stock of inward FDI, where this is estimated on the basis of cumulative flows. Since the discrepancy will be greater relative to profits than relative to the stock of investment, the rate of return will also be underestimated.

In general, overall net foreign exchange effects will not be affected in the short term. In the case of China, however, reinvested profits were included in new investment, but not in income on direct investment (until 1995), suggesting that the net foreign exchange effect is substantially inflated (IMF 1997a: Part 3, 157–8). The correction of this discrepancy illustrates the potential scale of the problem. China's reported FDI profits averaged $15 million per annum in 1988–92, rising to $231 million in 1993 and $400 million (less than 0.1 per cent of GDP) in 1994 (IMF 1997a). When reinvested profits started to be included in 1995, reported profits increased to $9,953 million, rising further to $11,679 million in 1996 (about 1.5 per cent of GDP in each year). The figures for earlier years still have not been amended.

In many instances, income on FDI is not reported at all, or only with a long time-lag; and this occurs even in some countries where FDI is substantial relative to the size of the economy. For example, no data are available for profits on inward FDI in Singapore, Guyana, Equatorial Guinea or the Gambia; and the final years of data are 1991 for Thailand, and 1992 for Togo.

As in the case of FDI inflows, some assessment of the scale of under-reporting of income on FDI can be made by comparing the data for total recorded global inflows and total recorded global outflows. This is done in Table 6.2. The discrepancy is substantially greater, and shows a much more marked pattern over time, than in the case of capital flows. It remains substantially positive throughout the period, increasing rapidly from $5.7 billion in 1985 to $40.8 billion in 1989, and remaining within a range of $37–46 billion per annum thereafter. The initial growth of the discrepancy is much faster than that of recorded outflows, either globally or from developing countries. As a result, the discrepancy increases from 13 per cent of total outflows in 1985 to a peak of 73 per cent in 1991, before falling back to 22–25 per cent in 1995–6. Relative to reported outflows from developing countries, it increases from 38 per cent to a peak of 214 per cent in 1989, falling to 83–90 per cent in 1995–6.

If we again consider the two extreme positions of the margin of error being equal in developed and developing countries, and the discrepancy arising entirely in the latter, this suggests that actual outflows of income on FDI from developing countries may be roughly double the reported levels on aggregate.[25] However, a substantial part of this (perhaps a quarter) is likely to arise from China.

Again, a comparison of the 1996 and 1997 editions of the *Balance of Payments Statistics Yearbook* suggests that future revisions might well increase the discrepancy in 1995–6, as both the 1994 and 1995 discrepancies were adjusted upwards by about $3 billion. As in the case of FDI flows, the credit figures were increased in both years as well as the debit figures (by $1 billion in 1994 and $9 billion in 1995), suggesting a larger upward adjustment in the level of FDI income outflows.

As in the case of FDI flows, the exclusion of reinvested profits from the data supplied by source countries means that the credit figures are likely to understate the true value of FDI income by a significant margin. A number of significant FDI source countries do not provide any data on direct investment income. These include Austria, Denmark, Singapore, Kuwait, and for historical data Belgium–Luxembourg (until 1994), Portugal (until 1992), Austria and Italy (both until 1988). In total, these countries accounted for around 5–10 per cent of total recorded FDI flows excluding reinvestment in each year from 1985 to 1996.[26] Other countries not providing data on reinvestment (as listed earlier in this chapter) account for 5–10 per cent of remitted profits during the same period. Correcting for these two sources of error therefore suggests that actual outflows of FDI profits may have been about a further 15 per cent above the recorded level.

Again, further upward adjustment would also need to be made for countries which use ownership thresholds above 10 per cent for FDI outflows, and for under-reporting of reinvested profits where these are included in the data; but these are not readily quantifiable.

Hidden Profits: Transfer Price Manipulation

As well as the underestimation or misreporting of profits, there is a risk that profits will be concealed by transfer price manipulation. By overpricing purchases from, and/or underpricing sales to, other parts of the same firm, a corporation can conceal profits made in a particular affiliate or transfer resources invisibly between its operations in different countries. This is illegal under most countries' tax regulations; but the ability to enforce such legislation is heavily dependent on the capacity of the tax administration, which is often limited in developing countries.

Transfer price manipulation is generally regarded as being widespread among transnational corporations. This was unquestionably the case in the past: Tang (1979; 1981) found that 92 per cent of US, 73 per cent of

Japanese, 85 per cent of Canadian and 79 per cent of British transnationals surveyed admitted to using some transfer price manipulation in the late 1970s. However, recent attempts to measure its significance have been very limited; and estimating the extent of over- and underpricing is problematic. As a result, 'we still remain largely ignorant about the actual transfer-pricing practices of TNCs and their possible deviation from prices that would prevail between unrelated parties' (Plasschaert 1996: 396).

The potential for corporations to manipulate transfer prices arises from the importance of intra-firm trade (that is, trade between different parts of the same corporation located in different countries). By controlling both ends of the transaction (the decision to purchase and the decision to sell), a transnational corporation with some degree of centralisation in its decision-making processes can effectively decide on what prices to apply to intra-firm transactions without regard to market prices.

The scale of intra-firm trade, both in imports and in exports, is very considerable – generally put at around 40 per cent of total world trade, implying a substantially larger proportion of the international transactions of transnational corporations. While these figures will vary considerably between sectors, investors and types of investment, they are likely to be substantial in most cases. For foreign affiliates of US-based TNCs, for example, intra-firm trade accounts for an average of 64 per cent of their total exports and 85.5 per cent of total imports; and only in the case of mining sector exports does the figure fall significantly below 50 per cent[27] (see Table 6.3.)

Table 6.3 • Shares of Intra-Firm Trade in Exports and Imports of Foreign Affiliates of US Firms, 1993 (per cent)

Sector	Exports	Imports
Petroleum	47.3	75.8
Mining	15.5	79.2
Manufacturing	74.2	82.5
Wholesale trade	57.0	93.4
All industries	64.0	85.5

Source: UNCTAD 1996: 104, Table IV.2.

Such high proportions of intra-firm trade mean that relatively small, and even undetectable, deviations of transfer prices from market prices can permit significant resource transfers. Based on the average figures in Table 6.1, for a company exporting all its output and with imported inputs equivalent to 50 per cent of its sales, a 1 per cent deviation could effect a resource transfer of 1.5 per cent of its turnover. Since market prices are often difficult to evaluate with any degree of accuracy, particularly where goods are traded only within the company (components or part-completed products in assembly operations, for example), even substantial deviations are often difficult to detect.

The classical explanations of transfer price manipulation cite the avoidance of taxation and of foreign exchange restrictions – they hypothesise that corporations price their intra-firm trade in such a way that their profits are concentrated in those countries which tax them the least, or as a means of transferring their profits out of countries from which they would otherwise be unable to remit them to the parent company. Reductions in corporate taxation, the widespread provision of generous tax concessions to foreign investors, and the relaxation of foreign exchange restrictions (particularly for foreign investors) in developing countries since the 1980s would imply a dramatic reduction in transfer price manipulation.

However, there are a number of other motivations for transfer price manipulation whose significance is less likely to have diminished significantly. In particular, it may be seen as desirable to limit the apparent rate of profit in a particular country, for example

- to avoid allegations of monopoly profits (which might lead to investigation or strengthened regulation);

- to protect the company's popular image in the country (the weakening of which could affect sales, or give rise to vandalism in politically unstable situations) or internationally;

- to retain political support or goodwill;

- to limit pressure for wage increases from the workforce;

- to avoid pressure from communities in which the company operates to support social or environmental projects; or

- to legitimise price increases in the local market (especially, but not only, where there are price controls).

Transfer price manipulation can also be used to avoid anti-dumping restrictions (measures by importing countries to prevent or retaliate against the sale of exports at prices below their production cost as a means of securing a foothold in the market or to drive out competitors). By underpricing inputs bought from other parts of the company, production costs can be made to appear lower, so that exports which are in fact being dumped appear to be sold at a profit. This could also occur in the case of sales within domestic markets: by underpricing inputs, a transnational company can reduce its apparent production costs as a means of undercutting domestic producers, in order either to drive them out of the market, or to weaken their financial position as a prelude to taking them over.

In either of these cases, a transfer of profits will be a by-product of the process; and it will result in an over-reporting of profits in the country where the final product is produced, and a corresponding under-reporting in the country where the inputs are produced. It should be noted, however, that there will also be harmful long-term effects in the country where the goods are being sold, due to the reduction of competition. Equally, transfer price manipulation can be used more positively – to bolster an ailing affiliate, for example, when the country in which it operates is encountering economic difficulties – but this will necessarily occur at the expense of other affiliates (or the parent company).

Clearly, transfer price manipulation will not always occur at the expense of developing countries. It can in principle be used to transfer profits into, out of, or between developing countries. However, the differences in the effectiveness of tax administrations between developing and developed countries are likely to skew the effects: developed countries are generally much better equipped than developing countries for the complex and resource-intensive task of preventing transnational companies' profits being transferred out of their reach by transfer price manipulation.

Given the lamentable lack of systematic evidence on the current scale and extent of transfer price manipulation, all that can be said with certainty is that it makes reported profit figures unreliable; but the general perception is that the net effect on developing countries is likely to be negative. The limited evidence which is available is consistent with this view, showing both over-pricing of imports (in some cases in excess of 100 per cent) and more limited underpricing of exports (see, for example, Dunning 1993: 512–24; Plasschaert 1996.) However, these results need to be treated with some caution, as they are based on data which are now quite old, and the situation has changed substantially in the interim in some important respects (notably relative tax rates and foreign exchange restrictions). It cannot therefore be assumed that these findings are representative of the current situation. There is also likely to be some selectivity in the results: cases where transfer price manipulation is thought to be occurring are more likely to be investigated; and the results are more likely to be seen as worth publishing, and to gain wider attention, than negative results. Nonetheless, the evidence does suggest that historically transfer price manipulation has been both widespread and in some cases on a substantial scale.

As noted above, even transfer price manipulation on a scale too small to be readily detected could distort reported profits significantly. The potential importance of such effects is demonstrated by an investigation by the British Monopolies Commission (1973) into Hoffman–La Roche's UK subsidiary between 1966 and 1972. This found that 76 per cent of the profits accruing on the investment took the form of transfer price manipulation, and that a further 12 per cent was in the form of contributions to the company's research and development spending. This suggests that the actual profits were around seven times the reported figure.

If transnational corporations are indeed using transfer price manipulation to transfer profits out of their operations in developing countries, then recorded figures for profits and remittances will understate the true picture, and possibly by a very considerable margin. (Reinvested profits will not be affected.) This in turn would imply that rates of return will also be understated. Brandt and Giddy (1977) found that the average rate of return for foreign-owned enterprises in Brazil in 1974 was increased by about one-fifth when the effects of transfer price manipulation were corrected.

FDI-Related Trade

Data on the trade of direct investment enterprises are not included in standard statistical sources. Estimates are occasionally reported for selected countries, but are often incomplete and/or very approximate. An example is UNCTAD (1997b), Table II.9, which attempts to estimate the balance of payments effects of FDI on China, Malaysia, Singapore and Thailand in 1990–5.[28] For Thailand, no trade figures are available. For Singapore, the only figures available are for manufacturing sector exports in 1990–2. For Malaysia, the estimates used are from a non-official source for 1990–2, and figures for subsequent years are estimated assuming the continuation of past growth trends. Only for China are the figures complete, and then only from 1992.

Even where data are available and accurate,[29] the exports and imports of direct investment enterprises are only part of the data needed to assess the effect of FDI on the balance of trade. As discussed in Chapter 7, it is also necessary to know to what extent domestic sales substitute for imports. This is (understandably) not included in routinely published statistics. More surprisingly, perhaps, it does not appear to have been the subject of systematic empirical research.

Conclusion: What Do We Know about Stocks of Inward FDI?

While the availability and quality of data for the public sector debts of developing countries has improved considerably over the last 10–20 years, we have little reliable information on the scale of private sector external liabilities, and especially on direct and equity investment. The World Bank publishes no data on the stocks of direct and equity investment in its major statistical sources – not even in those, such as *Global Development Finance*, to which it is of direct relevance. The IMF publishes data for only a handful of developing countries; these are sometimes out of date and in many cases appear to be of questionable reliability.

UNCTAD's heroic efforts to fill the data gap for stocks of direct investment are constrained by their reliance on primary data from the IMF; and methodological and measurement problems mean that the estimates they provide would almost certainly understate the true scale of external obligations substantially overall, even if data on capital inflows were reliable, which is unlikely to be the case. Rather, data on FDI flows are themselves likely to be substantially underestimated (as are those for profits); and this will add to the underestimation of stocks.

It is not obvious that any very great effort is underway to improve this situation. Nor is there evidence of any resolve to rectify the almost complete lack of data on the stock of inward equity investment, despite its dramatically increasing importance, both as a source of capital flows and as a source of financial instability.

Both the inadequacy of the published data and the very limited efforts to improve it may well be attributable – as in the case of public sector debt in the 1970s – to a failure to appreciate its potential significance. In the case of equity investment and private sector debt, the significance should have become apparent following the East Asian financial crisis, and improvements may conceivably follow.

The lack of information on the scale of external liabilities was an important factor contributing to the debt crisis of the 1980s, because lenders were insufficiently aware of the external liabilities of the countries to which they were lending. The same may be true for investors in and lenders to the private sector in developing countries today.

7

The Foreign Exchange Dimension
General Principles

Why Foreign Exchange Effects Matter

The availability of foreign exchange in a country is one of the key constraints on a developing economy, limiting both economic policies and the potential for economic growth. Over the long term, there must be as much foreign exchange coming into the economy in the form of export earnings and net capital inflows as there is going out to pay for imports, to service foreign debts, and to meet other commitments. It may be possible to sustain a net outflow for some time by drawing on foreign exchange reserves, but ultimately these will run out. This means that the level of imports which can be sustained is determined by export revenues and capital inflows, less debt-service outflows, profit remittances on FDI, and other payments.

Imports are indispensable to developing countries because they are unable to produce all the goods they need. Almost all developing countries need to import much of the equipment needed for investment, and other critical goods such as essential drugs. They also need to import many consumer goods and, in some cases, basic foods. Production is also dependent on imported inputs such as components in industry, and fertilisers and other agrochemicals in agriculture.

The constraint on the sustainable level of imports is important in two key respects. First, imports increase as the economy grows, as people have more money to spend. The import constraint therefore limits the pace at which the economy can grow. Second, when the availability of foreign exchange is reduced due to a reduction in export prices (as for many commodity-dependent countries in the 1980s and early 1990s) or a reduction in the availability of foreign loans (as after 1982), imports have to be reduced, often very dramatically. This means either that the level of demand has to be reduced, which generally means lowering living standards; or that demand has to be switched from imports to domestically produced goods (usually by devaluing the exchange rate, which makes imports more expensive). In either case, the reduction in imports is potentially very disruptive to the economy.

According to the proponents of direct investment, one of its major advantages over foreign borrowing is that it generates foreign exchange outflows only if profits are made on the investment. It seems often to be assumed (though generally implicitly rather than explicitly) that this ensures that FDI will not give rise to balance of payments problems.

However, there are two flaws in this view. First, as discussed in Chapter 12, the basic assumption that profits can be remitted only if profits are made, does not always seem to accord with reality. Second, even if an investment is profitable, there is no assurance that it will generate sufficient additional foreign exchange earnings to off-set the repatriation of profits.

Investigating this second issue requires an assessment of all the direct and indirect effects of direct investment on the host country's foreign exchange earnings and expenditure. Accordingly, this chapter establishes some general principles for assessing these effects, and a framework within which they can be considered; and the next produces some simple numerical simulations to illustrate the possible effects.

Types and Phases of Investment

As with any other economic issue, a key question in assessing the effects of direct and equity investment is the counterfactual – what would have happened if the investment had not occurred. When considering individual investments, the implicit counterfactual varies between the different types of investment distinguished in Chapter 2.

- In the case of *direct investment through construction (FDI(C))* – that is, where new productive capacity is created – the counterfactual is that the investment would not have been made in the absence of FDI. (However, this assumption needs to be considered in the light of the relationship between FDI and overall investment, as discussed in Chapter 9.)

- In the case of *direct investment by purchase (FDI(P))* – that is, the purchase from local owners of existing productive capacity, or of enough shares in a company to influence its production decisions – the counterfactual is that the company or facility concerned would have remained in local ownership, and continued to operate as it did before the purchase (that is, that no changes would have occurred after the time of purchase). It should be noted that this is a substantial simplification, as productive behaviour could be expected to evolve over time irrespective of ownership.

- In the case of portfolio equity investment – the purchase of shares in a company insufficient to confer influence over production decisions – it is assumed that the shares would have remained in local hands, but that the operations of the company are unaffected (that is, that the same changes would have occurred after the time of purchase).

The foreign exchange effects of direct investment also vary over time. In particular, it is important to distinguish between three distinct phases:

- the investment phase, when the investment is actually being made (the period during which the production facility is being built, or the point at which shares, a company or a production facility are bought);

- the production phase, when the investment is operational and in foreign ownership; and

- possibly a disinvestment phase, when the investment is sold to a local owner or liquidated.

This is something of an oversimplification, in that investment may well continue in parallel with production, to expand or modernise the production process. In addition, foreign exchange effects are likely to evolve over the course of the production phase, as the investment matures. For example, profits are likely to rise over time as efficiency improves and markets are developed; and local inputs may be substituted for imports, as domestic producers respond to the demand generated by the investment. Nonetheless, this is useful as a conceptual distinction.

Types of Foreign Exchange Effect

In each phase, the foreign exchange effects of direct investment can be seen as occurring on five levels.

- *Direct foreign exchange effects.* In investing and producing in a host country, investors transfer foreign exchange into the country to make the investment, earn foreign exchange for exports, spend foreign exchange on imported inputs, and transfer foreign exchange out of the country in the form of profit remittances and to service any foreign debts they may have incurred to finance the investment.

- *Substitution effects.* Some of the local sales of the TNC operation may sub-stitute for imports, so that the foreign exchange which would otherwise have been spent on the imports is saved. Conversely, some of the local inputs which are used might otherwise have been exported, so that the foreign exchange these exports would have earned is lost; or they might otherwise have substituted directly for imports, so that foreign exchange needs to be spent on additional imports when they are diverted to the TNC.

- *Feed-through effects.* The locally produced material inputs which are used by the TNC are themselves likely to require imports, import substitutes or exportable goods in their production, so that they have some foreign exchange cost to the economy as a whole. This is a continuous process: the locally produced inputs required to produce the TNC's locally produced inputs will also have some foreign exchange content, and so on. In addition, workers are likely to spend part of their income on imports; the locally produced goods they buy will have some foreign exchange content; and the recipients of the income generated by their local purchases will spend part of it on imports.

- *Macroeconomic effects.* The foreign exchange effects of the investment, coupled with effects on incomes, savings, domestic investment and domestic borrowing, will have an effect on the overall economy; and this in turn will affect economic policies on taxation, government spending, interest rates and the exchange rate. Both the effects on economic perfor-mance and the associated changes in economic policies will have knock-on effects on the balance of payments.

- *Global market effects.* Direct investment as a whole may have effects on global markets, which in turn affect developing countries generally, as well as the individual host countries. To the extent that direct investment increases the global production of a particular good which is traded inter-nationally, or reduces its production costs, the resulting increase in supply can be expected to reduce its price in the world market. This in turn will reduce the export revenues of other exporting countries and producers, and lower the prices paid by importing countries and consumers.

There is an important distinction between the first three of these effects and the last two. The first three effects relate essentially to an individual investment – the inputs it uses, the profits it generates and the location of its sales. Macroeconomic effects, by contrast, represent overall effects of direct investment in a particular country *as a whole*. While different investments may contribute to this process in different ways, or to different extents, the individual components are much more difficult to disaggregate. Similarly, global market effects relate to the overall investment in a particular sector throughout the world.

Accordingly, the first three effects (hereafter referred to as *immediate foreign exchange effects*) are considered together in Chapter 8, while global market effects are left until Chapter 10.

Macroeconomic effects are not considered in detail here. Essentially, these come down to two elements:

- the effects on the overall level of demand in the economy (and thus the demand for imports); and

- the knock-on effects of the balance of payments effects on the exchange rate (and thus on the production of exports and the consumption of imports).

These questions are sidestepped here by, in effect, modifying the question. As noted at the beginning of this chapter, the foreign exchange effects of direct and equity investment (or of other capital flows) are important because of the trade-off between the balance of payments and economic growth. The faster the economy grows, the faster the growth of imports; but there is a limit to how fast imports can grow without causing balance of payments problems. Where this limit lies depends on export earnings, capital inflows and the cost of servicing foreign liabilities.

Against this background, the relevant question is not the overall impact of direct investment on the balance of payments, but rather its effect on the balance of payments *for a given level of income and a given rate of economic growth*. If economic growth is an object of policy, then to regard the deterioration in the balance of payments which necessarily results from growth as a bad thing is inconsistent. Rather, the question is whether FDI improves or worsens the trade-off between economic growth and the balance of payments – that is, whether it tightens or relaxes the foreign exchange constraint on growth.

A similar logic can be applied in the case of exchange rate effects. An improvement in the overall net foreign exchange position will generally increase the exchange rate, and vice versa, so that the two can almost be regarded as synonymous.

What we are really interested in, therefore, is not so much the foreign exchange position as the foreign exchange position *for a given level of income and the exchange rate*. Posing the question in this way enables us to set aside foreign exchange effects which operate through changes in economic growth and the exchange rate.

Investment in Existing Capacity

The foreign exchange effect of the investment phase, whether of direct or portfolio equity investment, differs greatly between investment in existing capacity (equity investment in existing shares and direct investment through purchase) and investment which creates new capacity. The former entails a direct transfer of foreign exchange to the local seller of the shares or other assets involved; and the overall foreign exchange effect depends on what the recipient does with the proceeds. On average, some of the proceeds are likely to constitute foreign exchange outflows from the economy, so that the net foreign exchange effect will be less than the amount paid for the shares.

There are various ways in which the proceeds may be used.

• If they are invested locally in existing productive capacity (through the purchase of other local shares, or of production facilities), or saved in local currency (deposited in a local bank), they will remain wholly in the local economy, and the inward transfer of foreign exchange will remain equal to the original investment. In the former case, however, the seller of the shares or production facilities may also transfer some of the proceeds abroad, in which case there will be some indirect leakage of foreign exchange out of the economy.

• If the proceeds are invested locally in new capacity (by building new production facilities, for example) this is likely to entail some imports of capital equipment, reducing the initial net transfer. However, the longer-term effect will depend on what is produced: there should be a continuing net foreign exchange gain if the investment produces exports or import substitutes; but a net outflow (due to the purchase of imported inputs) if the investment is in non-tradeable goods or services.

• If the proceeds are invested in another country, the initial inflow will be neutralised, but there may be a continuing net inflow of income on the investment in the future. However, this will occur only if the income is ultimately repatriated to the host country of the original investment and converted into local currency, which will by no means necessarily be the case.

• If the proceeds are spent on locally produced consumption goods, there will be some outward transfer, equivalent to their import content (plus the profits of TNC producers).

- If the proceeds are spent on imported consumption goods, the foreign exchange will simply be transferred back out of the country, and the net inflow will be zero.

In aggregate, the proceeds of direct investment by purchase and equity investment in existing shares will be spent on a combination of these elements, although it seems likely that investment (the first three of the above options) will predominate. Since none of the possibilities increases the initial inward transfer, while most reduce it, the net transfer will necessarily be less than the amount paid for the shares.

Portfolio equity investment as part of a privatisation programme can be considered as similar in financial terms to the purchase of existing shares during the investment phase, except that the shares are sold by the government rather than by a private investor. This means that the proceeds may be used to relieve the government's fiscal constraint, and thus to increase government spending. This may have some import content, which would reduce the initial capital inflow without any direct effect on future foreign exchange earnings. (While productivity increases due to improvements in health services, education, infrastructure or administrative efficiency may have a significant indirect effect, this benefit is likely to accrue only over a very long period.)

Nonetheless, provided the government's priorities are appropriate, the imports should be of high social value; and the developmental benefits of relieving a severe fiscal constraint, such as exists in many low-income countries in particular, are likely to outweigh the importance of this leakage substantially. This does not mean that the net effects of foreign equity investments in the context of privatisation are positive; but it does suggest that the costs may be less than the very high rate of return on equity investments would imply.[30]

An exception will arise to the extent that privatisation proceeds are used to finance external debt-service payments which would otherwise not have been made (or not until later).

- If the debt service would otherwise not have been paid at all (as is likely to be the case in many of the highly indebted poor countries),[31] the foreign exchange inflow is simply lost.

- If the debt-service payment would otherwise have been made later, there will be a net cost over the long term, to the extent that the rate of return on the equity investment is greater than that on the debt it replaces. Effectively, using privatisation in this way is simply a potentially expensive way of refinancing foreign debts.

Investment in New Capacity

The use of direct or equity investment to create new productive capacity is very different from its employment in the purchase of new capacity. Rather than simply being paid to a local owner, the capital invested is used to finance the costs of construction, the installation of equipment and other productive components. The foreign exchange effects therefore need to be assessed differently.

Figure 7.1 provides a framework for considering these effects. The left-hand side shows the various sources of financing for direct investment through construction. As well as equity capital from the parent company (which may include the accumulated profits of existing operations), these may include intra-company loans, other external borrowing, and local borrowing. The first three will bring in foreign exchange (FE), while the last is in local currency (LC). In the case of portfolio equity investment, only equity financing is involved.

Figure 7.1 • Foreign Exchange Effects of Direct and Equity Investment in New Capacity: the Investment Phase

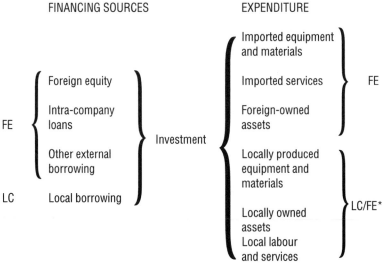

LC = Local currency costs.
FE = Foreign exchange costs.
*As discussed in the text, these elements will entail some indirect foreign exchange costs if the recipients spend some of the payments on imports.

The right-hand side of Figure 7.1 shows the uses of these funds. Part of the money invested goes directly into foreign exchange expenditure on imports of equipment, materials (construction materials, for example) and services (consultancy services, specialised services required to instal and operationalise equipment, and so on). The purchase of foreign-owned assets such as land and buildings also effectively constitutes foreign exchange expenditure; and there may also be other foreign exchange costs such as relocation allowances for expatriate staff.

Local currency expenditure includes wages for local labour (in work such as construction and the installation of equipment) and purchases of locally produced equipment and materials, locally provided services and locally owned assets. However, there may be some foreign exchange component of spending on local goods and services, to the extent that they have some import content; and there may be some loss of foreign exchange earnings if they would otherwise have been exported. The foreign exchange content of inputs will generally be greater where they are purchased from TNCs rather than locally owned companies, both because their profits constitute a foreign exchange cost and because they tend to use more imports in production. In addition, payments to local workers and for the purchase of locally owned assets are likely to entail some indirect foreign exchange costs, to the extent that the recipients spend the money on imports.

Disinvestment

Whether the investment takes place through purchase or construction, the production facility will remain in foreign ownership, and the income on it will constitute a foreign exchange cost, until such time as it is sold to a local investor. At this stage, the capital flow will be reversed: to buy the shares, the local investor will have to transfer foreign exchange back out of the economy. Since the foreign investor will then realise the capital gain on the investment, the amount transferred is likely to be much greater than the amount originally invested.

The potential for this transfer to be off-set by leakages back into the economy is much more limited than for initial outward leakages: only if the foreign exchange is used to import goods from the host country will the net outward transfer be reduced, and even then the reduction will be limited by the foreign exchange content of the goods purchased. (Investment in the local economy will merely defer the outward transfer until the new investment is sold.)

However, the counterfactual is again important: the money used to buy the shares would otherwise have been used in some other way; and the effect of this spending not taking place needs to be taken into account in assessing the overall foreign exchange effects. The possible alternative uses are essentially the same as for the money originally paid for investment in existing capacity, as outlined earlier – local investment in existing or new productive capacity, savings in local currency, investment abroad with or without repatriation of income, or the purchase of locally produced or imported consumer goods. The foreign exchange effects of each component are essentially the same in each case, although the balance between the various items may be different.

The Production Phase: Direct Investment

Figure 7.2 sets out a framework for assessing the foreign exchange effects of direct investment during the production phase.

- Company expenditure in local currency is limited to labour (excluding expatriate workers), interest payments on debts in local currency, and purchases from local firms and other TNC operations located in the country (net of their import content and profit remittances). Once again, wage payments may have some indirect foreign exchange effect to the extent that they are spent on imports. Conversely, any money spent by expatriate workers on locally produced goods and services (net of their foreign exchange content) will remain in the host country economy.

- On the receipts side, exports generate foreign exchange earnings for the company, while sales to the local market are in local currency. However, some of the local sales may substitute for imports, which would otherwise have had to be paid for in foreign exchange. From the perspective of the economy as a whole, these constitute a saving of foreign exchange.

    Thus even if the entire output of a TNC operation is exported or substitutes for imports, it is only the amount paid for local inputs (including wages and local debt servicing, but excluding the foreign exchange content of material inputs) and taxes which actually represent a net gain in the foreign exchange position of the wider economy. The less output is exported or substitutes for imports, the smaller the net gain becomes, becoming negative when the foreign exchange costs exceed exports and import substitution.

    Where foreign direct investment creates new productive capacity, all the foreign exchange receipts and expenditures in Figure 7.2 represent foreign exchange effects of FDI. However, where FDI takes the form of foreign purchases of existing productive capacity, its foreign exchange effects are

Figure 7.2 • Foreign Exchange Effects of Direct Investment: the Production Phase

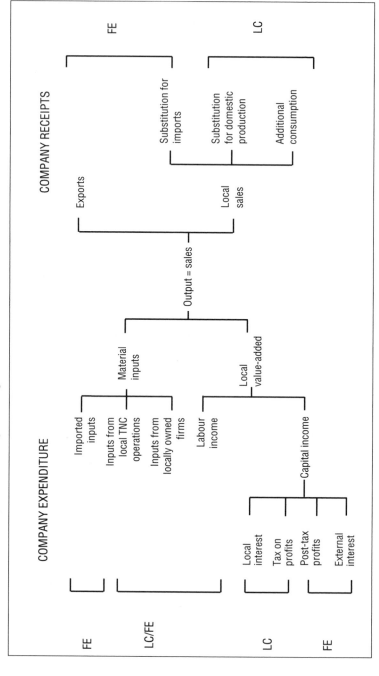

limited to the *changes* in these receipts and expenditures resulting from foreign ownership, plus the pre-FDI post-tax profits, which are transformed from a local currency cost to a foreign exchange cost.

An Alternative Perspective

A company's profit (before depreciation) is the money it receives from its sales which it does not spend meeting the costs of production or servicing its debts. This means that the total of the items on the left-hand side of Figure 7.2 (the company's expenditure and profits) is the same as the total of the items on the right-hand side (the company's receipts). At the same time, both the right- and left-hand sides are made up entirely of foreign exchange costs and local currency costs. This is illustrated in Figure 7.3.

What we are interested in is the net foreign exchange effect – that is, the difference between the foreign exchange component on the left-hand side, and that on the right-hand side. This is equivalent to the shaded part of the central column. However, as can be seen from Figure 7.3, this is also equal

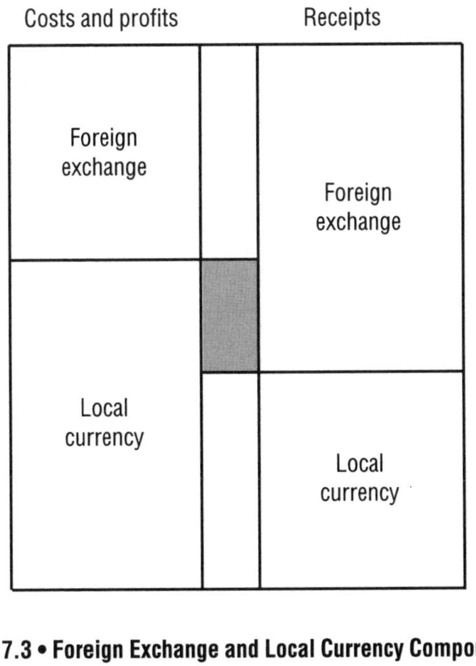

Figure 7.3 • Foreign Exchange and Local Currency Components of Receipts, Costs and Profits

to the difference between the local currency components of the left- and right-hand sides.

In other words, to determine the net foreign exchange effects of foreign direct investments, we can equally look at the balance between its receipts and costs in local currency.[32] (The profits attributable to foreign investors, it will be recalled, represent a foreign exchange cost.)

Since the company's local currency receipts and expenditure represent its transactions with the host country (as opposed to its transactions with other countries), this suggests an alternative way of looking at the issue. We can consider the productive activities financed by direct investment, not as part of the host economy, but as if it were another 'country'. For ease of reference, let us call this country Tiencia.

From a balance of payments perspective, it is as if the rest of the economy (individuals resident in the host country, locally owned companies and the government), were 'exporting' labour and other inputs and lending money to Tiencia, and 'importing' part of its output and receiving debt-service payments from it. There are also transactions within Tiencia, as the local subsidiaries of different TNCs (or different subsidiaries of the same TNC) trade with each other.

The only fundamental difference between the host country's economic relations with Tiencia and with a real foreign country is in the field of taxation: the government of the host country can levy taxes on profits, and on transactions between different parts of Tiencia (that is, between different TNCs operating in the country) as well as on imports and exports (labour and inputs produced by locally owned firms and outputs sold to local consumers). An additional complication, however, is the existence of companies which are only partly foreign-owned, so that they straddle the 'border' between Tiencia and the host economy. Nonetheless, this is, in some respects, a helpful way to conceptualise the issue.

Viewed in this way, one can say that the foreign exchange effect of direct investment is equivalent to the balance of payments of the rest of the economy with the artificial 'country' made up of foreign-owned production facilities. This suggests the following relatively simple criteria for the foreign exchange effects of FDI.

- the net foreign exchange effect of direct investment in new productive capacity during the production phase *equals*

> the company's spending on
> locally produced inputs
>
> *plus*   wages paid to local labour

plus	spending by expatriate workers on locally produced goods and services
plus	tax payments by the company[33]
minus	local sales (net of import substitution).

- The net foreign exchange effect of direct investment in existing capacity *equals* the net *change* in the above elements

minus	the profits prior to foreign ownership.

The Production Phase: Equity Investment

In terms of direct foreign exchange effects during the production phase, equity investment in existing capacity is at the opposite extreme from direct investment in new capacity. This is the most straightforward case, as it entails no additional production, and no change in the pattern of production, merely a transfer of ownership. The direct foreign exchange effects during the production phase are therefore limited to the transfer of the stream of dividend payments from a local recipient to a foreign recipient, and thus from a local currency to a foreign exchange cost.

Over the long term, there will be a second element of foreign exchange cost, namely the increase in the value of the shares. This is likely to represent the majority of the profit to the shareholder, and thus also of the potential foreign exchange cost; but it will be realised (both as profit and as a foreign exchange cost) only when the shares are eventually sold to a local resident. In the meantime, however, it will increase the overall value of external liabilities.

There is no assurance that the total foreign exchange costs of the investment (dividends plus capital gains) will be less than the company's net foreign exchange earnings (the relationship between the two being broadly as described for direct investment earlier in this chapter); but this relationship is at most of secondary importance. It makes little or no difference to a company's activities or performance who owns the shares in it – if the foreign shareholder had a sufficient stake to make a difference, the investment would be classified as FDI rather than as portfolio equity investment. Where existing shares are bought by foreigners from local investors on the stock exchange, the effect is simply to transfer the rights to the future capital gains and dividend income on the shares from the local investors to foreign investors, with no effect on the company's output, exports or imports.

In the case of equity investment in new capacity, new production is generated, so that the framework presented in Figure 7.2 can be applied, except that the treatment of profits is rather different. In this case, 'profits' are the profits to foreign investors of share ownership rather than the profits of the company itself – that is, dividend payments and the capital gains resulting from changes in share prices; but the latter cost is deferred until such time as the shares are sold to a local investor.

8

Foreign Exchange Effects of Direct and Equity Investment on the Host Country

Rates of Return on Direct and Equity Investment

The most obvious foreign exchange costs of foreign direct and portfolio equity investment are the profits and capital gains they generate for their owners. This cost is very substantial: because it is the investors who bear the risk, the rate of return required to compensate them for that risk is much higher than on less risky debt instruments.

However, it is difficult to estimate the actual rates of return, especially on direct investment, because of the limitations of the data available. To calculate the rate of return, it is necessary to know the value of the stock of direct investment, new investment flows, capital gains and profits for each country, over a period long enough to even out (possibly very wide) fluctuations over time. As discussed in chapters 5 and 6, the available data are subject to a number of serious shortcomings.

An added complication is that direct investment through construction often has a long gestation period, during which profits will not be made. Even after the construction period, profitability is likely to be relatively limited at first, increasing over time as the investment 'matures' – as markets are developed and production processes improved. When new direct investment is large relative to the previously existing stock (which may well be the case when FDI flows are increasing rapidly), this may result in the long-term rate of return being significantly underestimated. However, the extent of this discrepancy is impossible to evaluate, as direct investment for construction and for purchase are not generally distinguished, and the time-lags involved are very variable both between and within sectors.

Against this background, estimates of rates of return on direct investment must be treated with extreme caution. A rough guide is provided by World Bank (1997b: 34, Box 1.2), which puts rates of return at 16–18 per cent per annum for developing countries as a whole, and 24–30 per cent per annum for sub-Saharan Africa, between 1990 and 1994.

In principle, the rates of return on portfolio equity investment (and direct investment in quoted shares) are easier to estimate, by looking at the performance of the stock markets in the countries concerned. Even here, however, it should be noted that there is some room for error, in that the portfolios held by foreign investors may be significantly different from those held by domestic investors.[34]

The average rate of return on equity investments in 15 markets which had significant recorded inflows of portfolio investment from abroad was 29 per cent per annum between 1976 and 1992. In only two cases (Malaysia at 14 per cent per annum and Indonesia at -12 per cent per annum) was the rate less than 20 per cent per annum; and in the latter case the period covered by the data was only three years, suggesting that the figure may be unrepresentative of the longer-term picture. In three cases (Argentina at 68 per cent per annum, the Philippines at 45 per cent per annum and Colombia at 43 per cent per annum), the average rate was in excess of 40 per cent per annum (Woodward 1996: 46, based on data from World Bank 1995). The bulk of this return takes the form of capital gains, while dividend payments represent perhaps 1–2 per cent of the current value of shares per year. However, these rates of return will have been reduced substantially by the succession of financial crises, and the associated contagion spreading among 'emerging market' stock exchanges, since the end of 1994.

Direct Investment by Purchase: Export Sector

Direct investment by purchase has two effects:

- it represents a transfer of ownership of existing productive assets, converting the profits they generate from a local currency cost to a foreign exchange cost; and

- it may entail significant changes in the level and/or pattern of production, and thus in input use, profits and other factors.

The first element represents a clear foreign exchange cost (provided the enterprise or production facility which is bought is making a profit prior to the investment). For the overall foreign exchange effect of the investment to be positive, the effect of changes in production factors must be sufficiently positive to off-set this cost.

If the investment is in the export sector, any increase in output as a result of foreign ownership will increase the host country's foreign exchange earnings. In itself, this should lead to a favourable foreign exchange effect, as the additional foreign exchange earnings should be more than sufficient to finance the profits on the additional production and factors such as the cost of additional imported inputs.

However, it is essential to consider *how* production is increased, and particularly to distinguish between an increase in the *scale* of production (using more inputs) and an increase in the *efficiency* of production (using the same inputs to produce more output). To the extent that an increased scale of production is achieved by new investment, this element of the investment represents direct investment through construction rather than through purchase, and should be assessed separately as such, as discussed later in this chapter. If production is increased purely by an increase in the efficiency with which the existing capital stock is used – that is, if the use of labour and other inputs is increased by the same proportion as output – then the net foreign exchange effect will be the value of the increase in production, less the foreign exchange content of the additional inputs required.

If production is increased by improving the efficiency with which non-capital inputs are used, the picture is more complex, for two reasons.

- First, changes in efficiency affect the whole of production, not just the additional production following the investment. This means that the effects of changes in input use could, in principle, outweigh the effect of changes in production.

- Second, the main effect of increased efficiency (for a given level of output) is to reduce production costs, and thus to increase profits; and changes in profits represent a foreign exchange cost. This means that any reduction in local currency costs through improved efficiency effectively converts that cost into a foreign exchange cost (although part of this cost may be recovered through taxation on profits).

This can be illustrated by the alternative approach to foreign exchange effects suggested in Chapter 7, of considering direct investment enterprises as a separate 'country' called Tiencia, with which the host economy trades. Since we are assuming, in this instance, that none of the company's output is sold locally, the host country's balance of payments with Tiencia will improve only if its 'exports' to (and receipts from) the company increase. If the company increases its output purely by increasing the efficiency of its input use rather than the volume of inputs it uses, then the host economy's 'exports' are not increased, and there is no foreign exchange benefit. The only effect is an increase in the company's profits; and the foreign exchange benefit to the host country is limited to any increase in tax receipts which may result.

This makes changes in the *balance* between different inputs crucial to the foreign exchange effect. If there is substitution from inputs with a relatively low foreign exchange content (labour and non-tradeable goods and services with a low import content produced by locally owned firms) to inputs with a higher foreign exchange content (imports, import substitutes, exportable goods, goods with a high import content, and purchases from other TNCs in the host country), this will tend to make the foreign exchange effect less positive or more negative.

These changes are likely to be broadly unfavourable in most cases. In general, the scope for reducing the quantity of physical inputs used per unit of output is relatively limited. This is especially true for manufactured components – the number of wheels needed per car is relatively fixed, barring changes in design. It may be more feasible to reduce commodity inputs, for example to use less steel per car, or less rubber per tyre; but the potential for cost reduction in both cases is essentially limited to reducing wastage (again barring design changes).

The scope for reducing labour costs per unit of output is often much greater. Increasing labour productivity, for example by changes in the production process,[35] is often a major objective of foreign investors, particularly in the context of privatisation. Moreover, while the prices paid for inputs are generally beyond the control of the company (unless it can exercise monopoly power) it may be more able to reduce wage rates.

This implies that cost reduction is likely to be skewed strongly towards local currency costs rather than foreign exchange costs. The greatest reduction in expenditure is likely to be for labour, which has among the lowest foreign exchange contents of any input. Reductions in the use of physical inputs are likely to be more limited, and smallest for manufactured components, which are most likely to be imported. Price reductions are also more likely for labour and for locally produced non-tradeable goods (where the company may be able to exercise monopoly power), which also have a relatively low foreign exchange content.

A change to foreign ownership is also likely to be associated with a more direct switch from purchased inputs with a low foreign exchange content to those with a higher foreign exchange content. By their nature transnational companies tend to interact more with the international economy than locally owned companies. Their procurement policies are strongly influenced by a number of features which skew their purchases in this direction.

- Globalisation of production processes and the expansion of companies through vertical diversification (into industries which produce inputs and process outputs) promotes intra-company trade.

• Operations of the same TNCs in different countries often use the inputs from the same sources as a means of standardising their products or facilitating quality control.

• Many TNCs have network trading arrangements, under which their subsidiaries purchase a particular type of inputs from a particular company (usually another TNC), in return for more favourable terms or as part of a reciprocal arrangement.

All of these factors tend to increase the proportion of TNC inputs which are imported or purchased from other TNC operations in the host country.

These effects are illustrated in Table 8.1, which shows the local currency (LC) and foreign exchange (FE) income and costs of a particular production facility before FDI and in various post-FDI scenarios. It should be emphasised that the actual figures are illustrative, although they are at least partly based on actual data for developing countries (Box 8.1, pp. 98-9).

Table 8.1 • Net Foreign Exchange Effects of Direct Investment by Purchase in Export Production

	Before FDI		After FDI						
			Scenario (1)		Scenario (2)		Scenario (3)		Scenario (4)
Output/capital	0.60		0.60		0.75		0.75		0.75
Output/labour	6.00		6.00		600		7.50		7.50
Imports/purchased inputs	0.50		0.50		0.50		0.50		0.67

	LC	FE	LC	FE	LC	FE	LC	FE	LC	FE
Sales	0.0	+60.0	0.0	+60.0	0.0	+75.0	0.0	+75.0	0.0	+75.0
Labour costs	−8.0	−2.0	−8.0	−2.0	−10.0	−2.5	−8.0	−2.0	−8.0	−2.0
Local inputs	−12.0	−6.0	−12.0	−6.0	−15.0	−7.5	−15.0	−7.5	−10.0	−5.0
Imports	0.0	−18.0	0.0	−18.0	0.0	−22.5	0.0	−22.5	0.0	−30.0
Profit taxes	−2.8	0.0	−2.8	0.0	−3.5	0.0	−4.0	0.0	−4.0	0.0
Post-tax profit	−11.2	0.0	0.0	−11.2	0.0	−14.0	0.0	−16.0	0.0	−16.0
Total FE effect		+34.0		+22.8		+28.5		+27.0		+22.0
Change cf pre-FDI		n/a		−11.2		−5.5		−7.0		−12.0

> **Box 8.1 • Assumptions for Illustrative Figures on Net Foreign Exchange Effects of Direct and Equity Investment**

The numerical illustrations in this chapter assume an investment of $100 million In the case of investment which creates new productive capacity, it is assumed (arbitrarily) that half of this is spent on imported capital equipment.

The investment of $100 million is assumed to be associated with gross production after investment of $75 million, based on a comparison of the gross output of foreign affiliates in developing countries in 1994 (9.1 per cent of GDP, according to UNCTAD 1997b: 267, Table A.4) with the stock of investment in the same year (12.5 per cent of GDP, according to UNCTAD 1996: 262, Annex Table 6).

Value added after investment is set at $30 million, based on the average incremental capital–output ratio (ICOR) for developing countries as a whole of 3.2 in 1971–81 and 3.7 in 1982–92 (Agénor and Montiel 1996: 528, Table 15.5). This in turn is divided between capital and labour on the basis of the World Bank's estimate of a 16–18 per cent rate of return on FDI in developing countries as a whole in 1990–4 (World Bank 1997b: 34, Box 1.2). Allowing for 20 per cent taxation on profits, the lower end of this range implies post-tax profits of $16 million per annum per $100 million of investment, and $4 million of profit taxes, leaving $10 million for labour value added. The resulting share of pre-tax profits in value added (two-thirds) is broadly consistent with a range from 52.7 per cent to 81.0 per cent (arithmetic mean 70.7 per cent) for the manufacturing sector in 14 developing economies for various periods between 1974 and 1986 given in UNCTAD (1997a: 169, Table 44).[36] It is assumed that 20 per cent of wages are spent directly or indirectly on tradeable goods, and thus constitute a foreign exchange cost.

Deducting value added from gross production implies purchased inputs totalling $45 million. Two-thirds of these ($30 million) are assumed to be imported, based on the average figure for Japanese FDI in Latin America between 1981 and 1994 (UNCTAD 1997b: 104, footnote 63). The remaining $15 million of locally produced inputs are assumed to have a total direct and indirect foreign exchange content of $5 million, including the profits of transnational producers and the foreign exchange content of their own locally produced inputs, as well as imported and other tradeable inputs.

Where direct investment entails the construction of new productive capacity, it is assumed that the investment would not otherwise have occurred, so that the foreign exchange effects of the FDI are equal to the total net foreign exchange earnings of the investment itself. Where FDI takes the form of the purchase of existing productive capacity, the effect is measured as the change in net foreign exchange earnings from a hypothetical pre-FDI scenario. These effects are divided into four components, shown separately to illustrate the impact of each:

1   the transfer of ownership, converting post-tax profits from a local currency cost to a foreign exchange cost;

2   an increase in the efficiency of capital use, increasing output and all inputs by the same proportion (25 per cent);

3   an increase in labour productivity, reducing labour use (by 25 per cent) from scenario 2, while retaining the higher level of output; and

4   the substitution of imports for a proportion (one-third) of purchased inputs from local sources, keeping the total value of inputs as in scenario 3.

For simplicity, the pre-FDI figures are derived by working backwards from scenario 4, so as to allow the same baseline to be used throughout. It should once again be emphasised that the absolute and relative scale of these effects is arbitrary, and that the results are therefore illustrative.
The resulting assumptions are summarised below.

	Before FDI	**After FDI**
Initial investment:	n/a	$100m
Imported capital goods: (where new productive capacity is created)	n/a	$50m
Gross production:	$60m	$75m
Purchased inputs (pa):	$36m	$45m
imported:	$18m	$30m
locally produced (FE 33%):	$18m	$15m
Value added (pa):	$24m	$30m
labour (FE 20%):	$10m	$10m
capital (tax 20%):	$14m	$20m

The foreign exchange effect of foreign ownership as such is inevitably negative, as it represents only a change in post-tax profits from a local currency cost to a foreign exchange cost. The net impact based on the figures used here is a net foreign exchange loss of $11.2 million per annum per $100 million of investment. This is partly off-set by the increase in capital efficiency, as the use of labour and locally produced inputs (and, to a lesser extent, profit taxes) increases. However, as labour productivity is increased, and as imports are substituted for locally produced inputs, the negative impact again becomes stronger. The overall effect of all the changes hypothesised is to increase exports by $15 million per annum – but to worsen the country's balance of payments by $12 million per annum.

This suggests that the foreign exchange cost to the host country of FDI through purchase may be substantial even in what might appear to be the most favourable possible scenario – that of investment in the export sector which increases both output and productivity. The overall impact on the balance of payments will be positive only if the increase in efficiency of capital use is enough to off-set the foreign exchange cost of profits plus the negative foreign exchange effects of increased labour productivity and increased use of imported inputs. In the present example, this would require an increase in capital productivity of at least 50 per cent merely to off-set the effect of profits. With the hypothesised improvement in labour productivity and switch to imported inputs, capital productivity would need almost to double to avoid a negative foreign exchange effect.

In general, the annual net foreign exchange cost should be lower relative to the total amount invested than is implied by the rate of return on the investment (in this example, 10.4 per cent per annum compared with 16 per cent per annum). However, as the illustrative figures presented here demonstrate, it may nonetheless be at least as high as the cost of other (non-equity) types of capital inflow.

Moreover, the picture is made still worse by two other considerations.

- First, the actual foreign exchange inflow associated with the initial investment is likely to be less – and may be considerably less – than the value of the investment itself, depending on the uses to which the receipts are put by the recipient. (See the discussion of portfolio investment in existing shares later in this chapter.) This may greatly increase the ratio between the annual foreign exchange cost and the initial (net) foreign exchange inflow.

- Second, the effect will be more negative from the perspective of developing countries as a whole to the extent that the increase in production and/or reduction in production costs reduces the prices received by other developing country exporters, either by increasing the supply of primary commodities in the global market, or by intensifying price competition for manufactured goods (see Chapter 10).

Direct Investment by Purchase: Non-Tradeable Sectors

In the case of non-tradeable goods and services (retailing and fast-food outlets, for example), the net foreign exchange effect is more clearly negative, because the increase in production does not generate additional foreign exchange earnings. This is illustrated in Table 8.2, using the same illustrative scenarios of sales and costs as in the export case.

Table 8.2 • Net Foreign Exchange Effects of Direct Investment by Purchase in Non-Tradeable Production

	Before FDI		After FDI							
			Scenario 1		Scenario 2		Scenario 3		Scenario 4	
Output/capital	0.60		0.60		0.75		0.75		0.75	
Output/labour	6.00		6.00		600		7.50		7.50	
Imports/purchased inputs	0.50		0.50		0.50		0.50		0.67	
	LC	FE	LC	FE	LC	FE	LC	FE	LC	FE
Sales	+60.0	0.0	+60.0	0.0	+75.0	0.0	+75.0	0.0	+75.0	0.01
Labour costs	−8.0	−2.0	−8.0	−2.0	10.0	−2.5	−8.0	−2.0	−8.0	−2.01
Local inputs	12.0	−6.0	12.0	−6.0	−15.0	−7.5	15.0	−7.5 -	10.0	−5.0
Imports	0.0	18.0	0.0	18.0	0.0	−22.5	0.0	−22.5	0.0	30.0
Profit taxes	−2.8	0.0	−2.8	0.0	−3.5	0.0	−4.0	0.0	−4.0	0.0
Post-tax profit	11.2	0.0	0.0	11.2	0.0	14.0	0.0	−16.0	0.0	−16.0
Total FE effect		−26.0		−37.2		−46.5		−48.0		−53.0
Change of pre-FDI		n/a		−11.2		−20.5		−22.0		−27.0

Because the same level of profits is assumed as in the export case, the foreign exchange effect of foreign ownership as such is again $11.2 million per annum. Also as in the export case, the effect of increased labour productivity and of a switch from locally produced to imported inputs increases this effect. The key difference is that the increased output associated with more efficient use of capital compounds this negative impact rather than offsetting it, because the increased production brings no foreign exchange benefit, while increased profits and imports of inputs add to foreign exchange costs. The result is that every aspect of the effects of FDI is negative.

Based on the illustrative figures used here, the overall effect is to increase the net foreign exchange cost by $27 million per annum, more than doubling the pre-FDI level. The scale of this effect is noteworthy in two respects.

- First, it represents a much greater proportional increase than that in production (104 per cent compared with 25 per cent), implying a substantially higher foreign exchange cost per unit of output after investment than before ($70 per $100 of output, compared with about $43, an increase of around 60 per cent), despite increases both in the efficiency of capital use and in labour productivity.

- Second, the net foreign exchange cost is substantially greater relative to the amount invested than the rate of return (27 per cent per annum compared with 16 per cent per annum).

However, a slight complication arises in this case, to the extent that some of the extra money spent by consumers on the additional non-tradeable output might otherwise have been spent on imports (or exportable goods).[37] The effect is simply to reduce the negative foreign exchange effect by the amount of import substitution. Thus if 40 per cent of the additional sales ($6 million) substitute for spending on tradeable goods, the post-FDI foreign exchange cost is reduced from $53 million to $46 million. This moderates the negative impact of FDI to some extent, but by no means eliminates it. In the illustrative scenario presented here, even 100 per cent substitution would leave the foreign exchange cost at $12 million more than before FDI. The foreign exchange cost per unit of output could be reduced below the rate of return on the investment, but only if the import substitution effect of additional production were in excess of 73 per cent. Again, it is important to note that the actual foreign exchange inflow associated with the investment is likely to be substantially less than the value of the investment, depending on how the proceeds are spent.

All this suggests that the foreign exchange effect of direct investment through the purchase of existing productive capacity in the non-tradeable sector is consistently, unambiguously and strongly negative. In practice, however, there are likely to be some important exceptions to this negative impact, primarily in sectors which contribute substantially to the overall efficiency of the economy (such as transport and communications). If increased efficiency and reduced costs in these sectors improve the competitiveness of exports and import substitutes, the indirect positive effect on these sectors may be sufficient to outweigh the negative direct effect.

Direct Investment by Purchase: Import Substitutes

Direct investment by purchase in the production of import substitutes is an intermediate case between the export and non-tradeable cases. In principle, it follows the export case (as shown in Table 8.1), but with the foreign exchange benefits of increased production arising from reduced spending on imports rather than increased export revenues.

In practice, however, it is likely that the net effect of spending on imports will be less than the overall increase in sales, as the increase in sales is likely to substitute in part for production by other import-substituting producers rather than for imports, and in part to represent an increase in total consumption of the goods produced (if consumption is promoted by advertising, for example). In the latter case, the increase in consumption can be expected to substitute partly for spending on non-tradeable goods and/or savings, and only partly for imports. The result is likely to be an import substitution effect of additional production significantly less than 100 per cent.

The overall foreign exchange effect is therefore complex and ambiguous. On the whole, it is likely that the effect will be more negative (or less positive) than for investments in export production, because of the less than one-to-one relationship between output and net foreign exchange earnings. However, it will depend critically on the degree of foreign exchange savings arising from the additional production. This is illustrated in Table 8.3, using alternative figures for foreign exchange savings of 80 per cent and 60 per cent of additional sales.

The results for pure import substitutes are, by definition, identical to those for export production, as shown in Table 8.1. However, each 20 per cent reduction in the degree of import substitution makes the foreign exchange effect more negative by 20 per cent of the additional production ($3 million per annum) in each of the scenarios where output is increased. The result is that increased capital efficiency (scenario 1) reduces the negative

Table 8.3 • Net Foreign Exchange Effects of Direct Investment by Purchase in Import-Substituting Production

| | Before FDI | | After FDI | | | | | | | |
| | | | Scenario 1 | | Scenario 2 | | Scenario 3 | | Scenario 4 | |
	LC	FE	LC	FE	LC	FE	LC	FE	LC	FE
Output/capital	0.60		0.60		0.75		0.75		0.75	
Output/labour	6.00		6.00		600		7.50		7.50	
Imports/purchased inputs	0.50		0.50		0.50		0.50		0.67	
Sales:										
(a) 100% imp. subst.	0.0	+60.0	0.0	+60.0	0.0	+75.0	0.0	+75.0	0.0	+75.0
(b) 80% imp. subst.	+12.0	+48.0	+12.0	+48.0	+15.0	+60.0	+15.0	+60.0	+15.0	+60.0
(c) 60% imp. subst	+24.0	+36.0	+24.0	+36.0	+30.0	+45.0	+30.0	+45.0	+30.0	+45.0
Total costs (as Tables 8.1/2)	−34.0	−26.0	−22.8	−37.2	−28.5	−46.5	−27.0	−48.0	−22.0	−53.0
Total FE effect:										
(a) 100% imp.subst.		+34.0		+22.8		+28.5		+27.0		+22.0
(b) 80% imp.subst.		+22.0		+10.8		+13.5		+12.0		+7.0
(c) 60% imp. subst.		+10.0		−1.2		−1.5		−3.0		−8.0
Change cf pre-FDI:										
(a) 100% imp.subst.		n/a		−11.2		−5.5		−7.0		−12.0
(b) 80% imp. subst.		n/a		−11.2		−8.5		−10.0		−15.0
(c) 60% imp. subst.		n/a		−11.2		−11.5		−13.0		−18.0

impact in the case of 100 per cent and 80 per cent import substitutes, but increases it slightly in the 60 per cent case. The increase in labour efficiency and the substitution of imports for locally produced inputs again strengthens the negative effect in all three cases. Once again, there is a clear negative impact in every scenario, ranging between $12 million per annum and $18 million per annum in scenario 4, where all the potential effects of FDI are taken into account.

Thus the foreign exchange effects of direct investment through the purchase of existing productive capacity in import-substituting sectors is more negative (or less positive) than in the case of exports, and thus likely to be substantially negative overall; and the increase in the efficiency of capital use required to off-set the negative effects of foreign ownership is still greater than in the export sector. However, the impact on other producing countries, through the effect of increased production, is likely to be much more limited.

Direct Investment through Construction of New Productive Capacity

The foreign exchange effects of direct investment through construction are more straightforward than those of direct investment by purchase. Since the

---

Table 8.4 • Net Foreign Exchange Effects of Direct Investment through Construction of New Productive Capacity

1 Initial investment ($m)

Capital inflow:	+100
Imported equipment:	−50
Net effect:	+50

2 Operations ($m pa)

	Exports and pure import substitutes	Partial import substitutes				Pure non-tradeables
		80%	60%	40%	20%	
Sales (FE effect):	+75	+60	+45	+30	+15	0
Inputs/profits (FE):	−53	−53	−53	−53	−53	−53
Net effect:	+22	+7	−8	−23	−38	−53
% of initial FE inflow:	+44%	+14%	−16%	−46%	−76%	−106%

(why?)

counterfactual assumption is that the investment would not otherwise have taken place, the foreign exchange effects essentially correspond to the foreign exchange transaction of the direct investment enterprise itself, plus the indirect foreign exchange effects of its operations (such as import substitution and the foreign exchange content of locally produced inputs).

This is illustrated in Table 8.4, using figures consistent with those in the earlier illustrations, as outlined in Box 8.1. It is again assumed that the initial investment is of $100 million, of which half takes the form of imported equipment and related costs. Various scenarios are used for the degree of export orientation or import substitution of production, ranging from zero (pure non-tradeable goods) to 100 per cent (exports and pure import substitutes).

In the case of direct investment through construction for the production of exports and pure import substitutes, the net foreign exchange effect is inevitably positive over the long term (subject only to the earlier caveats about world-price effects in the case of exports). However, this benefit quickly evaporates as the degree of import substitution (or, equivalently, the proportion of output exported) declines.

While it should once again be emphasised that these figures are essentially illustrative, the results in this example are extremely sensitive to the assumptions made about the degree of export orientation or import substitution: a 20 per cent decline in import substitution (or export orientation) makes the annual net foreign exchange impact more negative by 30 per cent of the initial net foreign exchange inflow. Below about 70 per cent, the net foreign exchange effect becomes negative; and once it falls significantly below 65 per cent it becomes greater than the cost of commercial borrowing.

Direct Investment to Expand and Improve Existing Productive Capacity

Thus far, a clear dichotomy has been made between direct investment which entails the purchase of existing productive capacity, and that which involves the construction of new productive capacity. In reality, however, this distinction is less clear-cut. Often, the purchase of existing capacity will be accompanied or followed by the provision of new capital to the plant or subsidiary which has been purchased; this may well be essential to bring about the improvements in efficiency which the investment seeks to achieve.

To the extent that such investment increases the *scale* of the direct investment enterprise – that is, increases its output *without changing the inputs used per unit of output* – it is equivalent to an investment in new capacity. Each element of foreign exchange and local currency costs and benefits will increase in the same proportions as in the case of investment in new capacity, so that the net foreign exchange effect of a given increase in output of a particular good will be the same as in the last section. However, it may be that a given increase in output can be achieved with a smaller injection of capital, as start-up costs are avoided; or that a greater proportion of the capital will be spent on foreign exchange costs such as imported equipment because no construction costs are involved. In either case, the initial foreign exchange inflow will be reduced, so that the net foreign exchange costs (or benefits) during the production phase will be larger relative to the initial inflow.

However, the case is very different when investment in new capacity changes the relationship between output and inputs. This applies particularly to labour-saving technology. If a direct investment enterprise invests in new equipment which allows it to reduce its labour costs per unit of output – by mechanising production processes, for example – this will reduce its local currency expenditure; and if output is not increased, this will increase the foreign exchange cost (or reduce the benefit) in the production phase.

Table 8.5 • Net Foreign Exchange Effects of Direct Investment in Expansion and Improvement of Existing Productive Capacity (Export Sector)

	Pre-FDI		Expansion		Labour saving	
	LC	FE	LC	FE	LC	FE
Output	0.0	+75.0	0.0	+90.0	0.0	+90.0
Labour	−8.0	−2.0	−9.6	−2.4	−4.8	−1.2
Local inputs	−10.0	−5.0	−12.0	−6.0	−10.0	−5.0
Imports	0.0	−30.0	0.0	−36.0	0.0	−30.0
Profit/tax	−4.0	−16.0	−4.8	−19.2	−4.8	−19.2
Net FE effect		+22.0		+26.4		+19.6
cf pre-FDI		n/a		+4.4		−2.4

These two cases are illustrated in Table 8.5, for an additional investment of $20 million in a foreign-owned export production facility. The first part of the table shows the starting point, based on the illustrative figures used earlier in this chapter. The second part shows the effects of an investment to expand production, increasing the use of all inputs proportionally with the increase in output (by 20 per cent). The effect is to increase the foreign exchange benefits by the same proportion. As in the case of investment in new capacity, this figure falls as the foreign exchange content of output falls; the effect will become negative at the same threshold of import substitution (around 70 per cent). In short, the foreign exchange effects of a given increase in output are indistinguishable from those of investment in new capacity (although, as noted above, the initial injection of foreign exchange required to achieve this increase may be somewhat smaller).

The final part of Table 8.5 shows the effect of an investment of $20 million to reduce labour costs by 40 per cent ($4 million per annum) with no change in output or purchased inputs. This increases total profits by the same amount, from $20 million to $24 million (and post-tax profits by $3.2 million, providing a rate of return on the investment of 16 per cent per annum, as assumed in the previous illustrations). The impact on the foreign exchange effects of production is limited to $2.4 million by the saving on the indirect foreign exchange content of wages (workers' spending on imports), and taxes on profits. Nonetheless, the effect is clearly negative. It should be noted that the effect is the same irrespective of the sector involved: since there is no change in production, its foreign exchange content makes no difference to the result.

In practice, most investment in the expansion and improvement of existing capacity is likely to fall somewhere between these two extremes. Expansion will tend to affect the composition of inputs (and, for the reasons discussed earlier, this is likely to tip the balance towards those with a higher foreign exchange content); and the introduction of labour-saving technology can be expected to increase output as well as reducing labour inputs. Nonetheless, the general conclusion remains that investment in the expansion and/or improvement of existing capacity will, on the whole, have a less favourable (or more unfavourable) foreign exchange effect than investment which creates new capacity; and investment in labour-saving technology may have a negative foreign exchange effect even in the export sector.

Portfolio Investment in Existing Shares

The disparity between the foreign exchange flows associated with an investment and the effect of its production on the host country's net foreign exchange position is perhaps most obvious in the case of equity investment which entails the purchase of existing shares on the stock exchange. The money paid for the investment will not necessarily remain in the economy; and the capital gain, which represents most of the return to the investor, is related to the market valuation of shares rather than to the company's profits. There is therefore no reason to expect that any increase in net foreign exchange receipts associated with an investment will necessarily cover the foreign exchange cost.

As discussed in Chapter 7, the money paid for shares by foreign investors

Table 8.6 • Illustrative Net Foreign Exchange Effects of Portfolio Investment in Existing Shares

		Year 1	2	3	4	5	6	7/later
Capital flow		+10.00	0.00	0.00	0.00	0.00	−25.00	0.00
Dividends		−0.24	−0.29	−0.35	−0.42	−0.50	0.00	0.00
Local saving/investment in existing capacity		0.00	0.00	0.00	0.00	0.00	0.00	0.00
Local investment in new capacity	Exports	−0.50	+0.45	+0.45	+0.45	+0.45	+1.70	−0.67
	Import substitutes	−0.50	+0.30	+0.30	+0.30	+0.30	+1.55	−0.45
	Non-tradeable	−0.50	−0.15	0.15	−0.15	−0.15	+1.10	+0.22
Investment abroad	Income repatriated	−1.47	+0.03	+0.04	+0.05	+0.05	+3.73	−0.02
	Income not repatriated	−1.50	0.00	0.00	0.00	0.00	+3.75	0.00
Consumption	Imports	−0.50	0.00	0.00	0.00	0.00	+1.25	0.00
	Local products	−0.20	0.00	0.00	0.00	0.00	+0.50	0.00
Total		+4.59	+0.34	+0.29	+0.23	+0.15	−11.42	−0.92
Memo: Value of investment (end year)		12.0	14.4	17.3	20.8	25.0	n/a	n/a

is likely to be spent by the local recipients on some combination of local investment (either through the purchase of existing productive capacity or through the creation of new capacity) or savings; investment in another country; and purchases of imported or locally produced consumption goods. Similarly, spending will be diverted away from these uses when the foreign investor subsequently sells the investment back to a local resident.

Table 8.6 illustrates the possible effects of portfolio equity investment in existing shares on the host country's net foreign exchange position, taking account of these alternative uses of funds. This supposes that a foreign investor buys a small equity stake in a local company from a local investor for $10 million at the beginning of year 0, selling it back to another local investor at the beginning of year 6. The value of the stake increases by 20 per cent during the course of each year, reaching $25 million by the time it is sold; and a dividend is paid at the end of each year, equivalent to 2 per cent of the value at that time.

The local investor is assumed to divide the proceeds between the alternative uses outlined above:

- $3 million for local currency savings and investment in existing local shares and production capacity;

- $3 million for investment in new local productive capacity, equally divided between exports, import substitutes (with an 80 per cent import substitution effect) and non-tradeable goods (with a 20 per cent import substitution effect), in each case producing $0.75 million of output and using $0.3 million of imported inputs, 50 per cent of the amount invested being spent on imported capital goods, and production beginning after a 12-month gestation period;

- $3 million for investment abroad, the income and capital on half of it remaining abroad; the remaining half is assumed to receive income of 2 per cent per annum, all repatriated, with a further 15 per cent per annum in capital gains, realised and repatriated at the beginning of year 6;[38] and

- $1 million for consumption, equally divided between imports and local production with a 40 per cent foreign exchange content.

It is assumed that the money paid to repurchase the investment at the beginning of year 6 would otherwise have been divided between the same uses in the same proportions, and the effect of this expenditure not taking place is included in the analysis. It cannot be emphasised too strongly that these figures are purely illustrative and essentially arbitrary (although those for productive investment are broadly consistent with the assumptions used for inward FDI earlier in this chapter).

The initial capital inflow is simply the amount of the inward investment at the beginning of year 1, and an outflow of the value of the investment (including accumulated capital gains) at the beginning of year 6. The dividends begin at $0.24 million, increasing to $0.5 million in year 5, falling to zero thereafter, as the investment is no longer in foreign ownership.

Local saving and investment in existing productive capacity have no direct foreign exchange effects. Investment abroad represents an initial outflow, followed by a small but growing inflow of dividend income where this is repatriated. While this is reversed when the investment is repurchased, resulting in investment abroad being reduced, this is largely off-set by the value of the initial increase (including capital gains), so that the net investment position after year 6 is only $1.5 million lower than it would otherwise have been (with income remitted on only half of this).

Local investment in new capacity has a negative effect in year 1 (corresponding with the foreign exchange content of the investment), and a positive effect (corresponding with the foreign exchange content of the investment which would otherwise have occurred) in year 6. In the intervening years, the additional production of tradeable goods generates additional net foreign exchange earnings (production less import content), while production of non-tradeable goods increases foreign exchange expenditure (for imported inputs). Again, this is reversed after year 6.

The consumption options increase foreign exchange costs in year 0, by $0.5 million for imports and $0.2 million for locally produced goods (equivalent to their assumed foreign exchange content). Again this is reversed, on an increased scale, in year 6.

The result is an initial net capital inflow equivalent to just under half of the amount invested in year 1, followed by a very small and progressively declining positive foreign exchange effect in years 2–5. It should be noted, however, that the initial sign of the net effect is very sensitive to the assumptions about the uses of the proceeds of the initial sale of shares, while its tendency to become less positive (or more negative) over time, is much less sensitive.

The net effect becomes substantially negative after the original investment has been sold – in this case at a level of about 20 per cent of the original net foreign exchange inflow. This is primarily because money which would otherwise have been used for new investment in the production of tradeable goods has instead been used to buy back the shares from foreign investors. Since the price of the shares is much higher in year 6 than in year 1, the investment forgone to buy the shares back is greater than the amount of extra investment financed by their sale in year 1, so that the country's productive capacity for tradeable goods is reduced.

Again, the scale of this effect is sensitive to the assumptions about productive investment; but if the same assumptions are made about the use of the proceeds of the original sale of the shares and the alternative uses of the funds spent to buy them back, a smaller negative impact from year 7 would be associated with a smaller positive or a negative effect in years 2–5.

However, the most serious negative foreign exchange effect of portfolio equity investment in existing shares arises when the investment is sold, owing to the high rate of capital gain. In this illustration, the effective foreign exchange cost of the initial capital inflow is equivalent to a loan at an interest rate of about 23 per cent per annum (broadly in line with the rate of return assumed on the investment). In terms of overall foreign exchange flows, some safeguard is provided by the likely impact on share prices of a general exodus from the market: there can only be an overall outflow on inward portfolio investment if foreign investors sell more shares than they buy; and in these circumstances the increase in supply will depress prices. The resulting losses will at least partially off-set the accumulated gains. This issue is taken up in Chapter 11.

Nonetheless, even if the shares remain in foreign ownership, the rate of return arising from dividend payments alone may be very high over the long term, unless they are off-set by the investment of the proceeds of the initial sale of shares in the production of tradeable goods in the host country. If dividends are 2 per cent of the market value of the shares, and prices rise at 20 per cent per annum, the rate of return (excluding the ultimate repatriation of capital) becomes positive after 13 years, and exceeds 10 per cent per annum after 19 years. With price increases of 40 per cent per annum, the rate of return becomes positive after 9 years and exceeds 20 per cent per annum after 14 years. These assumptions are by no means far-fetched: it will be recalled from the beginning of this chapter that most 'emerging' markets provided average rates of return between 20 per cent per annum and 40 per cent per annum over the sixteen years from 1976 to 1992.

Portfolio Investment in New Share Issues

Portfolio investment in new share issues which are used to finance investment are similar in their foreign exchange effects to direct investment through construction, except that profits need to be treated differently. There is a key distinction here between the short-term effects of the investment, while it remains in foreign ownership (when only dividend payments represent a foreign exchange cost), and its long-term effects allowing for the sale of the shares to a local investor (so that capital gains arising from the increasing value of the shares are realised).

These foreign exchange effects are shown in Table 8.7, making the same assumptions as were used earlier for direct investment (Box 8.1), and again assuming dividend payments of 2 per cent per annum and capital gains of 20 per cent per annum. In the short term, because dividends are much lower than the profits on direct investment, the foreign exchange effect is more positive or less negative than that of direct investment, for a given level of export orientation or import substitution. As a result, the net effect becomes

Table 8.7 • Net Foreign Exchange Effects of Portfolio Investment in New Share Issues

1 Initial investment ($m)

Capital inflow:	+100
Imported equipment:	−50
Net effect:	+50

2 Operations ($m pa): Short-term effects

	Exports and pure import substitutes	Partial import substitutes 80%	60%	40%	20%	Pure non-tradeables
Sales (FE effect):	+75	+60	+45	+30	+15	0
FE content of inputs:	−35	-35	−35	−35	−35	−35
Dividends:	−2	−2	−2	−2	−2	−2
Net effect:	+38	+23	+8	-7	-22	-37
% of net FE inflow:	+76%	+46%	+16%	−14%	−44%	−74%

3 Operations ($m pa): Long-term effects

	Exports and pure import substitutes	Partial import substitutes 80%	60%	40%	20%	Pure non-tradeables
Sales (FE effect):	+75	+60	+45	+30	+15	0
FE content of inputs:	-35	−35	−35	-35	−35	−35
Dividends/cap. gains:	-22	−22	−22	−22	−22	−22
Net effect:	+18	+3	−12	−27	−42	−57
% of net FE inflow:	+36%	+6%	−24%	−54%	−84%	−114%

negative at a little over 50 per cent export orientation or import substitution (compared with 70 per cent for direct investment), and reaches the level of commercial borrowing at about 45 per cent (compared with 65 per cent).

In the long term, however, when allowance is made for the possibility of the shares being sold, the effect is more negative than for direct investment, as dividends plus capital gains are greater than FDI profits. As a result, the net foreign exchange effect is favourable only above about 75 per cent export orientation or import substitution. Once again, effects on international prices must be taken into account in the case of export production, and will make the impact on developing countries as a whole more negative or less positive than that on the host country.

Conclusion

It seems clear from the discussion in this chapter that the foreign exchange effects of direct and equity investment are much more negative than the optimistic view outlined in Chapter 3. Clearly positive effects arise only where new productive capacity is created in the export sector, and in very strongly import-substituting sectors (that is, where almost all the output substitutes for imports rather than for existing import-substituting production, non-tradeable goods or savings). Direct investment through the purchase of existing capacity in the export sector will have a negative foreign exchange effect even where the production of exports is increased, unless the efficiency with which capital is used increases sufficiently to off-set the other negative foreign exchange effects of foreign ownership. On the illustrative assumptions used in this chapter – which are far from extravagant – this might require the efficiency of capital to be at least doubled.

At lower levels of import substitution, the effect of direct and equity investment in new capacity is more ambiguous, and may well be negative even for some goods which might conventionally be regarded as import substitutes. The effects of foreign investment in existing capacity for import substitutes, and in new or existing capacity in the non-tradeable sector, are clearly negative.

Thus, unless direct investment through construction in the export sector is sufficient to outweigh the effects of equity investment and of other direct investment, the overall effect is likely to be negative, and may well be substantially so. As Box 8.2 demonstrates, direct investment in the export sector represents a relatively small proportion of the total in many developing countries – less than 40 per cent on average for investment by US transnationals. Adjusting this to exclude investment in existing capacity would reduce the figures further, possibly by a substantial amount.

Box 8.2 • Export Orientation of Direct Investment

Data are not readily available on the sectoral distribution of FDI as between export, import-substitute and non-tradeable production. However, some general observations can be made. While there are exceptions, it is likely that investment in primary production (minerals and agriculture) will be largely export-oriented, while services will be mainly non-tradeable, though possibly with an element of import substitution. Manufacturing will be split between exports and import substitutes; but the balance between the two varies considerably between host countries. The overall export orientation of production by US majority-owned foreign affiliates is shown in Table 8.8 below.

Table 8.8 • Share of Exports in Total Output of US Majority-Owned Affiliates, 1993 (%)

Latin America/Caribbean	22.2
Brazil	17.0
Mexico	32.1
Newly Industrialising Asia	67.0
Hong Kong	55.0
Korea	27.9
Singapore	85.9
Taiwan	38.8
Other Asia	64.4
India	4.1 (1986)
Malaysia	84.9
Philippines	37.3
Thailand	61.2
All developing countries	38.7

Source: UNCTAD 1996: 110, Table IV.7.

It is clear that a substantial proportion of FDI in all regions is not in export production. According to UNCTAD estimates, the sales of foreign affiliates located in Latin America and the Caribbean were nearly three times (293.6 per cent of) the region's total exports in 1993, suggesting that even if all exports were produced by foreign affiliates this would amount only to one-third of their production. The corresponding figure for sub-Saharan Africa was 157.7 per cent, and that for Asia 106.8 per cent. For developing countries as a whole, the figure was 133.5 per cent (UNCTAD 1996: 17, Table I.6).

The finding that investment which generates new export production is virtually the only element of direct and equity investment which brings a significant foreign exchange benefit to the host country has a further significance: as discussed in Chapter 10, this type of investment will in many cases impose foreign exchange costs on other developing countries, by reducing the prices of their exports in world markets; and these costs may well outweigh the benefits to the host country itself. If this is the case, the overall foreign exchange effect of direct investment on the developing world as a whole is likely to be strongly negative.

▶ 9
Other Effects at the National Level

Effects on Investment

The relationship between inflows of direct and equity investment and the overall level of investment in the host economy is more complex than it might at first appear. The complexity arises partly because the investment itself does not necessarily add to the country's capital stock; and partly because it may have indirect effects on local investors.

By definition, direct investment for construction and equity investment in new share issues to finance productive investment contribute directly to overall investment in the host country, in that they create additional productive capacity. However, this is not the case with portfolio investment in existing shares or direct investment through purchase, which merely represent a transfer of ownership of existing capacity. In these cases, the amount invested is paid to the previous (local) owner of the investment, and what happens to the payment depends on the previous owner's decision. In some cases it may be invested in local capacity; but, as discussed in Chapter 7, it could equally be spent on consumption, invested in financial instruments inside or outside the country (which may or may not finance productive investment indirectly), or it may be used for direct investment in another country. On average it is likely that substantially less than 100 per cent will be invested locally in new productive capacity.

Reinvested profits on FDI follow broadly the same pattern, depending on whether they are used for construction or purchase. However, it should be noted that (measured) reinvestment includes increases in inventories of inputs and outputs and cash held in the host country by the subsidiary, which do not contribute to productive investment.

The capital gain on portfolio investment does not directly represent an increase in productive capacity, although it may partly reflect it. Price changes are determined by the demand and supply conditions on the stock market; these in turn may reflect market conditions, openness to (and the sentiments of) foreign investors, and similar factors at least as much as the productive capital base of each company.

The effects of direct investment on decisions by local investors could, in principle, be positive or negative. On the positive side:

- direct investment may provide opportunities for investment in the production of the inputs it requires, or for processing the outputs it produces;

- if direct and portfolio investment contribute to faster economic growth, this will increase the attractiveness of investment in production for the local market (by increasing demand) and may also increase the resources available for it (by increasing local incomes and savings); and

- where direct investment entails a transfer of technology, this may increase the supply of specialist skills useful to other producers over the long term (although it may also have a contrary effect, as discussed later in this chapter).

However, other effects tend to operate in the opposite direction.

- Where direct investment for construction is large relative to the economy as a whole (as in some very small middle-income countries), it could crowd out locally owned investment by using scarce inputs needed for construction (skilled labour such as engineers or electricians, for example), or by pushing up their prices beyond the means of local investors.

- In the case of sectors based on natural resources (such as mining, forestry or fishing), even direct investment which creates new capacity may merely prevent local producers from taking the same opportunities. The same may also apply in other sectors which require the use of scarce inputs, like technologically intensive sectors where the necessary skills are in limited supply.

- Direct investment which serves the local market (retailing and fast-food outlets or soft drinks bottling plants) may displace established local producers, or limit the growth of their market.

- A similar crowding-out effect may occur to the extent that governments seek to sterilise the monetary effects of capital inflows, as recommended by the IMF and (prior to the Asian financial crisis) the World Bank. This reduces the supply of local capital to the private sector and increases interest rates, making investment in productive activities more expensive and less attractive relative to financial investments (see Box 9.1).

Box 9.1 • Capital Inflows, Sterilisation and Local Investment

If capital inflows into an economy are greater than its current account deficit (that is, there is an overall balance of payments surplus), then there is more demand for local currency than there is supply. In a floating exchange rate system, this will push the exchange rate up, which makes local production of tradeable goods less competitive. This helps to eliminate the overall surplus, by increasing the current account deficit and discouraging capital inflows (by making investment less attractive); but it also reduces employment, as tradeable production falls.

In a fixed exchange rate system (that is, where the exchange rate is set by the government rather than being determined by market forces), the exchange rate cannot appreciate, so this automatic adjustment does not occur. Instead, the Central Bank has to provide the extra local currency to buy the surplus foreign exchange at the official exchange rate. This allows the Central Bank to increase its foreign exchange reserves, which provides resources to meet any subsequent overall balance of payments deficit; but it also increases the money supply, which in turn fuels inflation. Inflation in turn increases production costs, which again weakens the competitiveness of tradeable production, and causes a deterioration in the current account deficit.

The orthodox response to this situation is *sterilisation*. This requires the Central Bank to borrow locally from the (non-bank) private sector, usually by issuing bonds. In effect, this means taking as much money out of the economy by borrowing as is put in to purchase the surplus foreign exchange, so as to avoid increasing the money supply, and thus inflation.

However, sterilisation has some important drawbacks. Of particular relevance in the present context is that it uses up local savings which might otherwise have been used to finance productive investment, and that it increases local interest rates (by increasing the demand for local savings). Higher interest rates further discourage productive investment, by making it less attractive relative to investments in financial instruments; by increasing the cost of borrowing; and by reducing companies' profits (by increasing the cost of servicing their existing local currency debts), and thus the resources they have available for investment without borrowing. The result is likely to be a lower level of locally owned productive investment than would have occurred without sterilisation.

Sterilisation also has other potential drawbacks, some of which may have knock-on effects on productive investment, although this is not their primary effect. First, while the Central Bank's foreign exchange reserves increase by as much as its debts, the interest rate on its borrowing is generally higher – often much higher – than that on its extra reserves. In effect, sterilisation entails the Central Bank borrowing at a high interest rate to invest at a lower rate, so that it incurs continuing losses. These losses add to the public sector deficit, and thus tighten the constraint on government spending and/or require increases in taxation, both of which further reduce investment. The increase in interest rates associated with sterilisation strengthens this effect, by increasing the cost of servicing the public sector's local currency debts more generally.

Sterilisation also makes foreign borrowing cheaper relative to local borrowing. Provided companies do not expect a devaluation, this encourages them to build up foreign rather than local currency debts (and to borrow abroad to refinance their existing domestic debts). At the same time, it makes it very profitable for foreign companies and banks to deposit money in the country's banking system, to take advantage of the high interest rate and the fixed exchange rate. This type of capital inflow, which was very important in Mexico and Thailand prior to their respective financial crises, is exceptionally volatile, as the money deposited can be (and almost inevitably will be) withdrawn very quickly once a devaluation is in prospect.

As a result, sterilisation in response to large capital inflows encourages a further increase in capital inflows, which requires further sterilisation, which increases capital inflows, and so on. The result may be a continuing spiral of increasing capital inflows, and accelerating accumulation of (particularly volatile) external liabilities. Each twist of this spiral increases the pressure on the public finances and reduces locally owned and locally financed investment in productive capacity.

The overall impact of direct investment will depend critically on the balance between these positive and negative influences.

To summarise:

1 new flows of direct investment for construction increase investment in productive capacity by 100 per cent of their value;

2 direct investment by purchase, portfolio investment and reinvested profits on FDI will increase investment in productive capacity on average by somewhat less than 100 per cent of their value; and

3 there may also be a positive or negative impact on local investment; but the direction as well as the size of this effect will depend heavily on local conditions.

This suggests that the overall effect of direct and equity investment inflows on productive capacity will be somewhat less than 100 per cent, *unless* the third consideration above is both positive and strong enough to outweigh the shortfall arising from the second. If the net effect on local investment is negative or only slightly positive, the scale of the net shortfall could be substantial, especially where inflows are dominated by equity investment and direct investment by purchase. The disparity between the growth of the stock of foreign-owned investment and that of the overall capital stock may be still greater, to the extent that the capital gain on equity investment is greater than the increase in productive capacity which underlies it.

One way of considering this issue is to compare the increase in direct and equity investment flows to a particular country with the increase in its total investment over the same period. This is done in Table 9.1, with respect to the experience of Mexico during the early 1990s. Between 1990 and the financial crisis at the end of 1994,[39] direct and equity investment increased from 9.2 billion pesos to 40.3 billion pesos at 1990 prices, an increase of 31.1 billion pesos. This is substantially greater than the increase in gross fixed capital formation (GFCF – that is, total productive investment), which amounted to only 22.5 billion pesos over the same period.

To assess the extent of additionality (that is, the net effect on total productive investment for each extra dollar of direct and equity investment), we would need to know what would have happened to gross fixed capital formation if the increase in direct and equity investment had not occurred.

Table 9.1 • Direct and Equity Investment and Gross Fixed Capital Formation in Mexico, 1990–93/4 (Billion Pesos, 1990 Prices)

	1990	Year to September 1994	Change
Direct investment	7.2	20.5	+13.3
Equity investment	2.0	19.8	+17.8
Total	9.2	40.3	+31.1
Gross fixed capital formation	127.7	150.2	+22.5

Source: Author's estimates, using data from IMF 1997b; 1998a.

Table 9.2 • Estimates of Additionality of Direct and Equity Investment in Mexico, 1990–93/4

Local investment assumption	Hypothetical GFCF	Actual minus hypothetical GFCF	% of increase in direct and equity investment
Zero growth	127.7	+22.5	72%
Constant per capita	136.5	+13.7	44%
Constant % of GDP	143.7	+6.5	21%
4.4% pa real growth	150.2	0.0	0%

Notes: GFCF = gross fixed capital formation. All figures are the author's estimates, based on data from IMF 1997b; 1998a. The baseline for local investment assumes 100 per cent additionality of direct and equity investment in 1990, except for the final line, which assumes zero additionality.

This is clearly unknowable. However, it is reasonable to assume that it would have increased, as the external economic environment improved considerably over this period, due to debt reduction under the Brady Plan and the North American Free Trade Agreement (NAFTA).

Some indication of the possible extent of additionality can be obtained by comparing the actual gross fixed capital formation in 1993/4 with what it would have been on certain illustrative assumptions about the growth of local investment over this period. This is done in Table 9.2. For simplicity, it is assumed here that all direct and equity investment in 1990 added directly to total productive investment, so that local investment can be estimated by deducting them directly from gross fixed capital formation (giving 118.5 billion pesos in 1990 prices). Relaxing this assumption would imply a somewhat lower figure for additionality than the estimates given.

The results, even on the basis of very conservative assumptions about local investment growth, suggest that $1 of direct and equity investment increases productive investment by substantially less than $1, and possibly by as little as $0.20.

- If local investment would otherwise have remained unchanged (in real terms), additionality is around 72 per cent.

- If local investment would otherwise have increased in line with population growth, additionality is around 44 per cent.

- If local investment would otherwise have increased in line with overall GDP growth – by no means an extravagant assumption – additionality is only about 21 per cent.

As shown in the final line, GFCF growth without increased direct and equity investment over this period in excess of 4.4 per cent per annum would be consistent with negative additionality – that is, with direct and equity investment actually reducing total productive investment. This compares with average GDP growth during the period of 3.2 per cent per annum.

It should be emphasised once again that these figures are essentially illustrative; and that, even if the conclusions are valid for Mexico in the early 1990s, they cannot necessarily be extended to other countries or other periods. Nonetheless, this does seem to suggest that $1 of direct and equity investment contributes considerably less than $1 to total productive investment in at least some cases.

If the additionality of direct and equity investment in terms of total productive investment is indeed below 100 per cent, then the stock of locally owned investment will grow more slowly with such investment than would have been the case without it. In other words, foreign direct and equity investment is at least partly a substitute for locally owned investment.

Moreover, if the stock of locally owned investment is lower as a result of direct and equity investment, this implies that the total profits on such investment are also likely to be reduced. Since this is a critically important source of future investment, this will tend both to extend and to intensify the negative effect on locally owned investment over the longer term.

Effects on Employment

The effects of direct investment on employment are in some respects comparable to its effects on aggregate investment. The two extreme cases are relatively straightforward, at least in terms of their direct effects.

- Direct investment through construction and equity investment in new share issues to finance the creation of new capacity can be expected to have a positive direct effect on employment, by creating jobs.

- Equity investment in existing shares is unlikely to have any significant direct impact.

FDI through the purchase of existing capacity is more complex. Its direct effect on the productive capacity is, in principle, neutral, at least in the short term, as it represents only a transfer of ownership. However, it may be made more negative, to the extent that the new (transnational) owners of the company seek to increase efficiency by reducing labour costs. While this may be partly or wholly off-set by a more positive effect over the longer term, if that increased efficiency allows an expansion of production, this is likely to require additional investment to increase capacity; and the increase in employment might more appropriately be attributed to this additional investment than to the original purchase (although the latter may be a necessary condition for the investment in expansion to occur).

Once again, the indirect effects of the investment are also important. Generally speaking, the positive and negative indirect effects of direct and equity investment on investment will also apply to employment: if locally owned investment is reduced by direct investment, it is also likely to reduce employment by locally owned enterprises. However, the indirect effects are likely to be stronger relative to the direct effects in the case of employment, to the extent that local production is more labour-intensive than that of transnational companies. This may make the overall impact on employment less positive or more negative than that on investment.

A partial exception to this general rule is the sterilisation of capital inflows (as discussed in Box 9.1). While sterilisation is likely to reduce local investment in new capacity by increasing interest rates, it can also be expected to contribute to a shift towards (or a slower shift than might otherwise have occurred away from) more labour-intensive production methods. This implies a more ambiguous effect on overall employment by locally owned companies, so that this element of the indirect impact will be less negative than the effect on investment, and could in principle even be positive.

To summarise, it is far from certain that the overall effect of direct and equity investment on employment will necessarily be favourable. The direction and strength of the effect will depend critically on:

- the balance of direct and equity investment between the creation of new capacity and the purchase of existing capacity;

- the extent of labour-saving efficiency gains in the case of direct investment by purchase;

- the labour intensity of the new productive capacity which is created;

- the extent to which additional production for the local market substitutes for existing production by foreign-owned and locally owned enterprises, and the relative labour intensity of the latter; and

- the extent of sterilisation and its relative impact on the level and labour intensity of production.

Simply to assume that direct investment necessarily contributes to increased employment is a serious, and potentially misleading, oversimplification.

The Development and Transfer of Technology [40]

A major part of the purported benefit of direct investment is the transfer of technology from developed to developing countries, which is seen as allowing a process of 'catching up' with developed countries in productivity and thus incomes.

In practice, however, the extent to which the transfer of technology increases growth depends on the extent to which it is actually *transferred* to the local economy rather than merely being used by a single (foreign-owned) producer — what Rao (1997) terms the 'localisation of development'. Various mechanisms are put forward by proponents of FDI as assisting this process, for example 'learning by doing' by employees who then work for other, locally owned, companies, or who establish their own enterprises.

However, there are some important constraints on this process. In particular, the extent to which transferable technological skills are developed depends on the level at which local employees are engaged in the development and application of technology; and this in turn depends in part on the local availability of workers with high-level technical skills – which is often very limited, especially in low-income economies.

At the same time, the transfer of sector-specific technologies in this way depends on locally owned firms coexisting or being established in the same sector as the foreign-owned enterprise. This is likely to be limited, in the former case, by their ability to compete with the TNC which introduced the technology; and, in the latter case, by the availability and cost of initial capital. At best, there will be a time-lag between the introduction of technology and the percolation of its benefits through to the local economy, as local employees are recruited, learn the technology, leave the company, and establish production using the new technology elsewhere.

The TNC concerned can be expected to resist this process at every stage, so as to limit the competition it faces. Measures used to this end may include, for example,

- the employment of expatriate staff in key managerial and high-level technical positions;

- ensuring that local technical staff work only on isolated parts of the technical process, to limit the transferability of their skills;

- inducements to technical staff to remain with the company ('golden handcuffs');

- legal conditions on staff to prevent them 'pirating' technologies for future employers;

- legal action against actual or prospective competitors on such issues as infringement of patents; and

- anti-competitive measures such as undercutting competitors, incurring losses which are implicitly absorbed by the parent company.

Against this background, the prospect of technology actually being absorbed by the local economy, against resistance from the originating company, before it becomes obsolete, seems remote. Even if it were transferred successfully, the adopting company would need to keep pace with the further progress and adaptations made by the TNC to remain competitive, which in most cases would be equally problematic in view of the limited resources available to the latter. Faced with such long odds, technical staff and potential competitors would have little incentive to embark on this unequal struggle. The problem is likely to be compounded by the WTO agreements on Trade-Related Intellectual Property Rights (TRIPs) and Trade-Related Investment Measures (TRIMs), and by the General Agreement on Trade in Services (GATS). These may, as has been argued by their proponents, lead investors to provide more investment embodying technology; but it will further strengthen the hands of TNCs in ensuring that it is not transferred into the local economy, and that they thus retain the incomes associated with the application of those technologies.

If transnational companies are successful in retaining local employees with specialist technological skills, and in preventing the leakage of technological advances into the wider economy, the effect on indigenous technological progress of using local employees in such positions could well be negative. The returns to technological advances accrue, not to the individual employees involved in their development, but to the company which employs them. There is therefore a danger that, by recruiting the most able technologists, transnational companies will in part transfer technological progress from locally owned to foreign-owned enterprises. While greater technological progress may be made within the country (because technologists have greater access to resources, for example, or a more favourable working environment), the benefits will accrue to the transnational company rather than to the local economy. As in industries based on natural resources, direct investment may displace local investment which might otherwise have occurred, by absorbing a scarce input (in this case technological human capital) essential to production.

Politics and Economic Policy

Large-scale flows of direct and equity investment can have a major effect on economic policy in two ways. Firstly, reliance on these flows imposes an important constraint on policy, because of the need to avoid policies which might discourage continued inward investment. This constraint is likely to become progressively stronger as the stock of direct and equity investment becomes larger (see Chapter 12). As the stock, and thus the total profits, of direct investment increase, so the inflow of new investment needed to maintain an inward net resource transfer is also increased. In the case of portfolio investment, the stock represents a potential outflow of funds (and a source of domestic economic instability if this should occur, because of the impact of large-scale selling on the value of locally owned shares). As the stock grows, so the potential impact of disinvestment increases commensurately.

Second, in the case of direct investment, the growing stock of investment represents an increasing presence and economic interest of transnational companies in the economy. As the experience of the developed countries clearly demonstrates, transnational companies represent an immensely powerful interest group. In many cases, they are larger, richer and better-resourced than the governments of the countries (especially developing countries) in which they operate. Combined with their economic power within the host country, as employers, as taxpayers, as exporters, as investors, as owners of productive capacity, as providers of capital inflows – and quite possibly as financiers of the ruling party – this gives them considerable political power.

This suggests considerable scope for direct and indirect influence on policy, which increases in line with the stock of equity, and especially direct, investment. The result is likely to be a shift in the objectives of policy towards the priorities of transnational companies and foreign investors. While there may be some overlap with the interests of the population and of the economy as a whole, there are also many areas of direct conflict – for example, on wage levels, environmental regulations, and the competitive position of transnational companies relative to local producers. It seems likely that the overall effect on indigenous development and the welfare of the population will be negative.

10

The Global Dimension
Competition for Direct Investment
and Export Markets

Effects on Export Markets and Prices

The discussion so far has considered the effects of direct and equity investment in a purely national context – that is, from the perspective of the
individual country which receives them. In practice, however, both the
investments themselves and the goods and services they produce (where
these are internationally tradeable) form part of a global market. It is therefore important to take account of their effects on these markets, and the
implications for other developing countries.

The effect on export markets is of particular significance because it is
strongest for direct investment through construction in the export sector –
the one case which (based on Chapter 8) has a clearly positive foreign
exchange effect at the country level. It also applies to direct investment
through purchase in the export sector, where this entails an increase in
output; and, to a more limited extent, to investment which increases the
production of import substitutes. The effect will be at best to limit, and
potentially even to reverse, any positive foreign exchange effect from the
perspective of developing countries as a whole; and to intensify any negative
impact.

The discussion of the foreign exchange effects of direct investment in
Chapter 8 effectively assumed that the prices of exported outputs were
unaffected by the investment. This is generally appropriate from the perspective of an individual country's decision as to whether to accept a particular
investment, as most investments are too small for any price impact to affect
that country significantly.[41] In considering the overall effect of direct investment in developing countries, however, the effect may be substantially
greater, and significantly affect the calculus of costs and benefits.

To the extent that direct investment increases the world supply of the (tradeable) goods it produces, it will tend to reduce their prices in the international market. This is most apparent in the case of primary commodities, such as unprocessed agricultural produce and minerals: when supply in the world market is increased without a corresponding increase in demand, the result is a fall in the market price. However, a very similar effect can arise in the case of manufactured goods exported by developing countries, as an increase in supply to the world market intensifies price competition among producers.

Where the demand for the product concerned is price inelastic – that is, where a 1 per cent increase in supply leads to a fall of more than 1 per cent in the price – producers as a whole will receive less income as a result of the price fall, even allowing for the increase in production. In other words, other producers will lose more gross revenue than the total value of production resulting from the investment. Many primary commodities produced largely or wholly by developing countries (such as coffee, cocoa, tea or copper) fall into this category.

However, from the perspective of net foreign exchange effects, even if demand is price-elastic (and the price effect much smaller), increased production of exports by transnational companies may cause a deterioration in the position of developing country producers as a whole, because the net benefit to the host country is much smaller than the overall increase in the value of its production. To take the pure export example presented in Chapter 8 (Table 8.3), the net foreign exchange benefit of a $75 million increase in annual export production was only $22 million per annum. This implies that the net foreign exchange effect on producers as a whole would be negative if the extra production led to a price fall sufficient to reduce the gross revenues of other producers in excess of $22 million – that is, if the price elasticity of demand were 3.4 ($75 million divided by $22 million) or less. Most major developing country commodity exports – basic manufactures such as textiles, wood products and leather goods as well as primary commodities – have price elasticities of demand well below this level.

The impact on world supply (and thus on world market prices) can only be averted if the additional exports produced as a result of the investment displace those of existing producers. However, if the producers concerned are in developing countries, this will have a similar effect, in that the foreign exchange earnings of the country concerned will be reduced. In practice, the outcome is likely to be some combination of these two elements: a reduction in the output of other producers sufficient to limit, but not eliminate, the negative effect on the world price.

As noted above, the effect of a single investment on the world market may at first appear minimal, and it is not likely to affect the calculus of costs and benefits from the perspective of the host country. However, what matters from the perspective of developing countries as a whole is not the size of the effect, but rather the relationship between the change in output and the world price; and this is independent of scale.

Suppose, for example, that a 1 per cent increase in the world supply of a particular commodity leads to a 1 per cent fall in its price on the world market. If a particular investment increases the world supply by 0.01 per cent, the price will fall by 0.01 per cent. The overall revenues generated will therefore be unchanged, and the (gross) revenues generated by the investment will be exactly off-set by a loss to other producers because of lower prices. This will impose some degree of foreign exchange loss on other developing country exporters, depending on their share of world supply and the degree of local ownership.[42]

Where exports are close substitutes for other goods (as in the case of tropical fruits and vegetables), demand is likely to be relatively price-elastic, so that the overall foreign exchange effects of increased production for producing countries will be less negative, and could in principle even be positive. In such cases, however, increased production will also reduce the prices of other goods for which it is a substitute; and the effects on developing country producers of these goods also need to be taken into account. Where substitutes are produced largely in developing countries, the overall effect is again likely to be negative.

In other words, even where direct investment generates a net foreign exchange benefit to the host country, this will often be at least partly off-set by net foreign exchange costs to other developing countries who have locally owned companies exporting the same product. The importance of this effect will depend on the price elasticity of demand for the product concerned; the cross-price elasticities of demand of other developing country exports (that is, the responsiveness of their markets to a reduction in the price of the export whose production is increased); the share of developing countries in the world supply of the export itself and of substitutes for it; and the extent of foreign ownership in the sectors concerned in developing countries as a whole.

At best, this will reduce the potential foreign exchange benefits of FDI to developing countries as a whole, and could well reverse them in the only scenarios where potentially significant benefits exist. However, since the costs are imposed on countries other than the host country, who have no control over the investment decision, they will not influence whether a particular investment takes place. As in the case of export promotion in response to debt problems (Woodward 1992: Vol. I, Ch. 2), developing countries acting individually have a strong incentive to act against their own collective interests.

Competition for Direct Investment

The growing importance of direct investment as a source of capital has led to a process of intense competition among developing countries for FDI flows. Attracting such investment is, by its nature, largely a competitive process: investment decisions are primarily about *where* to invest rather than *whether* to invest. While total direct investment flows to developing countries have increased greatly in recent years, any individual host country's success in attracting a particular investment must therefore be regarded as occurring at least partly at the expense of alternative locations.

A number of widespread features of developing countries in the contemporary world economy act to intensify this competition. These include, in particular:

- tight foreign exchange constraints, accentuated in many middle-income countries by recent financial crises, and in many low-income countries by continuing debt problems;

- limited domestic savings and the absence or declining availability of other forms of international capital flows (particularly commercial bank loans and aid) to finance investment, or their high cost (bond issues, for example);

- high levels of unemployment and poverty in many countries, and the failure of structural reforms to generate increased employment, creating an urgent social and political need for investment to create jobs; and

- (arguably) an over-optimistic assessment of the short-term benefits and long-term costs of inward direct investment.

These factors combine to increase the long-term cost countries are willing to accept in order to attract direct investment flows.

Host-country efforts directed wholly or partly to attracting direct investment have broadly taken a combination of four forms:

1 deregulation (the relaxation of restrictions on foreign ownership, approval requirements for new investments, local content and export orientation of production, employment of expatriate staff, repatriation of capital, profit remittances, etc);

2 the introduction of new measures designed to protect the interests of companies undertaking direct investment: the strengthening or more effective enforcement of patent and copyright protection; or mechanisms to protect foreign investors from expropriation of their assets;

3 direct or indirect subsidisation or the reduction of costs (as through the provision of infrastructure specific to the project at public expense, temporary tax concessions to foreign investors, or the establishment of export processing zones); and

4 policies benefiting producers as a whole, to create a conducive environment for investment in general (such as deregulation of labour and product markets, or a general reduction of corporate taxation).

The first three of these incentives benefit foreign investors specifically, strengthening their position relative to local companies. Some measures of the fourth type may also benefit foreign investors disproportionately as new entrants to the market – the relaxation of restrictions on advertising, for example.

From the point of view of the individual host country, the effect of such measures is to increase the amount of direct investment which is received; but potentially to reduce the long-term benefit per dollar of investment, in terms of development and the welfare of the population. Such potential costs take a number of different forms, notably:

- fiscal effects (due to lower rates of general corporate taxation, tax concessions specific to direct investors, or the skewed provision of infrastructure);

- balance of payments effects (through removal of restrictions on profit remittances, capital repatriation, export orientation and local content);

- the quantity and quality of employment (the effects of labour market deregulation, including workplace health and safety);

- technology transfer into the local economy (affected by such factors as patent protection or the removal of restrictions on expatriate staff); and possibly

- environmental standards (compromised by the deregulation of goods markets and production processes).

Such effects may be greatly increased to the extent that policy changes apply to the existing stock of direct investment and/or domestic investment as well as new foreign investment.

For the individual country, such costs are presumably seen by the government as a price worth paying for the new investment they can attract – otherwise the concessions would not be offered. However, even at the country level, three critically important caveats need to be taken into account.

First, in assessing the overall impact of direct investment, it is necessary to take account of the costs of the measures taken to attract it, as well as the potential benefits of the flows themselves. If there are some economic or social costs entailed, the net benefits may be substantially less than the value of the investment.

Second, if the orthodox view of direct investment is indeed over-optimistic, as has been argued in this book, host-country governments are likely to overestimate the benefits of direct investment; and they may therefore be willing to incur greater costs in order to attract such investment than is in fact warranted. This risk is increased by the vociferous promotion of the pro-FDI view and active support for pro-FDI policies by powerful and influential agencies such as the World Bank, as discussed later in this chapter.

Third, governments generally have a relatively short time horizon, because of their limited periods in office. Even if the orthodox view is valid, governments may still take an artificially positive view of the overall effects of direct investment if its benefits arise largely in the short term (because of the initial capital inflow) while the costs are incurred further into the future.

From the perspective of developing countries as a whole, the picture is much more negative. As in the case of export revenues, the additional investment received by one country as a result of the government's promotion efforts is likely to come at least partly at the expense of others. As noted above, the main consideration facing transnational companies in making investment decisions is not so much *whether* to make an investment as *where* to locate it; and the nature and motivation for investments in developing countries (access to regional markets or low labour costs, for example) mean that the competition is largely between alternative developing countries.

Even if an investment which is induced by policy concessions is beneficial to the host country, it will only lead to a benefit for developing countries as a whole if the investment would not otherwise have occurred, or if it would otherwise have been located in a developed country. To the extent that concessions to foreign investors influence decisions on the location of investments between alternative developing countries, there will be no genuinely additional investment in developing countries to off-set the reduction in developmental and welfare benefits arising from the policy changes made and inducements offered in order to attract it.

Because this process is competitive, each concession made by one developing country increases the need for concessions by other developing countries. As the process continues, and more and more countries offer more and more concessions, so the baseline against which each country has to compete is shifted further and further in favour of investors and against host countries. In the process, developing countries are effectively forced to bid

away the developmental benefits of direct investment merely in order to maintain their share of the flows available.

The effects of this competitive process are likely to be particularly acute for poorer developing countries. As noted above, their foreign exchange constraints are particularly tight, their domestic savings rates particularly low, their access to commercial loans extremely limited, and the prospects for official flows are poor due to chronically declining aid budgets. This means that their need for such capital flows as are available is generally more acute than for most middle-income countries.

At the same time, however, they are also less able to compete for the available investment. The factors identified as being conducive to direct investment inflows include, for example, a stable macroeconomic environment; large markets with sustained rapid growth of demand; open trade régimes; effective legal protection for investors; a skilled and educated workforce; and reliable access to quality inputs and business services (Bergsman and Shen 1995). These features are the polar opposite of conditions in most low-income countries – especially those in sub-Saharan Africa and other least-developed countries.

- Most of these countries are anything but stable in macroeconomic (and in some cases political) terms, because of structural economic weaknesses and chronic debt problems, with little prospect of immediate improvement.

- With a few obvious exceptions, low-income countries' markets are both small (with relatively small populations as well as low per capita incomes), and slow-growing because of their macroeconomic problems. Again, long-term growth prospects are generally substantially weaker than for most middle-income countries.

- Progress in trade liberalisation has been relatively limited (Dean *et al.* 1994) and is seriously constrained by low government revenues, heavy reliance on import tariffs and/or export taxes, and limited capacity to raise revenues from other sources.[43]

- Legal systems are often critically weak, due to limited administrative capacity, chronic lack of resources, and in some cases wider problems in governance (such as limited legitimacy of government institutions, profound ethnic divisions, political instability and conflict). None of these problems is conducive to a speedy resolution.

- Educational attainment at all levels, from basic literacy to university graduation, is generally much lower in low-income than in middle-income countries. Once again, the time-lags inherent in education, coupled with continuing tight resource constraints on education systems at all levels, mean this is unlikely to improve dramatically in the near future.

- Access to supply of quality inputs is generally more limited than in most middle-income countries, due to the lack of local production capacity and often high transport costs (and, possibly, unreliability of supply) for imports, particularly in the case of landlocked countries.[44]

In short, the basic economic conditions of most low-income countries put them at a considerable disadvantage in the competition for direct investment relative to middle-income countries. In principle, there are two ways in which they could overcome (or at least reduce) these fundamental weaknesses as direct investment locations: to improve their infrastructure and human development; or to make their policy régimes more favourable to foreign investors.

Unfortunately, the scope for most low-income countries to pursue the first option is limited, because the financial cost of improving infrastructure, and the cost and long time-lags entailed in increasing the educational attainment of the workforce are incompatible with their tight fiscal constraints and the urgency of increasing foreign exchange inflows and productive investment.

This suggests that the only instruments of competition available to most low-income countries (or, to a great extent, to many middle-income countries) is to intensify their policy efforts in those areas which are within the government's control, and which can be expected to yield a reasonably rapid increase in inflows of direct investment – essentially the elements of deregulation, financial inducement and broader economic reforms outlined above.

This process has been continuing apace.

In each of 1991 and 1992, according to UNCTAD, over 30 developing and 'transitional' countries introduced over 75 changes to their investment regimes, none of them in the direction of more control. (Crotty *et al.* 1997: 8)

Tax incentives of various kinds (holidays, exemptions, rebates, reliefs and so on) are also widespread (Crotty *et al.* 1997: Table 4).

As noted above, all of these policies have potentially significant costs in developmental terms, which need to be taken into account in assessing the effects of direct investment. However, neither direct financial inducements nor policy concessions have had a major effect on flows of direct investment. 'The empirical literature suggests that investment incentives have not been effective in attracting direct investment flows' (Crotty *et al.* 1997: 29) and 'any attempt in [poor developing] countries to improve cost advantages by easing their entry conditions for FDI, or by reducing wages further, will almost certainly fail to offset other disadvantages' (UNCTAD 1997a: 92).

The result is an intense competition for direct investment inflows, which is potentially harmful in developmental terms, but largely ineffectual in increasing overall investment. In consequence,

> Many [developing] countries may be making large and costly changes in their economies and government policies, such as following IMF austerity programs or liberalizing their financial sectors, to attract FDI, yet receive little. (Crotty *et al.* 1997: 28)

Official Encouragement

The competitive process outlined in the previous section has been greatly exacerbated – indeed actively promoted – by international efforts to encourage direct investment. The catalogue of bilateral and multilateral actions to promote direct investment flows, primarily from developed to developing countries, is truly spectacular, as shown by the following account from the International Finance Corporation (IFC, part of the World Bank Group).

> Since the end of World War II, the industrial countries have encouraged private capital flows as a prime policy objective.... [The establishment of the IFC in 1956] was one of the international community's first initiatives to channel the flow of foreign direct investment (FDI) to developing countries. To improve the policy framework for FDI, including investment in developing countries, bilateral and multilateral legal agreements were also implemented. To protect investors from political risks in developing countries, bilateral and multilateral guarantee programs were established. Individual industrial countries set up financial institutions alongside bilateral and multilateral investment promotion programs....

> Altogether, 155 countries have been involved in one or more [bilateral investment treaties (BITs)]. These treaties aim to improve the conditions for investment by firms of each signatory country in the other.... The number of BITs has expanded rapidly, reaching nearly 1,130 by May 1997.... Several of the most recent multilateral treaties contain closely similar provisions to those of the BITs....

> The Multilateral Investment Guarantee Agency (MIGA), also part of the World Bank group, provides political risk insurance to investors in developing countries. In addition, several agreements reached during the Uruguay Round trade negotiations limit aspects of host-country policies toward foreign direct investors that would adversely affect international trade....

A Multilateral Agreement on Investment (MAI) is now being negotiated among the OECD countries.... Nearly 15 [*sic*] of the OECD governments have established national financing institutions with mandates to support national firms' investments in developing countries.... The European Union supports International Investment Partners to promote FDI in developing countries. The Inter-American Development Bank has its Inter-American Investment Corporation whose activities parallel those of the IFC. Many industrial countries operate investment promotion programs to encourage their national firms to invest in developing countries. (IFC/FIAS 1997: 21–2)

A curious omission from this list, particularly in view of its source, is the role of structural adjustment programmes supported by the World Bank. These have regularly promoted the liberalisation of all manner of restrictions on direct investment flows, on a country-by-country basis, as well as large-scale privatisation programmes, which often represent an important channel for direct investment.

Privatisation may also take the form of portfolio equity investment, which has also been promoted more directly by structural adjustment programmes through the establishment of stock exchanges (or the opening of existing exchanges to foreign investors), partly as a means of attracting inflows of equity investment. Equity investment has been further encouraged by changes in financial regulations in developed countries, as well as by relatively low real interest rates in developed countries in the early 1990s, which encouraged investors to seek higher returns elsewhere.

Looking ahead, there are two key proposals which could move this agenda substantially further forward: the proposal to extend the IMF's mandate to encompass capital account liberalisation (that is, the removal of restrictions on international capital flows); and the proposed Multilateral Agreement on Investment (MAI).

If the IMF were to adopt a role in capital account liberalisation (CAL) similar to its current approach to current account transactions, it would essentially represent a ratchet mechanism: existing exchange restrictions would remain (largely) protected, but the introduction of new restrictions (including the reintroduction of restrictions once they have been removed) would be heavily proscribed.[45] The definition of capital account restrictions in this context remains vague: capital inflows and outflows on direct and equity investment are clearly affected (and profit remittances are already covered by the arrangements for restrictions on current account transactions); but it is possible, at least, that the definition will be drawn sufficiently broadly to encompass policies towards direct investment and transnational companies' operations more generally. If this were the case, capital account liberalisation could closely resemble, and thus enforce, the MAI (as discussed below).

At the time of writing the status of the capital account liberalisation proposal is unclear. Although the Asian and Russian financial crises and their aftermath raised serious doubts about the appropriateness of universal capital account liberalisation, the IMF is still pushing the idea, conceding only a need for greater rigour in requiring each country to establish a strong financial system first. The leading government proponents of CAL (the US and the UK) have become less active in promoting it; but this is widely seen as no more than a tactical withdrawal, motivated by a fear that the proposal would be watered down if implemented now, due to the concerns raised by the financial crisis.

The MAI proposal aims primarily to promote direct investment as such, by protecting the interests of investors. This would have the effect of institutionalising the current high level of demand for direct investment, by locking in place the policy concessions which developing countries have made or are willing to make at the height of competition for direct investment flows. The result would be to limit the ability of governments in the future to adopt a more selective approach to FDI inflows, or to implement policies aimed at increasing their developmental benefits.

If it is successful (in its own terms), the MAI will create a large pool of countries which offer favourable conditions to investors in order to attract direct investment inflows, at the expense of accepting more limited developmental and welfare benefits per dollar of investment. Once participation reaches a certain critical mass, direct investors will be able simply to choose between MAI participants in their locational decisions. As a result, any country which is not within the ambit of the MAI, or which withdraws from it, can expect to receive little in the way of new inflows. If the country already has a substantial stock of inward direct investment, this is almost certain to imply outward net resource transfers on a scale which few countries could sustain.

Three key features stand out in the overall process of direct investment promotion:

- first, it focuses heavily on the demand side (that is, the substantive changes which it promotes are directed at encouraging developing countries to seek investment rather than at encouraging transnational companies to make investments in developing countries);

- second, a major part of the process is directed at changing the policies of individual developing countries towards direct investment, particularly in adjustment programmes and bilateral investment treaties; and

- third, it seeks to entrench any concessions which are made unilaterally by developing country governments towards foreign investors through international agreements.

These features have critically important implications for the process of competition for direct investment among developing countries.

By operating on the demand side rather than the supply side, the promotion of direct investment tends to increase its cost to developing countries. It is a basic result of economics that increasing demand while supply is unchanged will almost inevitably shift the balance of advantage towards suppliers (in this case foreign investors), allowing them to increase the price which they receive (in this case the rate of return). If similar pressure were instead applied on transnational companies – through regulatory and tax régimes, for example – to encourage them to invest in developing countries, the reverse would be the case: supply would increase without a corresponding increase in demand. There might then be an equal increase in the total amount of investment flows; but the cost would be reduced rather than increased.

In practice, however, the opposite has been the case, as developed country governments have themselves sought to compete for TNC investment, often by providing inducements to potential investors on a scale that the vast majority of developing countries can only dream of. This amounts to an active discouragement of direct investment in developing countries offering competing sites. In some cases, there is even a competitive process between localities within a single developed country, as for example between individual states in the US.

Crotty *et al.* (1997, Table 2) cite numerous examples of direct and indirect subsidies provided to transnational investors by national and local governments in developed countries to attract them away from alternative locations between 1983 and 1995. These show a strong upward trend, both in absolute terms (from an average of $80 million in 1983–6 to $140 million in 1993–5) and still more markedly in the cost per job (from an unweighted average of $32,500 to $98,000 over the same period).[46] Such subsidies are likely to have more than off-set the largely superficial efforts by developed country governments to promote outward direct investment in developing countries by their own transnational companies, through mechanisms such as the EU's International Investment Partners.

By operating on the country level, the promotion of direct investment in developing countries encourages their governments to act in their individual interests, without regard to the costs they impose on others. This has been a key factor in the creation of the competitive bidding process outlined above, in which developing country governments bid away the potential benefits of inward investment in order to keep up with the terms others are being encouraged to offer.

If promotion efforts took place instead within a global framework which sought to protect the interests of host countries, this could avert what is widely seen as a 'race to the bottom' in terms of developmental benefits, employment and wages, health and safety standards, and environmental costs. The amount of investment might be somewhat lower; but this would be off-set by an increase in the net benefits per dollar of investment to the recipients.

The use of international agreements to entrench the policy concessions which are made towards foreign investors, limit the choices available to future governments, by attaching considerable costs to policy reversals. Coupled with escalating stocks of inward investment, the effect is to seal in any limits to the benefits and increases in the costs of direct investment to host countries which governments may concede.

This is particularly important because of the timing of this phenomenon.

- As discussed in Chapter 3, the general perception of direct investment is at present exceptionally optimistic − and arguably unrealistically so. Should the balance of opinion shift away from FDI, this might well imply a need to redress the balance of policy.

- The need for direct investment inflows as a source of capital, foreign exchange and employment has also been particularly acute in many countries at different times over the last decade, due to the effects of debt and other financial crises, slow growth, or weak export markets. If and when the external environment for developing countries improves, their needs will be less acute, and the extent of policy concessions which are worth making to attract investment will be more limited.

- The intense competition for direct investment further increases the need to make policy concessions to attract it. If no other country had made concessions to foreign investors, the extent of concessions needed in any individual country to attract $1 million of additional direct investment would be relatively limited. In a period of general (and competitive) easing of policies, the baseline is continuously falling, and substantial changes are needed simply to maintain the country's existing competitive position relative to alternative locations. Again, if the competitive environment were to improve, either due to a general reduction in the perceived need for direct investment, or due to a change in the international regulatory framework, the concessions which have been made might no longer be appropriate.

- Many of the policy changes of developing country governments in recent years – particularly under structural adjustment programmes – have been made under some degree of duress. The terms of such programmes may mean that policy changes are necessary, not to attract FDI flows, but to secure urgently needed financial packages, without which the economy could face near-disaster. (The concessions extracted from Korea in return for its 1998 'rescue' package are a clear case in point.) This means that governments may have made concessions towards foreign investors which were not justified in terms of the (perceived) benefits of the direct investment they were expected to attract.

For all these reasons, the operation of international agreements not only places a ratchet on policy concessions towards foreign investors, but also does so at a time when the circumstances enforce policy concessions which are unlikely to be justified over the long term. The MAI and CAL proposals would institutionalise this ratchet mechanism in a much stronger form than at present.

Conclusion

Part of the reason for the over-optimism of the prevalent view of direct investment is the tendency to look at the effects on the host country in isolation from the developing world as a whole. Because of the global nature of the markets, both for direct investment itself and for the exports it produces, this is erroneous; and because the spill-over effects on other developing countries are clearly negative, a serious bias becomes apparent in the prevailing optimism. These costs may be considerable, in terms of export prices and the developmental benefits of direct investment, and may well outweigh any benefits to the host countries themselves in the limited number of cases where such benefits can be expected to accrue.

Moreover, the competitive process is particularly skewed against the poorest and least developed countries.

> To a great extent, developing countries have to compete for the fruits of globalization (exports and [inflows of direct and portfolio equity investment])…. This competition can be costly, depressing the prices received for exports, limiting the developmental benefits of FDI for host countries and reducing tax revenues; and it is almost inevitable that those least able to compete will lose. The key factors which inhibit effective competition – social and political instability, weak government revenues and tax bases, lack of administrative capacity, inadequate physical, economic and human infrastructure, etc. – are generally most acute in smaller and poorer countries. (Woodward 1996: 69–70)

Far from contributing to development, the efforts of developed country governments to promote direct investment have compounded and institutionalised this competitive process, entrenching the developmental costs. If implemented, the major current policy proposals concerning direct investment – the proposed Multilateral Agreement on Investment and the extension of the IMF's mandate to cover capital account liberalisation – will intensify this process still further, to the detriment of the developing world as a whole.

11

Net Transfers and the Build-Up of Investment Stocks

Equity Investment

The capital which is transferred into an economy in the form of direct and equity investment, like capital which is borrowed, creates external liabilities – that is, it entails a commitment to make payments in foreign exchange to the owners of the capital in the future.

However, the amount of this commitment is less clearly defined than in the case of a loan. When a loan is made, the borrower takes on a fixed schedule of principal payments, and undertakes to pay interest on the outstanding amount at a clearly defined interest rate; and these payments define the amount of foreign exchange which will leave the economy as a result of the loan in each subsequent year.

In the case of equity investment and direct investment in quoted shares, by contrast:

- the year-to-year outflow of foreign exchange (equivalent to the interest on a loan) is determined by the amount paid in dividends each year, which is entirely at the discretion of the company and cannot necessarily be forecast with any accuracy even over a relatively short period;

- the timing of the eventual repatriation of the capital investment (equivalent to the repayment of a loan) is determined by when the shares are sold to a local investor, which is entirely at the discretion of the owner; and

- the amount of the eventual capital outflow depends on the price of the shares concerned when they are sold to a local investor, which will depend both on the timing of the sale and the performance of the market.

In practice, the situation is simplified somewhat from a balance of payments perspective, because it is the totality of share purchases and sales which matters rather than each individual transaction. Nonetheless, there is a high level of uncertainty, particularly about the timing and amount of capital repatriation; and this depends crucially on the 'herd instincts' of investors, as discussed in Chapter 12.

As noted in Chapter 8, most of the return to foreign investors on equity investments takes the form of capital gains resulting from increases in share prices. This limits the outflow of foreign exchange (so long as foreign investors buy more shares in total than they sell); but it means that the rapid increase in share prices which attracts foreign investors to emerging markets translates directly into an equally rapid increase in the stock of inward investment.

Most of the potential cost of equity investment is incurred when foreign owners sell shares to local investors and repatriate the capital (or invest it elsewhere). However, if this occurs on a substantial scale – as during the recent Asian financial crisis – this can be expected to cause a substantial drop in prices and potentially a substantial devaluation, which will at least partly off-set the capital gains which have been made. From this perspective, a progressive sale of stocks by foreign investors will have a worse direct impact in balance of payments terms than a sudden one – although the wider effects of the latter are likely to be much more serious.

Nonetheless, even if there is a major withdrawal of foreign investors from the market, and the prices they receive are dramatically reduced as a result, the rate of return they realise may nonetheless be very high if they have held the stocks for a long period. If share prices were to rise by 25 per cent per annum, even if they were then halved by a general exodus of foreign investors, the rate of return would be positive on any investment held for three years or more, increasing rapidly to 10–11 per cent per annum after five years, and 18–19 per cent per annum after ten years.[47]

In terms of the overall impact, the weaker performance of shares which had been held for a shorter period would reduce the average rate of return. Nonetheless, assuming a constant level of net investment inflows, the average rate of return on shares sold would be 6 per cent per annum after seven years of inflows, 14 per cent per annum after ten years, and 20 per cent per annum after 15 years (Woodward 1996: 47).

Direct Investment

As in the case of portfolio equity investment, the foreign exchange liabilities a country incurs as a result of direct investment inflows are something of a blank cheque. The profits which they generate are not predictable with any accuracy over the long term; and it is difficult to evaluate when (or whether) the investment as a whole or particular assets may be sold to a local investor, how much will be raised as a result, or how much of the proceeds will be repatriated.

As discussed in Chapter 8, a much greater proportion of the total return on direct investment is generally repatriated than in the case of equity investment (except in the case of direct investment through the purchase of shares, which from this perspective is virtually identical to portfolio equity investment). This means that a host country is much more heavily dependent on attracting new inflows, and encouraging existing investors to reinvest their profits locally rather than repatriating them, if it is to maintain an inward net resource transfer (that is, to ensure that more foreign exchange flows into the economy in new investment than flows out in profits).

Clearly, it is possible for a country to attract enough new direct investment to receive an inward net transfer of resources. In principle, it is even possible to maintain inward net resource transfers for a prolonged period. (It should be noted, however, that the net resource transfer does not reflect the totality of the foreign exchange effects of direct investment, because of the effects on exports and imports, as discussed in Chapter 7.)

However, there may be a high cost attached to attracting inward net transfers: in general, any individual inward investment will ultimately require an outward net transfer much larger than the initial capital inflow; and the longer outward net transfers are avoided, the greater they will be when they do occur. Even if a country could simply keep on attracting an amount of new investment greater than the amount of profits in each year, the stage would eventually be reached where the entire economy was owned by foreigners and the opportunities for new productive investment were less than the profits – or, more realistically, where the extent of foreign ownership became unacceptable politically.

The problem may be summarised as follows. The profits on direct investment are equal to the existing stock of investment multiplied by the average rate of return. In order to avoid an outward net resource transfer, the host country therefore needs to attract this amount of new direct investment each year. However, this new investment increases the stock of investment in the following year, the growth rate being equal to the rate of return; and this increases the profits in the following year, and thus the amount of investment required to avoid an outward resource transfer, by a similar amount. This process is repeated every year, as illustrated in Box 11.1.

This means that outward net resource transfers can only be avoided so long as both the annual flows and the stock of direct investment are increased at an annual rate at least equivalent to the overall rate of return on the

Box 11.1• Rates of Return, Net Resource Transfers and the Stock of Inward Investment: a Numerical Illustration[48]

Suppose that a country starts with a stock of inward investment of $100 million, and that the average rate of return on that investment is 20 per cent per annum. In the first year, the profits will be $20 million. To avoid an outward net resource transfer (that is, to keep as much foreign exchange coming into the economy in new investment as goes out in profits), the country will need to attract new investment of at least $20 million.

However, this new investment will add directly to the stock of investment, increasing the total to $120 million (the original $100 million, plus $20 million) at the end of the first year. The profits in the second year will then be $24 million (20 per cent of $120 million), requiring at least $24 million of new investment to avoid an outward net resource transfer. Again, this new investment adds directly to the stock of investment, increasing the total to $144 million; and this increases the profits to $28.8 million. This process continues every year, as shown in the table below.

Year	Stock of investment at start of year ($m)	Profit ($m)	New investment ($m)
1	100.0	20.0	20.0
2	120.0	24.0	24.0
3	144.0	28.8	28.8
4	172.8	34.6	34.6
5	207.4	41.5	41.5
6	248.9	49.8	49.8

The result is that the stock of investment, the outflow of profits, and therefore the amount of new investment required to avoid an outward net resource transfer all increase at 20 per cent per annum – that is, at the rate of return on the investment.

existing stock of investment. The problem is that the rates of return on direct investment are much greater than any plausible expansion of the economy – 16–18 per cent per annum for developing countries as a whole, and 24–30 per cent per annum for sub-Saharan Africa in 1990–4, according to the World Bank (1997b).

The implications are demonstrated in Tables 11.1 and 11.2.[49] These simulate the flows and stocks of direct investment, and the profits they generate, over a 20-year period, using annual rates of return of 16 per cent per annum (the lower estimate for developing countries as a whole) and 30 per cent per annum (the upper estimate for sub-Saharan Africa) respectively. Three scenarios are considered:

1   a one-time inflow of $100 million in year 0, with one-third of profits reinvested in each subsequent year (roughly in line with the average for developing countries);

2   a one-time inflow of $100 million in year 0, with new investment in each subsequent year equal to profits (just enough, that is, to avoid an outward net transfer); and

3   an inflow sufficient to achieve an inward net resource transfer of $100 million in every year.

At a rate of return of 16 per cent per annum, the situation is clearly problematic. In scenario 1, with one-third of all profits reinvested, there is by definition a continuing and increasing outward net transfer. By the end of year 8, more has been transferred out of the economy than the initial inward transfer. By year 18, more than three times as much has been withdrawn from the economy than was initially injected, and a further quarter is transferred out of the economy every year.

In scenario 2, by definition, net transfers are zero. However, this is achieved only by rapidly increasing new investment, adding to the capital stock. By year 20, the total stock of inward investment is nearly $2 billion, twenty times the initial inward transfer; and the amount of new investment required each year to avoid an outward net transfer is $268 million.

In scenario 3, where inward net transfers are maintained at $100 million per annum, the new investment needed to off-set profit remittances escalates still more rapidly. By year 20, the total stock of inward investment is $13.5 billion, and inflows of nearly $2 billion are required each year – nearly as much as the total inward resource transfer over the whole 20-year period.

At a rate of return of 30 per cent per annum, the situation is far more serious. If one-third of profits are reinvested (scenario 1), the cumulative outward net transfers exceed the initial inflow by year 5; and more is transferred out every year than was originally invested after year 17. Over the whole 20-year period, outward transfers total $1.15 billion – 11.5 times the initial inward transfer, and the remaining external liabilities (the stock of investment) are $673 million, nearly seven times the amount originally invested.

In order to avoid outward net transfers (scenario 2), the stock of investment must be allowed to rise to $19 billion by year 20 – nearly 200 times the original inward transfer – requiring new investment of $4.4 billion per annum. An inward net transfer of $100 million per annum throughout the period (scenario 3) increases the stock of investment in year 20 to $82

Table 11.1 • Simulated Cost of FDI (Rate of Return 16% pa)

($m)	(1) 33% reinvestment				(2) Zero net transfer		(3) $100m pa net transfer		
Year	Capital	Profits	Remitted	Reinvested	Capital	Profit (all reinvested)	Capital	Profit	Investment
0	100.0				100.0		100.0		
1	105.3	16.0	10.7	5.3	116.0	16.0	216.0	16.0	116.0
2	111.0	16.9	11.2	5.6	134.6	18.6	350.6	34.6	134.6
3	116.9	17.8	11.8	5.9	156.1	21.5	506.6	56.1	156.1
4	123.1	18.7	12.5	6.2	181.1	25.0	687.7	81.1	181.1
5	129.7	19.7	13.1	6.6	210.0	29.0	897.7	110.0	210.0
6	136.6	20.7	13.8	6.9	243.6	33.6	1141.4	143.6	243.6
7	143.9	21.9	14.6	7.3	282.6	39.0	1424.0	182.6	282.6
8	151.5	23.0	15.3	7.7	327.8	45.2	1751.9	227.8	327.8
9	159.6	24.3	16.2	8.1	380.3	52.5	2132.1	280.3	380.3
10	168.1	25.5	17.0	8.5	441.1	60.8	2573.3	341.1	441.1
11	177.1	26.9	17.9	9.0	511.7	70.6	3085.0	411.7	511.7
12	186.5	28.3	18.9	9.4	593.6	81.9	3678.6	493.6	593.6
13	196.5	29.8	19.9	9.9	688.6	95.0	4367.2	588.6	688.6
14	207.0	31.4	21.0	10.5	798.8	110.2	5166.0	698.8	798.8
15	218.0	33.1	22.1	11.0	926.6	127.8	6092.5	826.6	926.6
16	229.6	34.9	23.3	11.6	1074.8	148.2	7167.3	974.8	1074.8
17	241.9	36.7	24.5	12.2	1246.3	172.0	8414.1	1146.8	1246.8
18	254.8	38.7	25.8	12.9	1446.3	199.5	9860.3	1346.3	1446.3
19	268.4	40.8	27.2	13.6	1677.7	231.4	11538.0	1577.7	1677.7
20	282.7	42.9	28.6	14.3	1946.1	268.4	13484.1	1846.1	1946.1

Table 11.2 • Simulated Cost of FDI (Rate of Return 30% pa)

($m)	(1) 33% reinvestment				(2) Zero net transfer		(3) $100m pa net transfer		
Year	Capital	Profits	Remitted	Reinvested	Capital	Profit (all reinvested)	Capital	Profit	Investment
0	100.0				100.0		100.0		
1	110.0	30.0	20.0	10.0	130.0	30.0	230.0	30.0	130.0
2	121.0	33.0	22.0	11.0	169.0	39.0	399.0	69.0	169.0
3	133.1	36.3	24.2	12.1	219.7	50.7	618.7	119.7	219.7
4	146.4	39.9	26.6	13.3	285.6	65.9	904.3	185.6	285.6
5	161.1	43.9	29.3	14.6	371.3	85.7	1275.6	271.3	371.3
6	177.2	48.3	32.2	16.1	482.7	111.4	1758.3	382.7	482.7
7	194.9	53.1	35.4	17.7	627.5	144.8	2385.8	527.5	627.5
8	214.4	58.5	39.0	19.5	815.7	188.2	3201.5	715.7	815.7
9	235.8	64.3	42.9	21.4	1060.4	244.7	4261.9	960.4	1060.4
10	259.4	70.7	47.2	23.6	1378.6	318.1	5640.5	1278.6	1378.6
11	285.3	77.8	51.9	25.9	1792.2	413.6	7432.7	1692.2	1792.2
12	313.8	85.6	57.1	28.5	2329.8	537.6	9762.5	2229.8	2329.8
13	345.2	94.2	62.8	31.4	3028.8	698.9	12791.3	2928.8	3028.8
14	379.7	103.6	69.0	34.5	3937.4	908.6	16728.6	3837.4	3937.4
15	417.7	113.9	75.9	38.0	5118.6	1181.2	21847.2	5018.6	5118.6
16	459.5	125.3	83.5	41.8	6654.2	1535.6	28501.4	6554.2	6654.2
17	505.4	137.8	91.9	45.9	8650.4	1996.2	37151.8	8550.4	8650.4
18	556.0	151.6	101.1	50.5	11245.5	2595.1	48397.3	11145.5	11245.5
19	611.6	166.8	111.2	55.6	14619.2	3373.7	63016.5	14519.2	14619.2
20	672.7	183.5	122.3	61.2	19005.0	4385.8	82021.5	18905.0	19005.0

billion, and the annual investment required in the same year to $19 billion.

In view of these results, it is not surprising that the stock of inward FDI in sub-Saharan Africa increased from about 7 per cent of GNP in 1980 to 20 per cent in 1994, while net resource transfers remained substantially negative throughout this period.

Net Transfers and the Stock of FDI: Two Country Examples

The effect on the stock of direct investment of increasing inflows to limit or reverse outward net transfers is well illustrated by the recent experiences of Malaysia and Swaziland. As shown in Figure 11.1(a–c), Malaysia received FDI inflows averaging about $600 million per annum between 1986 and 1988; but profits on the existing stock of FDI were nearly double this level, so that there was an outward net transfer of around $500 million per annum. Over the following four years, inflows increased rapidly, to peak at just over $5 billion in 1992 – enough to achieve a substantial inward net transfer – declining slightly to $4–4.5 billion in 1994–5, before returning to just over $5 billion in 1996–7.

Even while outward net transfers were increasing, the stock of inward FDI increased, not only in absolute terms (by 7 per cent per annum in

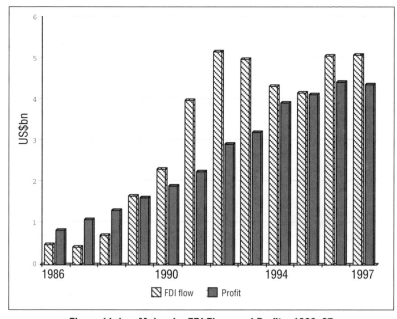

Figure 11.1a • Malaysia: FDI Flows and Profits, 1986–97

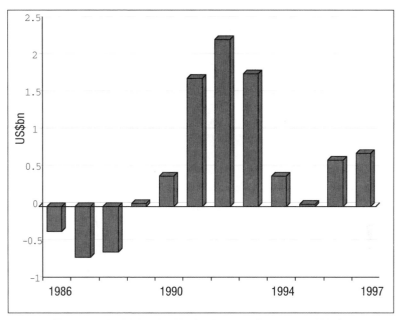

Figure 11.1b • Malaysia: FDI Net Resource Transfers, 1986–97

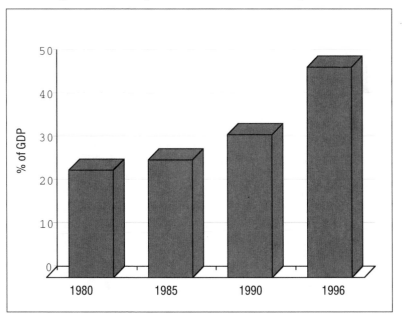

Figure 11.1c • Malaysia: FDI Stock, 1980–96

1980–5), but also relative to GDP (by nearly 2 per cent per annum, increasing the ratio to GDP from 25 to 27 per cent). This trend accelerated in 1985–90, despite overall outward net transfers in the period of $1.2 billion: the growth rate of the stock of FDI rose by half to 10.5 per cent per annum, and the growth rate relative to GDP doubled to just under 4 per cent. As a result, the stock of inward FDI increased from 27 to 33 per cent of GDP.

However, the effect of the inward net transfers of 1990–4 was much more dramatic, as the growth rate of the stock of FDI doubled again, to more than 21 per cent per annum in 1990–5. Despite impressive economic growth, this was twice as fast as the increase in GDP, so that the FDI stock increased by more than half as a proportion of GDP, from 33 to 52 per cent.

Inevitably, the growing stock of inward FDI meant an increase in the base for profit remittances by foreign investors, and profits increased from a trough of $830 million in 1986 to $4.4 billion in 1996. As a result, even though the dramatic increase in inflows in the early 1990s had been broadly sustained, the inward net transfer virtually disappeared in 1995, and was only $600 million per annum in 1996–7. The scale of the effect can be shown by comparing the two years in which net transfers were only just positive. In 1989, this was achieved by an inflow (and therefore an increase in the stock) of just $1.7 billion. In 1995, just six years later, it required an inflow nearly 2.5 times as great ($4.1 billion).

This case is likely to understate the scale of the effect for developing countries in general, for two reasons. First, Malaysia was considered to be one of the most attractive and lowest-risk locations for FDI during the late 1980s and early 1990s, and is therefore likely to have had one of the lowest rates of return. This is confirmed by the profit and FDI stock figures, which suggest an average rate of return in 1990–4 of around 14 per cent per annum, somewhat below the World Bank's estimate for developing countries as a whole of 16–18 per cent. In sub-Saharan Africa, especially, where the equivalent figure is 24–30 per cent, the increase in FDI stocks and future profits associated with a given level of inward transfers would be far greater.

Second, as noted above, the growth rate of the Malaysian economy was exceptionally high over the period. While this may have been partly because of the high level of FDI inflows, it is unlikely that the same level of inward net transfers would generate a similar rate of growth in most other countries. The effect is magnified by the strength of Malaysia's exchange rate against the dollar over the period, which further increases the dollar GDP figure which is used to calculate the ratio. The picture has changed dramatically since 1995, as the exchange rate has proven to be unsustainable. As a result of the Asian financial crisis, Malaysia's exchange rate has fallen by about one-third against the dollar since 1995. Adjusting the 1995 dollar GDP figure accordingly would imply an FDI/GDP ratio of around 80 per cent in 1995, rather than 52 per cent.

The implications of a higher rate of return are demonstrated by the case of Swaziland, as shown in Figure 11.2. Swaziland was successful in increasing direct investment inflows from $5–10 million per annum in 1984–5 to around $60–80 million per annum (7–9 per cent of GDP) in 1987–94. However, the effects of changes in inflows were eclipsed by changes in profit remittances. The initial increase in inflows was entirely off-set by an increase in profits, so that net transfers remained slightly negative in 1986–8. Profits then increased dramatically to a peak of $138 million in 1994, leading to a massive outward net transfer ($75 million or 7 per cent of GDP), before returning to a more moderate level. However, inflows declined from a peak of $83 million per annum in 1991–2 to just $16 million in 1996, turning negative in 1997. The result was a continued outward net transfer of $25–40 million per annum (2–3.5 per cent of GDP) in 1995–7. It seems likely that the increase in profits between the mid-1980s and the mid-1990s was partly a result of an increase in the rate of return, which also clearly caused the 1989–90 peak. However, the increase in the stock of investment also made a major contribution. The increased inflows from 1986 meant that the stock of inward FDI more than trebled in dollar terms between 1985 and 1990, from $104 million to $336 million, increasing further to a peak of $507 million in 1995. This suggests that around four-fifths of the profits in 1996–7 were attributable to investments made from 1986 onwards. Without this element of profits, net resource transfers would have remained positive in 1995–6, and the outward transfer would have been just $8 million, or slightly more than 0.5 per cent of GDP, in 1997.

While the rate of return is substantially higher in Swaziland than in Malaysia, it should be noted that it is still somewhat *below* the World Bank's estimate for sub-Saharan Africa as a whole, averaging 20 per cent per annum in 1990–4, as compared with 24–30 per cent. Once again, therefore, this case is likely to understate the scale of the potential problem from the perspective of the region as a whole.

As these illustrations demonstrate, it may be possible for countries to avoid or limit outward net transfers on direct investment, and even to attract substantial inward net transfers, by attracting new inflows. However, this comes at a very high price in terms of the build-up of inward investment stocks, both in absolute terms and – unless dollar GDP is increasing very rapidly – relative to the economy as a whole. This in turn increases future profits more or less proportionally, which greatly increases the level of new investment (and thus the increase in the stock of investment) required to achieve a given net transfer in the future.

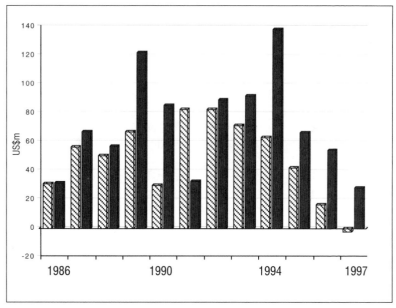

Figure 11.2a • Swaziland: FDI Flows and Profits, 1986–97

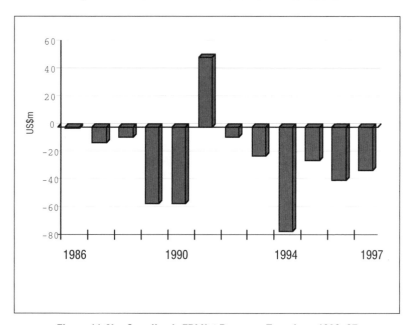

Figure 11.2b • Swaziland: FDI Net Resource Transfers, 1986–97

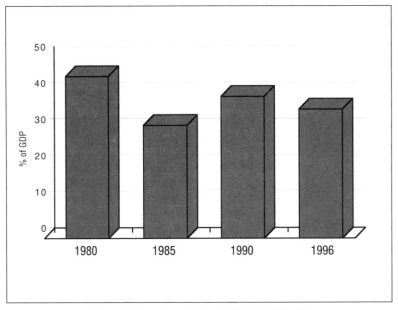

Figure 11.2c • Swaziland: FDI Stock, 1980–96

12

Surges and Cycles

The 1990s Surge in Equity Investment

As discussed in Chapter 4, the early 1990s saw a massive surge of equity investment flows to the 'emerging' markets, net inflows increasing from $3.2 billion in 1990 to $45 billion in 1993, and remaining between $32 billion and $46 billion per annum from 1993 until the Asian financial crisis in 1997 (World Bank 1998a: Vol. II, 14).

There were a number of reasons for this very rapid increase, on both the demand side and the supply side. The most obvious factor increasing the 'emerging' markets' demand for equity capital was the development of stock exchanges in a number of developing countries, and their opening to foreign investors, as part of the process of structural adjustment and financial liberalisation. The number of countries recording portfolio equity investment flows increased from eight in 1991 to 42 in 1994, slowing down thereafter (probably as a result of the Mexican crisis) to reach 48 in 1996 (World Bank 1998a: Vol. II).

A second element of structural adjustment promoting the demand for equity investment was privatisation, which occurred on a considerable scale across the developing world in the late 1980s and early 1990s. In many middle-income countries, this entailed offering large volumes of shares in formerly state-owned enterprises to foreign investors. Portfolio investment in privatisation share issues amounted to $26.4 billion (an average of $4.4 billion per annum) between 1990 and 1996 (World Bank 1998a: Vol. I, 110, Table A4.9).

At the same time, the supply of equity capital from the developed countries to 'emerging' markets also increased considerably, for a combination of reasons.

- Savings in developed countries became increasingly institutionalised, largely as a result of their own financial liberalisation. Reliance on private pensions and insurance increased, and households sought higher returns through mutual funds and unit trusts, rather than keeping their savings with banks, building societies and credit unions. The result was to create large pools of savings, actively managed to seek high rates of return, primarily through trading in financial instruments such as equities, bonds and derivatives.

- Real interest rates in the major developed countries fell to historically low levels, strengthening the incentive for investors to seek higher rates of return elsewhere, particularly in equity markets.

- Restrictions in developed countries which prevented investors (including institutional investors) from investing in developing countries were relaxed (SEC Rule 144A in the US, for example).

- As the credit ratings of a number of 'emerging' markets reached 'investment grade' in the early 1990s, they were seen as a much safer investment than previously, encouraging institutional investors to increase their exposures (IMF 1998b: 23). This was at least partly a result of the Brady Plan of 1989, which allowed the major debtor countries some degree of reduction of their debts to commercial creditors, although the actual debt reduction provided appears to have been at best very limited (EURODAD 1995), and the effect was probably more psychological than real.

- The apparent resolution of the debt problems of the major Latin American economies following the Brady Plan in the late 1980s also stimulated a substantial return of flight capital, much of it into equity investments.

Virtually all of these factors, on both the demand side and the supply side, can be divided into three broad categories. The first is made up of factors which are, by their nature, temporary and liable to be reversed. This includes, in particular, the low real interest rates in the major developed countries, which began to be reversed in 1994 (although rates fell again after the Russian crisis of 1998). In the light of subsequent financial crises, the achievement of 'investment grade' credit ratings may be also be put in this category, although it might at the time have been considered more permanent.

The second set of factors are those which represent a switch of a finite pool of resources from one form into another. This imposes a limit on how long the process can continue; and is likely to mean that the process will slow down progressively after a certain point, as the pool of resources in their original use diminishes. This category includes:

- privatisation, which represents a shift of ownership of the stock of state-owned assets, from the public to the private sector;

- the institutionalisation of savings, which represents a shift in the form in which assets are held; and

- the return of (a fixed stock of) flight capital to its country of origin.

Clearly, the timescale in which these processes will near completion varies considerably (being shortest in the case of privatisation); and the continuing growth of the overall level of savings would imply a continued increase in the resources available for equity investment after the proportion controlled by institutional investors had stabilised. Nonetheless, all three processes exhibit the same fundamental characteristic of shifting a finite pool of resources from one location or one form of ownership or control to another.

The third category is made up of effects which represent a one-time shift in the nature of the market. These include the establishment of stock exchanges and their opening to foreign investors; and the removal of developed country restrictions which previously limited investment in 'emerging' markets.

Temporary changes in market conditions, such as low real interest rates, can be expected to give rise to a similarly temporary increase in the volume of investment, possibly with a very sharp beginning and end (as in the case of the achievement and subsequent loss of investment grade credit ratings by 'emerging' markets). Finite processes such as those included in the second category can be expected to have a similarly temporary effect, although this may tend to be sustained over a longer period, and is likely to disappear more gradually.

The effect on capital flows of many one-time changes in the market – particularly those affecting who can invest in which countries – are also likely to be essentially temporary in nature. This is because their main influence is on the level of the stocks of investment held by foreign investors rather than the flows themselves. If restrictions prevent investors in a particular country from investing in 'emerging' markets, and then these restrictions are removed, investors will try to move quickly from having no investments in those markets to what they see as the appropriate proportion of their portfolios.

This stock adjustment means buying a large volume of shares in a relatively short period, followed by a much lower, or even zero, level of investment, as this proportion is kept broadly constant thereafter – that is, a large but temporary surge of portfolio equity investment flows. The surge will be sustained only as long as more countries of origin deregulate; and eventually there will be no more countries to do so.

The removal of restrictions in the host country might be expected to have a broadly similar effect (though concentrated on a single market), as investors seek to increase their portfolios in newly accessible markets to what they see as the appropriate level. In practice, however, this pattern has been much less marked than one might expect: while some 'emerging' markets have indeed experienced a decline in portfolio investment flows after the first year, most have seen continuing increases in inflows for at least two or three years, and many have sustained high levels of inflows for substantially longer.

Various possible explanations can be advanced for this. The stock adjustment process may be slowed down if investors wait for the market's credibility to be established; the expected decline may be off-set by other temporary factors (such as privatisation programmes), or by a secular or cyclical increase in equity investment for other reasons; or the initial surge in investment could be self-sustaining for a period because of herd-like behaviour by investors, as discussed in the next section.

Herd-like Behaviour

A critical factor influencing the pattern of equity investment flows over time is the herd-like tendency of investors to move into or out of the same markets at the same time. A strong fashion developed for investment in 'emerging' equity markets in the early 1990s, particularly in East and South East Asia, but also in Latin America; and this induced many institutional investors to shift a substantial part of their portfolios into these markets in the early and mid-1990s. This trend was by no means unrelated to the temporary factors and one-off changes in the markets described earlier in this chapter, and the investment opportunities they provided. However, it also had a major effect on the nature of their impact, allowing what might otherwise have been a very short-lived surge in equity investment flows to be sustained over a much longer period.

Herd-like behaviour arises partly from the nature of equity markets in general. Share prices are determined by demand and supply; but the demand for shares is itself determined primarily by investors' *expectations* of prices, while the supply of shares is relatively fixed. The result is that investors' expectations are, to a great extent, self-fulfilling. If investors as a whole expect, however irrationally, that share prices will rise, they will purchase shares; and this will increase demand, bringing about the price increases they expect. Conversely, if they expect the market to fall, they will sell shares, pushing prices down.

This creates a strong incentive for investors to move with (or ideally just ahead of) the herd. When other investors are moving into a market, it is rational for each investor to invest, almost irrespective of the economic fundamentals, even if prices have already been pushed up beyond the level which could possibly be sustained over the long term. Once the herd changes direction, however, it is rational for every investor to withdraw from the market by selling stocks as quickly as possible, before prices fall too far.

This is potentially very destabilising, greatly exaggerating what might otherwise be relatively modest rises or falls in the market. The destabilisation becomes considerably greater if investment decisions are based on current market performance – that is, if investors invest in markets when prices are rising, and sell when prices are falling. Investors first rush in, pushing share prices up and drawing more investors in until the market reaches an unsustainable level, creating a speculative bubble; then they panic and rush back out, bursting the bubble and causing market values to collapse.

The problem is compounded by the way in which competition operates between institutional investors – particularly mutual funds and unit trusts – and the incentives facing fund managers.

> Another source of potential instability comes from the mutual funds. Fund managers are judged on the basis of their performance relative to other fund managers, not on the grounds of absolute performance. This may sound like an arcane point but it has far-reaching implications as it practically forces fund managers into trend-following behaviour. As long as they keep with the herd, no harm will come to them even if the investors lose money, but if they try to buck the trend and their relative performance suffers even temporarily, they may lose their job. (Soros 1998: 142)

This is arguably what happened in the first half of the 1990s. The supply-side surge in equity investment flows to 'emerging' markets – particularly that arising from stock adjustments in the portfolios of institutional investors – entailed substantial purchases of shares. The resulting increase in demand, when virtually no international investors were reducing their holdings in these markets, pushed prices up quickly, providing large capital gains to those holding shares. The exceptionally high rates of return which resulted made these markets look even more attractive, drew still more investors in (or increased the proportion of their portfolios investors were willing to put in), and pushed prices up still further.

The result was to extend the effect of changes in the market which would otherwise have been very short-term in nature, increasing both their scale and their duration. They also pushed share prices (and to a lesser extent real exchange rates) up to unsustainable levels, forming a speculative bubble in equity markets. The series of financial crises from the end of 1994 demonstrated the fragility of the 'emerging' markets, causing the herd to change direction and, as investors withdrew *en masse* from markets, bursting the bubble they had largely created.

Direct investment is not generally seen as suffering such sharp reversals, as its primary motivation is long-term rather than speculative. However, some significant elements of direct investment – most notably investment in property – may be prone to similar instability. Like shares, commercial and residential property is often treated at least partly as a speculative investment. This is partly because it is relatively easily saleable (compared with production facilities and businesses), with limited transaction costs, giving the potential for capital gains as well as generating rental income.

Once property is seen as profitable as a speculative investment, it is bought by more overtly speculative investors, foreign and domestic; and their purchases push prices up further, bringing about the anticipated capital gains. The resulting upward trend in prices may attract new investors, pushing prices up still further; then, as it becomes apparent that the boom will not continue, buying turns to selling, and the market is in danger of collapse. However, while this may have a very disruptive effect on the property market, it is likely to have a relatively limited direct effect on overall flows of FDI, as investment in residential and commercial property is generally a relatively small proportion of the total.

Thus in both equity and property markets, there is a considerable potential for herd-like behaviour to generate unsustainable financial inflows and speculative bubbles, followed by major outflows and the collapse of market values. Similar patterns can also arise without an international dimension, fuelled mainly or even solely by domestic investors – the UK property market in the 1980s and the recent performance of internet stocks (and arguably the US stock exchange as a whole) provide noteworthy examples.

However, the involvement of international capital gives rise to two important differences. First, the potential scale of the problem is much greater, as the capital available to inflate the bubble is almost unlimited; and, second, the introduction of a foreign exchange dimension to the problem complicates and compounds the economic effects.

A broadly similar pattern of herd-like behaviour can be seen in the case of bank deposits. Depositors place their money in 'emerging' market banks to take advantage of higher interest rates than they can obtain domestically, coupled with (generally) fixed exchange rates; and the resulting foreign exchange inflows strengthen the overall balance of payments, allowing the fixed exchange rate to be maintained. However, if inflation in the host country is faster than in the country against whose currency the exchange rate is fixed, the exchange rate may become increasingly overvalued in real terms, as relative production costs rise and competitiveness is eroded.

At some point, it will become apparent that a devaluation will be necessary. However, governments are generally resistant to devaluation – not least because of the importance of the fixed exchange rate to the continuation of financial inflows. They therefore tend to put off a devaluation as long as possible by raising interest rates further or taking other measures to reduce inflation. As long as depositors believe that the government can maintain the fixed exchange rate – even temporarily – they will continue to deposit their money, often in increasing amounts. The moment they think that a devaluation is imminent, however, they will withdraw. In other words, the expectations of depositors are largely self-fulfilling: if they expect the fixed exchange rate to be maintained, they deposit more, allowing it to be maintained; if they expect a devaluation, they will withdraw their deposits and so precipitate a devaluation.

Fixed exchange rates can be sustained in this way for a surprisingly long time after a devaluation is widely seen as inevitable. *The Economist* warned of a possible Mexican devaluation – and of its potential impact on the banking system – nearly two years before the crisis at the end of 1994.[50]

Temporary Factors Promoting Direct Investment

As discussed in Chapter 4, direct investment flows to developing countries also enjoyed a major boom in the 1990s, although this was somewhat less spectacular than in the case of equity investment as it started from a higher initial level. Nonetheless, total FDI in developing countries increased five-fold between 1990 and 1996, from $23.7 billion to $119 billion (World Bank 1998a: Vol. II, 14).

Again, this largely reflects changes in the market for direct investment which have, in some respects, been similar to those affecting equity investment.

• Many developing countries have removed or relaxed restrictions on inward investment, particularly as part of structural adjustment programmes, although this has generally occurred progressively over a number of years rather than as a single 'big bang'.

• Privatisation programmes have been a major source of FDI as well as of portfolio equity investment, bringing in an average of $6.2 billion of FDI per year to developing countries as a whole between 1990 and 1996 (World Bank 1998a: Vol. I, 110, Table A4.9).

- Some flight capital (or resources classified as flight capital) may also have re-entered its country of origin as direct investment, although this is likely to represent a relatively small element of total FDI in most countries (except in specific cases, as in Uganda).

An additional element promoting direct investment in a number of 'emerging' markets, particularly in Latin America, in the late 1980s and early 1990s was debt–equity conversion. This is a mechanism which allows prospective investors to exchange hard currency debts owed by the government for local currency, usually at less than face value, provided the proceeds are used for investment (in new or existing capacity) in the country concerned. Since the conversion rate is generally higher than the price at which the debt can be bought in the secondary market, this effectively allows investors to acquire productive capacity at less than market price. Debt–equity conversions totalled $36.7 billion (an average of $5.2 billion per annum) during their peak period from 1987 to 1993 (World Bank 1998a).[51]

A critically important, if unquantifiable, factor in the rapid growth of FDI in the 1990s has been the globalisation of production processes – the relocation of specific operations in the production of a particular product in different countries according to where the cost of each operation is lowest. This is closely related to the liberalisation of FDI (and trade) régimes in developing countries, but has also been facilitated by advances in information technology and communications.

These factors exhibit similar characteristics to those promoting portfolio equity investment. Debt–equity conversion was a clearly temporary phenomenon; privatisation and the return of flight capital, as in the case of portfolio investment, are finite conversion processes; and reform of FDI régimes represent a one-time shift in the nature of the market, though generally a more gradual one than the establishment and opening of stock exchanges.

The globalisation of production processes is more difficult to interpret. This can also be seen as a finite conversion process, as existing productive operations are relocated out of their countries of origin. (Once this has happened, any subsequent relocation has no net effect on FDI, as investment in the new country is off-set by disinvestment in the previous one.) However, the greater complexity of the process, and the less clearly defined 'stock' of investment to be relocated, suggest that this will be a more prolonged process than in the case of portfolio diversification by institutional investors.

These factors can thus be expected to give rise to a temporary surge in FDI. However, the resulting cycle has been more muted than for portfolio equity investment, partly because of the more extended nature of the liberalisation of FDI régimes and the globalisation of production; partly because debt–equity conversion and most of the privatisation-related FDI occurred before globalisation neared its peak; and partly because of the absence of herd-like behaviour and self-fulfilling expectations, except in the special case of investment in property. It is also difficult to assess, without further research, whether we have yet reached the peak of FDI flows, because of the complexity of the globalisation process.

Procyclical Flows

Apart from the time-specific factors which contributed to the surge of FDI and portfolio equity investment in the early and mid-1990s, these forms of financing are subject to marked cycles over the longer term. These are important in themselves, as the variability of capital inflows represents an important challenge in macroeconomic management. Equally important, however, is the phasing of these cycles relative to the performance of the economy as a whole – *when* foreign exchange flows into and out of the economy, and when inflows increase and decline, relative to other developments in the economy.

Specifically, direct and equity investment tend to be procyclical in nature. This is clearest in the case of equity investment, and has been amply demonstrated by the experience of the Mexican, Asian and Russian financial crises, as discussed in Chapter 14. While the problems of procyclical flows are less widely acknowledged in the case of FDI, they nonetheless exist (though in attenuated form). When a country is performing well in a relatively problem-free economic climate, investors will be only too happy to invest. When problems arise, they will become more reluctant, and therefore will at best reduce their rate of investment, or even disinvest, and repatriate more of their profits. The effect is to compound the effect of external (and internal) shocks to the economy, in terms of their impact on the balance of payments, investment, output and income.

This can be illustrated by the level of FDI flows to Latin America before and after the Mexican debt crisis of 1982. As shown in Figure 12.1a, FDI flows to Argentina, Brazil and Mexico (at 1990 prices) fell from a peak of nearly $8.5 billion in 1981 to less than $3 billion in 1983, remaining at around that level for five years. Not until 1991 did they regain the pre-crisis level. Figure 12.1b shows the experience of three smaller Latin American

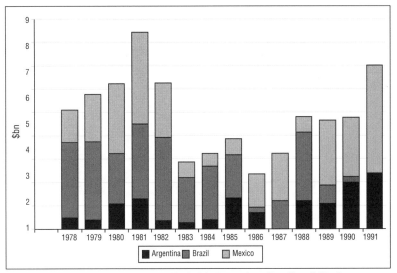

Figure 12.1a • FDI Flows, 1978–91: Argentina, Brazil and Mexico

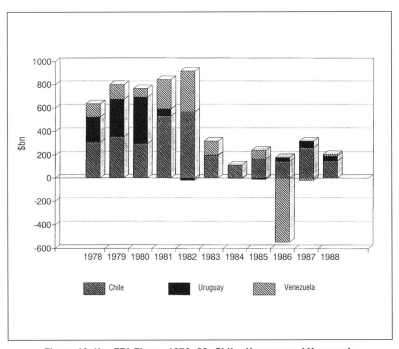

Figure 12.1b • FDI Flows, 1978–88: Chile, Uruguay and Venezuela

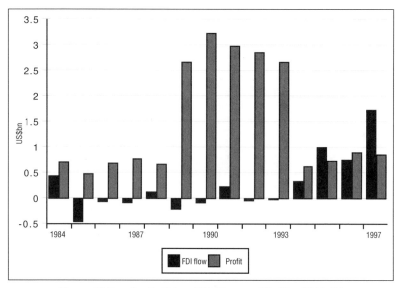

Figure 12.2a • South Africa: FDI Flows and Profits, 1984–97

countries (Chile, Uruguay and Venezuela) over the same period. Here, the effect was still stronger, FDI falling from $900 million in 1982 to around $200 million in 1983–8 (apart from 1986, when it was −$400 million, due to heavy disinvestment in Venezuela). In both cases, FDI had been growing by at least 10 per cent per annum in the period immediately prior to the crisis.

According to the optimistic view of FDI, this should be at least partly off-set by a reduction in profit remittances during times of economic difficulty: when the economy performs poorly (as during the 1980s in Latin America), foreign investors will also perform less well, make less profit, and therefore, it is argued, have less to remit.

However, this is not necessarily the case; and, in some cases at least, profit remittances may actually compound the problem. This is illustrated by the case of South Africa in the late 1980s and early 1990s.[52] Here, the outward net transfer of resources – the difference between the outflow of profits and the inflow of new investment in a given year – increased more than tenfold, from $265 million in 1984 to a range of $2.8–3.3 billion in 1989–93, before returning to about $0.3–0.4 billion in 1994–5 (Figure 12.2b). However, the change in investment was a relatively minor factor – the difference between the peak of inward investment in 1984 and the peak of disinvestment in 1989 amounted only to about $636 million. Rather, the increase in outward net resource transfers occurred almost entirely because recorded profits were 4–5 times higher in 1989–93 than either before or after (Figure 12.2a).

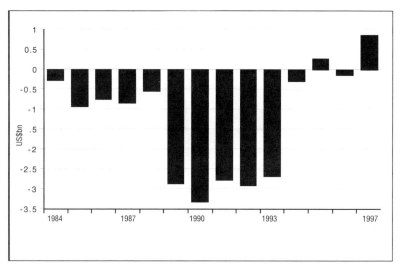

Figure 12.2b • South Africa: FDI Net Resource Transfers, 1984–97

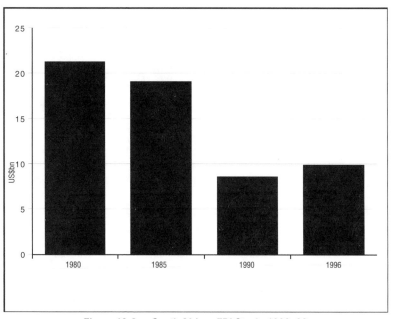

Figure 12.2c • South Africa: FDI Stock, 1980–96

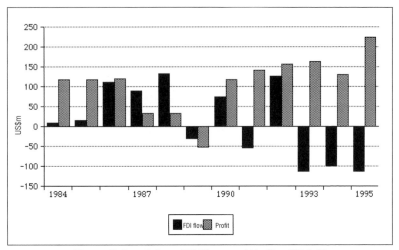

Figure 12.3a • Gabon: FDI Flows and Profits, 1984–95

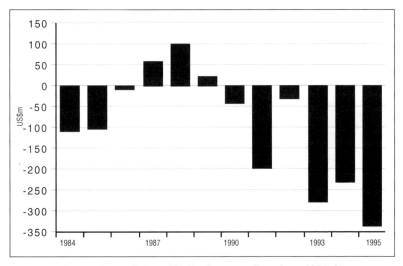

Figure 12.3b • Gabon: FDI Net Resource Transfers, 1984–95

Actual disinvestment is unusual, but by no means unknown, and may be sustained for some years. An example is Gabon, as shown in Figure 12.3, where substantial disinvestment occurred in 1989, 1991 and 1993–5. Coupled with profit remittances, this led to an outward net transfer averaging around $280 million per year in 1993–5. However, falls in investment and/or increases in profit remittances are the more usual scenario.

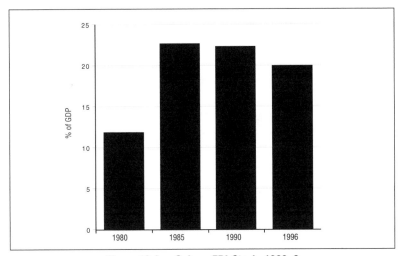

Figure 12.3c • Gabon: FDI Stock, 1980–6

Whatever the cause, an outward net resource transfer of the order of 10 per cent of exports – as in the cases of South Africa and Gabon – at a time of acute economic difficulties is a serious complication; and it is all the more problematic for a country which previously had been reliant on net inward transfers. The sheer volatility of transfers – in Gabon's case, from a net outflow of 3.5 per cent of GNP in 1984 to an inflow of 4 per cent of GNP in 1988, and back to a net outflow of 6–8 per cent of GNP in 1993–5 – raises serious problems of macroeconomic management.

However, the composition of the net outflow (or of changes in the net flow) may make an important difference. As noted in Chapter 7, inward investment in the construction of new capacity typically has a large import component; so the net foreign exchange inflow associated with an investment is substantially less than the headline amount. The effect of a reduction in investment on the availability of foreign exchange to the rest of the economy is therefore likely to be less than that of an increase in remitted profits.

It is at least arguable that FDI is quicker to recover than other forms of capital flow, and may thus help crisis-affected countries to recover more quickly than might otherwise be the case. One of the effects of a financial crisis such as the African and Latin American debt crises or the Mexican, Asian and Russian crises of the 1990s is to weaken the financial position of local businesses. This in turn reduces their market value, making both companies and productive facilities cheaper for investors to buy, while the ability of potential local investors to buy them is seriously impaired.[53] Foreign investment is made still cheaper by the devaluation associated with financial crises. Once the country's economic prospects seem set to improve, the result may be a renewed rush to invest in the country.

This is likely to result in an upturn in the level of FDI inflows from their post-crisis trough; and this in turn will almost certainly mean an acceleration in the rate of increase of foreign ownership of productive capacity in the economy. However, it is much less clear that the capital inflow will return quickly to the pre-crisis level. In practice, more companies and facilities may be bought for less money. Thus, as discussed in Chapter 14, while foreign investors were expected to pick up the pieces following the Asian crisis, IMF projections showed net FDI inflows remaining nearly one-third below their 1997 levels in 2000 (IMF 1999: 40, Table 2.5).

Again, the composition of the inflow is critically important. Following a financial crisis, the ready availability of existing companies and productive facilities at 'fire-sale' prices means that there is little incentive for investment in the construction of new capacity. The result is that most of the increase in FDI in the immediate post-crisis period will be in mergers and acquisitions, for which the long-term foreign exchange effects are the least favourable (as discussed in Chapter 8). Moreover, the artificially low prices paid for the investment will further reduce the initial capital inflow relative to the subsequent balance of payments costs. The result may be merely to accelerate the rate of progress towards the next crisis (see Chapter 14).

Echoes of the Past

As in the case of the other issues related to direct and equity investment, there are important parallels with the commercial lending of the 1970s; but there are also some important differences. Commercial lenders in the 1970s also exhibited marked herd-like tendencies, first rushing into lending to developing countries, then stopping their lending abruptly when the unsound basis of their lending decisions became apparent in the early 1980s. Moreover, as in the case of direct and equity investors in the 1990s, the rationality of the original decisions of commercial lenders relied on the fact that they were moving with the herd rather than on the economic fundamentals of the recipient countries: the main assurance that debt-servicing obligations would be met was that others would be willing to lend.

Equally, the effect of the herd changing direction fulfilled the expectation on which it was based, in that the foreign exchange required to service existing debts could no longer be borrowed. This in turn meant that debtor countries had to generate balance of payments surpluses; and this required large devaluations, which increased the budgetary cost of interest payments, further increasing the difficulty of debt servicing.

As in the 1990s, herd-like behaviour was also an important channel of contagion between countries. Mexico's default in 1982 led to a virtual cessation of lending, not only to Mexico, but, over the following months, to almost every country in Latin America and many in other regions. This both extended debt-servicing difficulties to other countries and made the adjustment process still more difficult, as the simultaneous attempts of a large number of countries to increase their exports to service their debts reduced the prices of their exports in the world market, sabotaging their efforts.

However, a key difference between the 1980s and the 1990s arises from the nature of the liabilities created by loans and by equity investments. The obligations arising from loans are determined by their repayment schedules and interest rates, limiting the amount of the liabilities and the rate at which foreign exchange can be withdrawn from the economy. In the case of direct and especially equity investment, the scale of the liability is determined by the market; and the herd-like rush of investors into the market inflates the value of the assets – and thus the scale of existing obligations – considerably. At the same time, there is no fixed schedule of payments to limit the rate at which foreign exchange can flow out of the economy; and, because the liabilities involved are those of the private rather than the public sector, the government cannot limit the outflow by renegotiating or suspending payments on its debts.

Conclusion

This chapter has discussed some of the reasons for the surge in direct and equity investment flows to developing countries in the 1990s. This discussion suggests that this surge is essentially temporary, as a result of time-specific circumstances, time-limited processes and one-time changes in market conditions which give rise to a stock adjustment in international investment. It is not clear whether FDI flows have yet reached their peak, but they can be expected to fall below their recent levels in the medium or long term.

More generally, the stock adjustment interpretation means that FDI and equity flows are related, not only to the *state* of the economic environment for investors, but also to a great extent to the *rate of change* in this environment – and particularly in policy régimes. This is problematic because there is limited scope for further liberalisation in the major source countries (the developed countries); and there is a limit to how much more favourable the environment for investors can become. Most developing countries which are open to inflows of equity investment already have broadly equal treatment of local and foreign investors; and FDI régimes may already have reached the point where such investment becomes counterproductive from a developmental perspective (see Chapter 10).

However, if the rate of improvement, from the investors' perspective, is slowed, this can be expected to reduce the level of inward investment substantially; and, given the existing stock of direct investment in developing countries, this is likely to give rise to a potentially damaging outward net resource transfer, possibly on a considerable scale (see Chapter 11.)

The cyclical nature of direct and equity investment over the longer term raises further problems, tending to compound the impact of other economic shocks. While FDI flows may help to accelerate the process of recovery from financial crises, this is also likely to hasten the onset of the next crisis. The net effect is to increase both the frequency and the amplitude of financial cycles. It seems all too likely that this process will be demonstrated over the coming years by the experience of crisis-affected countries in East Asia, as discussed in chapters 13 and 14.

13

Was that it? (I)

Direct Investment and Current Account Deficits in
the Mexican and Asian Financial Crises

The Mexican and Asian Crises

The Mexican crisis of 1994 was seen by some as 'the first financial crisis of
the next millennium', and the Asian crisis of 1997 as the second. Both of
these cases indeed represented a marked paradigm shift compared with the
1980s debt crisis, in that the foreign exchange liabilities of the private sector
played a decisive role. Moreover, both Mexico and the crisis-affected
countries of East Asia had been major recipients of direct and equity investment, and both crises were characterised in part by the drying-up or reversal
of equity investment inflows.

So are these cases illustrations of the potential for financial crises arising
from direct and equity investment? The answer is yes – and no. Direct and
equity investment did not, by themselves, *cause* the crisis; but they do appear
to have contributed significantly to it, and, in the case of FDI at least, they
played a greater role than is generally recognised. While the significance of
this role varies considerably between different countries, there is some
reason to believe that the crisis should have given rise to second thoughts
about direct investment rather than reinforcing the earlier complacency.

The idea of a generic 'third-millennium' – or even of a 'twenty-first-
century' – financial crisis suggests an unduly long timeframe. Alex Weber is
reported to have observed at a recent Centre for Economic Policy Research
(CEPR) conference that 'the sources of crises appeared to have changed
from decade to decade' (Chote 1998: 27). In this context, the Mexican and
Asian crises might be better regarded as the 1990s-type crises – the last of the
twentieth century rather than the first of the new millennium, and a transition between the old (1980s-style) and new (early twenty-first-century)
paradigms of financial crises in developing countries.

The Asian financial crisis is generally characterised as one of an underlying fragility giving rise to the possibility of crisis, which was turned into an actual crisis by a sharp deterioration in the external situation, caused partly by a realisation in the financial market that this fragility existed. This interpretation clearly benefits from a large element of hindsight – few would have argued even two years before the crisis that most of the rapidly growing economies of East Asia were in any sense 'fragile'. Nonetheless, it is a useful framework within which to view the crisis, and the possible role that direct and equity investment might have played in its genesis.

A key element of the hypothesised 'underlying fragility' of most of the economies affected by the Asian crisis was a weakness of the balance of payments current account, characterised by large and in some cases increasing deficits. Other factors have been given greater emphasis in some retrospective commentaries – notably weaknesses and inadequate regulation in the financial system, and questionable relationships between financial and non-financial companies and (especially in Indonesia) between governments and the private sector. Nonetheless, as in Mexico, current account weaknesses were of particular significance as an indicator that the region's fixed exchange rates might be overvalued, and were recognised as a key factor at the time.

Direct investment may have contributed directly to this weakness in three main ways:[54]

- ·the rapidly growing stock of inward direct investment may have generated similarly growing profits;[55]

- the inflow of direct investment may have directly fuelled an increase in imports of capital goods (such as equipment), for investment projects; and

- imports of other inputs by affiliates of transnational corporations may have exceeded the foreign exchange generated by their exports and saved by import substitution (or the opposite may have been the case, limiting or reversing other negative effects).

Other, less obvious factors may also have been significant. For example, foreign affiliates, particularly in the retailing sector, may have contributed to a shift in consumption patterns towards imports through advertising, promotion and less tangible cultural effects. However, while direct investment in retailing was very substantial in many East and South East Asian countries (notably Hong Kong, Malaysia and Thailand), the effects on consumption patterns can only be guessed at.

The remainder of this chapter discusses first the contribution of profit remittances and (more speculatively) FDI-related imports of capital goods on the current account deficits of the crisis-affected countries, before going on to assess the effect of imports of inputs and exports in Malaysia (the only country where adequate data are available to make such an assessment). Chapter 14 looks at the effects of changes in capital flows of FDI and portfolio equity investment during the crisis period.

Profits and Imports of Capital Goods

Profit remittances are the most obvious and, in principle, the most easily measurable foreign exchange cost of inward direct investment (subject to the data problems discussed in chapters 5 and 6). While the imports of capital goods associated with inward investment are not directly measurable, some indication of their possible contribution to the current account deficit may be estimated from the level of capital inflows in each year. For simplicity, it is assumed here that each $100 of inward investment is associated with $50 of imports of capital goods (or equivalently the diversion of $50 of domestically produced capital goods which would otherwise have been exported).[56]

The implications of the impact of direct investment on the current account deficits in the crisis-affected countries are shown in Figures 13.1–13.6.[57] This suggests a very wide range of experiences.

- At one extreme, the impact of FDI on Korea's current account appears to have been minimal, averaging only 0.25 per cent of GDP (Figure 13.1).

- In the Philippines, direct investment had a moderate impact in the order of 1.5 per cent of GDP (Figure 13.2). Without FDI, the current account deficit would have averaged about 3.5 per cent of GDP in 1996–7, as compared with 5 per cent.

- In Indonesia, IMF data suggest an average effect of 2 per cent of GDP, partly due to a substantial drop in profits after 1992 (Figure 13.3a). However, World Bank data do not show such a drop, implying an increase in the effect to 3.25 per cent of GDP by 1996, so that profit remittances and FDI-related imports of capital goods were almost entirely responsible for the deficit (Figure 13.3b). According to the IMF data, they accounted for slightly more than half of the deficit.

At first sight, the two countries with chronically large current account deficits (Malaysia at 6.2 per cent of GDP in 1991–7, and Thailand at 6.8 per cent in 1991–6) present very contrasting pictures.

- The published data for Thailand suggest a very limited impact of direct investment on the current account deficit, averaging around 1 per cent of GDP (Figure 13.4a).

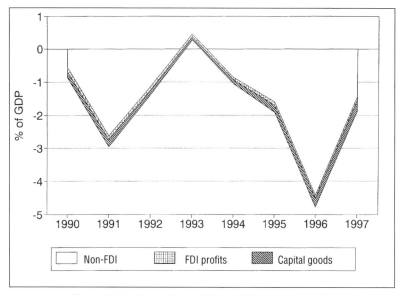

Figure 13.1 • Korea: Current Account Balance, 1990–97

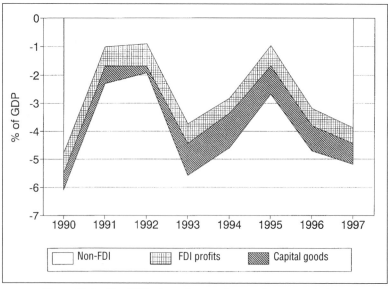

Figure 13.2 • The Philippines: Current Account Balance, 1990–97

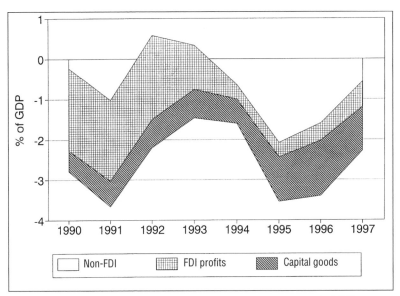

Figure 13.3a • Indonesia: Current Account Balance, 1990–97 (IMF)

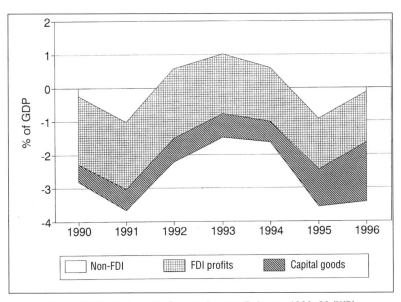

Figure 13.3b • Indonesia: Current Account Balance, 1990–96 (WB)

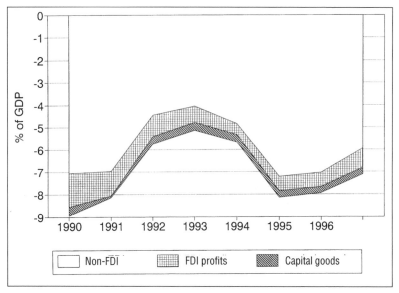

Figure 13.4a • Thailand: Current Account Balance, 1990–96 (IMF)

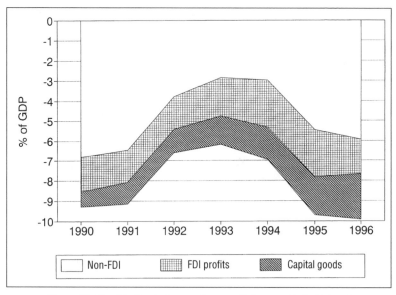

Figure 13.4b • Thailand: Current Account Balance, 1990–96 (DW)

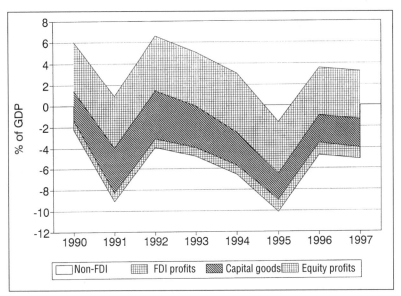

Figure 13.5 • Malaysia: Current Account Balance, 1990–97

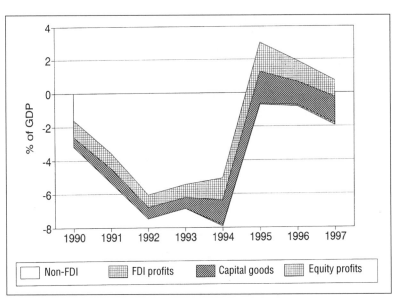

Figure 13.6 • Mexico: Current Account Balance, 1990–97

- Malaysia, by contrast, exhibits by far the greatest effect of direct investment on the current account deficit, averaging around 9 per cent during
  the 1990s (though falling somewhat over the course of the period)
  (Figure 13.5). Without FDI, this suggests that Malaysia would have had a
  current account deficit only in 1995; and there would have been a
  current account surplus of 3.5 per cent of GDP in 1996 rather than a
  deficit of 4.5 per cent.

However, the results for Thailand are potentially misleading because of
the serious data problems noted in Chapter 6 (particularly the non-recording
of reinvested profits and the misclassification of FDI flows). In view of the
central importance of Thailand, as the country which initiated the Asian
crisis, an attempt is made to rectify these data problems in Appendix I (and
illustrated in Figure 13.4b). This suggests a substantially greater effect, averaging around 4 per cent of GDP in 1994–6.[58]

- In Mexico, FDI also appears to have had a substantial impact on the
  current account deficit, averaging around 2.25 per cent of GDP between
  1990 and 1997 (Figure 13.6). The effect is to increase the deficit in the
  immediate pre-crisis period (1992–4) from 5–6 to 7–8 per cent of GDP.

In the case of Mexico, the phasing of the FDI effect is also significant. It
increased dramatically from an average of 1.5 per cent of GDP in 1990–93 to
2.75 per cent in 1994, as direct investment increased by 150 per cent (largely
in anticipation of the NAFTA agreement) and profit remittances nearly
doubled. It increased further to 3.5 per cent in 1995, as GDP fell sharply in
dollar terms due to devaluation, before stabilising well above the pre-crisis
level at 2.5 per cent in 1996 and 1997. The increase in 1994 more than fully
accounted for the increase in the deficit in that year: without the FDI effect,
the deficit would have declined by 0.25 per cent of GDP instead of increasing
by more than 1 per cent. This is in marked contrast with the crisis-affected
countries in East Asia, where there was no systematic tendency for the effect
to intensify prior to the crisis.

The methodology used here means that this assessment is at best indicative – in particular because of the exclusion of day-to-day transactions of
direct investment enterprises and the arbitrary assumption that 50 per cent of
capital inflows are used for imports of capital equipment. Nonetheless, the
following (necessarily tentative) conclusions emerge:

- profit remittances and FDI-related imports of capital goods appear to
  have played a decisive role in Malaysia, and almost certainly accounted
  for the entire (very large) current account deficit in most years between
  1990 and 1997;

- there is also likely to have been a considerable current account effect in Thailand, although this is concealed by shortcomings in the official data;

- in Korea, by contrast, the impact appears to have been minimal, clearly demonstrating than Asian-style crises can occur in the absence of this type of effect;

- in the other crisis-affected countries, the effect was more moderate, but nonetheless substantial (in the order of 2 per cent of GDP), and may have made otherwise sustainable deficits unsustainable;

- the strengthening of the FDI effect may have been decisive in the increase in the current account deficit in Mexico immediately prior to the crisis at the end of 1994, but there does not appear to have been a corresponding increase in the crisis-affected Asian economies.

Trade Effects of Foreign Affiliates' Operations

As noted above, profit remittances and imports of capital goods represent only part of the balance of payments effects of direct investment: the day-to-day operations of foreign affiliates will entail exports, import substitution, and the use of imports, import substitutes and exportable goods as inputs for production. Here the data problems are much greater. Nonetheless, taking account of these effects, UNCTAD found in its annual report on direct investment (dated July 1997, the very month of the Thai crisis):

> Indications are that FDI has played an important role in [Thailand's] large trade deficit, which constitutes the bulk of the current account deficit.... The sharp increase in the import to GDP ratio from 25 per cent in 1985 to 40 per cent in 1991 ... was largely due to a rise in import dependency, which was related to the growing role of FDI. Foreign investment projects imported 90 per cent of all machinery and equipment and over 50 per cent of raw materials. (UNCTAD 1997b: 92)

UNCTAD (1997b) also reports the findings of a dynamic simulation (Jansen 1995) which found that the effect of FDI on imports and profit remittances was greater than the inflow of FDI itself, suggesting a negative impact on the overall balance of payments (including capital flows) as well as on the current account. This suggests that FDI inflows actually increased the need for other capital inflows rather than reducing it; and that the interest payments due on this additional borrowing represent an additional foreign exchange cost of FDI over the long term. It is possible, however, that this is based on the official (underestimated) figures for FDI inflows, in which case a more accurate estimate might show capital inflows to be greater than the negative effect on the current account.

Data are more reliable for Malaysia, which appears to provide a clear illustration of an FDI-driven current account deficit, as shown in Table 13.1. The trade balance of foreign affiliates is estimated to have deteriorated markedly during the early 1990s, moving from a surplus of $0.8 billion in 1990 to a deficit of $2 billion in 1994. Royalty payments also increased, from $176 million in 1990 to $273 million in 1993; and profit remittances on FDI increased from $1.9 billion in 1990 to $4.5 billion in 1996.[59]

Table 13.1 • Malaysia: FDI-Related Balance of Payments Transactions, 1990–96 ($bn)

	1990	1991	1992	1993	1994	1995	1996
FDI-related							
Exports	15.5	18.3	22.3	26.2	34.4	44.3	49.7
Imports	14.7	19.6	22.0	26.3	36.5	48.4	52.8
Trade balance	0.8	-1.3	0.3	-0.2	-2.2	-4.1	-3.1
Royalties	0.2	0.2	0.3	0.3	0.3	0.4	0.4
Profits	1.9	2.3	2.9	3.2	3.9	4.1	4.5
FDI-related current account	-1.3	-3.8	-2.9	-3.7	-6.4	-8.6	-8.0
(% of GDP)	*-3.1*	*-8.1*	*-5.0*	*-5.7*	*-9.0*	*-10.0*	*-8.1*
Total current account	-0.9	-4.2	-2.2	-3.0	-4.5	-8.5	-4.6
(% of GDP)	*-2.1*	*-8.9*	*-3.8*	*-4.6*	*-6.4*	*-9.9*	*-4.6*
Non-FDI current account	0.4	-0.4	0.7	0.7	1.9	0.1	3.4
(% of GDP)	*1.1*	*-0.8*	*1.2*	*1.0*	*2.6*	*0.1*	*3.5*
FDI inflows	2.3	4.0	5.2	5.0	4.3	4.2	5.1
FDI-related overall balance	1.0	0.2	2.3	1.3	-2.0	-4.4	-2.9
(% of GDP)	*2.4*	*0.4*	*4.0*	*2.1*	*-2.9*	*-5.1*	*-3.0*

Sources: Figures for exports and imports in 1990–4, and those for royalties in 1990–93 are from UNCTAD 1997b: Table II.9. Figures for royalties in 1994–6 are based on the extrapolation of their growth rate in 1990–93 (15.8 per cent per annum). Figures for imports and exports in 1995–96 assume imports of capital goods equivalent to 50 per cent of FDI inflows in each year, and extrapolate the average growth rate of affiliates' exports and other imports relative to total exports and total imports (net of the imputed value of capital goods imports) in 1990–94 (2.3 per cent per annum and 4.5 per cent per annum respectively). Figures for FDI inflows and profit remittances are from IMF 1998c, as a more recent source; and this is also the source for the total current account balance. It should be noted, however, that the UNCTAD table gives a slightly lower figure for profits in 1994 ($3,846 million); a substantially higher figure for profits in 1995 ($5,350 million); and a significantly higher figure for FDI inflows in 1995 ($4,700 million). It also assumes zero growth of royalties in 1994.

This suggests that foreign affiliates had a current account deficit through-out 1990–94, and that this increased rapidly, not only in absolute terms (from $1.3 billion to $6.4 billion) but also relative to GDP (from 3.1 per cent to 9 per cent). Deducting these figures from the country's actual current account balance over this period suggests that the remainder of the economy had a small current account surplus on average during this period.

The increasing current account deficit of foreign affiliates was off-set by growing inflows of new direct investment in 1990–92, so that the effect of foreign affiliates on the overall balance of payments (including the capital account) peaked at +$2.3 billion (4 per cent of GDP) in 1992. However, as inflows declined thereafter, the positive balance fell sharply in 1993, and became substantially negative at −$2 billion (2.9 per cent of GDP) in 1994.

The final two columns of Table 13.1 extend the analysis to 1995 and 1996, by including subsequent data for profit remittances and FDI inflows, and by projecting TNC exports, imports and royalty payments on the basis of their respective growth rates between 1990 and 1994 and total export and import figures in 1995–96. For consistency with the earlier analysis, it is assumed that part of the imports, equivalent to 50 per cent of the value of new FDI, is made up of capital goods. The estimated value of these imports is based on the figures for FDI inflows, while exports and other imports are assumed to grow at the same rate relative to total exports and imports, respectively, as in 1990–94.

Based on these assumptions, the deteriorating trend would have con-tinued in 1995, the current account deficit of foreign affiliates increasing to $8.6 billion (10 per cent of GDP), and the negative impact on the overall balance to $4.4 billion (5.1 per cent of GDP). In 1996, the situation would have been comparable to that in 1994, with an FDI-related current account deficit of $8 billion (8.1 per cent of GDP), and an effect on the overall balance of −$2.9 billion (3 per cent of GDP).

At first sight, these figures would seem to suggest that foreign affiliates were solely responsible, not only for the increase in Malaysia's current account deficit between 1990 and 1996, but even for the very existence of the deficit throughout the period. It would also seem inevitable that the large negative effect on the overall balance of payments – 3–5 per cent of GDP for three years immediately prior to the crisis – would have been a major factor precipitating the crisis.

However, there is a need for some caution in interpreting these figures, partly because some of the assumptions underlying the projections are essen-tially arbitrary, but also, more importantly, because some important positive effects (notably import substitution) are not included.

The implications of these caveats are discussed in Appendix II. To summarise this discussion, the projections are not significantly affected by changes in the assumed ratio of direct investment to the associated imports of capital goods, or to the assumptions regarding exports and other imports. Import substitution could have a much greater effect, although this would be partly off-set by the use of inputs which could otherwise have been exported. The net effect would be to reduce the overall effect on the current account deficit substantially, although it would almost certainly remain economically significant.

Profits on portfolio equity investment, which increased from $350 million (0.8 per cent of GDP) in 1990 to $1,128 million (1.1 per cent of GDP) in 1996, are additional to these effects. Including portfolio investment in the analysis would thus strengthen the negative effect on the current account deficit, but the larger capital inflows after 1993 (averaging $2.9 billion per annum or 3.1 per cent of GDP in 1994–6) would make the effect on the overall balance significantly positive.

In short, despite initial appearances, direct investment is unlikely to have been *solely* responsible for Malaysia's current account deficit, or for its deterioration between 1992 and 1995. Nonetheless, it appears to have been a crucial factor, and was almost certainly a primary cause of the deficit reaching a level seen as being unsustainable. It is also possible, at least, that direct investment gave rise to a significant negative effect on the overall balance of payments, and increased the need for financing from other sources in the mid-1990s. This would have increased the risk of a shortfall in financing and a balance of payments crisis, and thus of speculative attacks on the exchange rate.

FDI-Financed Production and Export Prices

An additional factor, if a still less quantifiable one, is the impact of FDI on world prices for the goods it produces. A key element in the deterioration of current account deficits in the East Asian region in the period leading up to the 1997 crisis was a substantial fall in the prices of a number of major exports, most notably electronic goods and components. As in other contexts, there is an implicit assumption in most discussions of the crisis that these price changes were exogenous (that is, independent of the crisis itself, and of other factors contributing to the crisis); but, as in the case of the 1980s debt crisis (Woodward 1992: Vol. I, Ch. 2), while this may be correct from the point of view of each individual country, it may be seriously misleading in the broader context of the crisis as a whole.

As discussed in Chapter 10, where FDI increases the production of an internationally tradeable good, this will tend to reduce its price in the world market, and thus the export revenues of other producing countries. For an individual investment project, the price effect will be small in absolute terms; but in the case of price-sensitive products, the revenue effect will be substantial relative to (and may well be greater than) the value of the additional output produced by the investment.

The electronics industry is highly internationalised, with a substantial proportion of total capacity being financed through direct investment – much of it in the East Asian region, especially during the 1990s. The World Bank cites two 'pull' factors hastening the rapid shift toward high-technology exports in the 'second generation' newly industrialising economies in East Asia (primarily Thailand and Malaysia) between 1990 and 1996: foreign direct investment from industrialised countries ('the driving force behind the pull factor'), and the relocation of production from Korea, Hong Kong, Taiwan and Singapore, also through FDI, as their own labour costs rose.[60] These factors led, *inter alia*, to 'specialization in high-technology exports, mainly electronics' (World Bank 1998c, Ch. 2: 6–7). As a result,

> 64 per cent of the world's production of hard disk drives ... now takes place in Southeast Asia, with intense geographic concentration in Singapore, Malaysia, and Thailand, and 38 per cent of global production of semiconductors takes place in East Asia. (World Bank 1998c, Ch. 2: 10)

Such a rapid increase in exports to such a dominant position in the world market has inevitably had a major impact on the market itself. 'East Asian countries have been aggressive in expanding capacity', contributing to 'price wars and intense competition ... [arising] from ... a persistent trend towards overcapacity' in the global electronics industry (World Bank 1998c, Ch. 2: 10).

This is not to say that direct investment is solely responsible for the decline in prices of electronic goods. On the contrary, national companies within the region represent a substantial proportion of total capacity, and no doubt of the recent increase in capacity. However, this is, in a sense, part of the problem: if the production of electronic goods within East Asia were made up solely of the output of foreign affiliates of multinationals based outside the region, the primary effect of falling prices would have been on their profits, and the net effect on current account balances would have been relatively limited (unless the enterprises ceased production). It is the coexistence of national and transnational producers, and the expansion of production by the latter, which leads to the greatest impact on the balance of payments.

Conclusion

There are a number of reasons to believe that direct investment contributed substantially to the current account deficits of a number of East Asian economies and of Mexico prior to their respective financial crises. In Mexico, Malaysia and possibly Indonesia, FDI also appears to have made a major contribution to increases in the deficit prior to the crises. While the role of FDI was probably not decisive in most cases (with the possible exception of Malaysia), the widely drawn conclusion that direct investment *reduces* the risk of financial crisis is at best premature, and may well be dangerously misleading.

Just three years before the Asian crisis, in a high-profile publication series claiming to emphasise 'the policies and practices that hold the most promise of success in the effort to reduce poverty in the developing world', the World Bank proclaimed, in large, bold, italicised print: 'Malaysia and Thailand are the FDI-led miracles in East Asia' (World Bank 1994: 47). Five years later, a case can be made for the proposition that Malaysia may also have experienced the first FDI-led financial crisis; and that Thailand had the second crisis, after that of Mexico, in which FDI was a significant contributory factor.

14

Was that it? (II)
Capital Flows of FDI and Equity Investment in the Mexican and Asian Financial Crises

Speculative Bubbles

Equity investment played three distinct roles in the financial crises in Mexico, East Asia and Russia, although their relative importance varied markedly:

- it helped to inflate speculative bubbles in asset markets;

- it contributed to the reversal of capital flows which precipitated and intensified the crises; and

- it was a key factor in the contagion process spreading crises between countries.

It is widely accepted that the speculative bubble in asset prices played a major role in the Asian crisis, especially in Thailand. 'The story is one of unsustainable bubbles in asset prices, fuelled by inflows of private sector capital into economies with weak and poorly regulated financial systems' (Chote 1998: 30). This bubble gave rise to a boom–bust cycle: relatively cheap and plentiful capital gave rise to a surge of essentially speculative investment, mainly in the property market, as it exceeded profitable opportunities for productive investment. This speculative investment pushed prices up to unsustainable levels, and the acceptance by banks of property at inflated prices as collateral for their loans made the whole financial system vulnerable to the inevitable bursting of the bubble.

The oversupply of capital was, to a great extent, a result of large capital inflows on top of the region's unusually high savings rates. The result was very high investment as a proportion of GDP – 42 per cent in China, 41 per cent in Thailand and Malaysia, 38 per cent in Korea, and 32 per cent in Indonesia in 1996. The average for the East Asia and Pacific region as a whole was 39 per cent, half as high again as the next highest region (North

Africa and the Middle East, at 26 per cent) (World Bank 1998b: Table 4.8).

The crisis was, in this sense, a 'crisis of success'. Where other countries have struggled to raise their savings ratios and to attract foreign capital to finance investment in infrastructure and productive capacity, East Asia saved and attracted foreign savings too well. Given their high savings ratios, most of the countries in the region did not need to attract large volumes of foreign capital as well; by doing so they created speculative bubbles, unnecessary foreign exchange liabilities which did not add commensurately to productive capacity, unsustainable current account deficits – and, ultimately, financial crises.

The Reversal of Portfolio Equity Investment Flows in the Asian Crisis

The role of the reversal of equity flows in precipitating the crisis is more difficult to assess, largely because of data problems. IMF (1999) data show a substantial, but hardly devastating, decline in portfolio investment flows to the five Asian economies worst affected by the crisis in 1997 (Indonesia, Korea, Malaysia, the Philippines and Thailand) – from $20 billion to $12.6 billion, a reduction of less than 1 per cent of GDP.

However, this may greatly understate the scale of the change in equity flows. First, as shown in Table 14.1, the aggregate figures appear seriously inconsistent with the IMF's own country data, and with World Bank data, both of which suggest a much more serious deterioration. The IMF (1998c) country data show a reduction in net flows of $10 billion (excluding Malaysia, for which no figures are provided) between 1996 and 1997. Moreover, the reduction is limited to this level only by the singularly implausible tripling of net inflows into Thailand between 1996 and 1997, to a level nearly 50 per cent higher than the previous peak ($3.9 billion, compared with $2.7 billion in 1993).

World Bank (1998b and 1999) data, using different sources and methodologies, show a reversal of net flows between 1996 and 1997 both for Thailand (from +$1.6 billion to −$0.3 billion), and still more strongly for Malaysia (from +$4.4 billion to −$0.5 billion), although the reduction/reversal of flows for the Philippines and especially Indonesia is much smaller in these data. Using the World Bank data to fill the gap for Malaysia in the IMF country data implies an overall reduction of $15 billion (1.5 per cent of GDP) in net portfolio equity flows to the five countries between 1996 and 1997, while substituting the Bank data for Thailand for the implausible IMF figures suggests an overall reduction of $19.5 billion (2 per cent of GDP).

Second, because the crisis struck in the middle of 1997, annual data

Table 14.1 • Equity Investment Flows to Five Asian Countries, 1996–2000 ($bn)

(a) Country data, 1996–97

	BOPSY		WDI	
	1996	1997	1996	1997
Indonesia	1.8	−5.0	3.1	2.1
Korea	5.9	2.5	n/a	1.3
Malaysia	n/a	n/a	4.4	−0.5
Philippines	2.1	−0.4	1.3	0.1
Thailand	1.2	3.9	1.6	−0.3
Total	11.0	1.0	10.4	2.7

(b) Aggregate estimates and projections, 1996–2000

	BOPSY+M	BOPSY+M/T	WDI+K	WEO
1996	15.4	15.8	16.3	20.0
1997	0.5	−3.7	3.9	12.6
1998				−6.5
1999				−3.3
2000				5.9

Notes: BOPSY = Balance of Payments Statistics Yearbook; WDI = World Development Indicators; WEO = World Economic Outlook; M = Malaysia; T = Thailand; K = Korea. Figures are for net flows of inward equity investment. BOPSY data are from IMF 1998c: Table B-28; WDI data are from World Bank 1998b: Table 6.8 and 1999: Table 6.7; and WEO data are from IMF 1999: Table 2.5. Totals in part (a) exclude countries for which data are unavailable. In part (b), BOPSY+M uses IMF 1998c data for Indonesia, Korea, the Philippines and Thailand, and World Bank 1998b and 1999 data for Malaysia; BOPSY+M/T uses IMF 1998c data for Indonesia, Korea and the Philippines, and World Bank 1998b and 1999 data for Malaysia and Thailand; and WDI+K uses IMF 1998c data for Korea, and World Bank 1998b and 1999 data for Indonesia, Malaysia, the Philippines and Thailand.

combine a continued large inflow in the first half of the year with a much smaller inflow, or more probably an outflow, in the second half. This would imply a much greater reduction between 1996 and the second half of 1997 than between the annual data for 1996 and 1997. Thus if the net inflow to each country had continued in the first half of 1997 at the same annual rate as in 1996, the reduction/reversal between the first and second halves of the year would have been equivalent to $14.8 billion per annum (1.5 per cent of GDP) using the IMF aggregate data; $30 billion (3 per cent of GDP) using the IMF country data and the World Bank data for Malaysia; or $39 billion (4 per cent of GDP) also using the World Bank data for Thailand.

The Reduction of Direct Investment Flows in the Asian Crisis

Data for direct investment are somewhat more (though not entirely) consistent (Table 14.2). The IMF (1999) aggregate figures show a continued increase in inflows in 1997, from $9.5 billion to $12.1 billion. However, the IMF (1998c) country data show a higher starting point, roughly halving the increase,[61] and imply that the change in net flows was almost entirely attributable to a reduction in outward investment rather than an increase in inward investment. As in the case of equity investment, it is also likely that the annual figure combines a continued increase in the first half of the year, with a reduction in the second half. However, the reduction is likely to have been limited by the continuation or completion of ongoing investments.

The IMF (1999) estimate for 1998 shows a much greater reduction in FDI flows, from $12.1 billion to $4.9 billion, a fall of 60 per cent, or 0.7 per cent of GDP. Moreover, this almost certainly understates the scale of the reduction in the net flow of inward investment, as locally based companies will have reduced their outward direct investment substantially in 1998, as a result of much lower profits. Allowing for a reduction in outward investment of the order of 50 per cent would imply a reduction in net inward investment in 1998 of the order of $10 billion, or 1 per cent of GDP.

Table 14.2 • Direct Investment Flows to Five Asian Countries, 1996–2000 ($bn)

(a) Country data, 1996–97

	BOPSY						WDI	
		1996			1997		1996	1997
	in	out	net	in	out	net		
Indonesia	6.2	0.6	5.6	4.7	0.2	4.5	8.0	4.7
Korea	2.3	4.7	−2.4	2.8	4.4	−1.6	2.3	2.8
Malaysia	5.1	n/a	5.1*	5.1	n/a	5.1*	4.5	5.1
Philippines	1.5	0.2	1.3	1.3	0.1	1.1	1.4	1.2
Thailand	2.3	0.9	1.4	3.7	0.4	3.3	2.3	3.7
Total	17.4	6.4	11.0	17.6	5.1	12.4	18.5	17.5

(b) Aggregate estimates and projections, 1996–2000

	WDI (in)	BOPSY (in)	BOPSY (net)	WEO (net)
1996	18.5	17.4	11.0	9.5
1997	17.5	17.6	12.4	12.1
1998				4.9
1999				8.6
2000				8.3

Notes: Figures are for net flows of direct investment: 'in' refers to inward investment in the named country; 'out' to outward investment originating in the named country; and 'net' to inward investment net of outward investment. BOPSY data are from IMF 1998c: Table B-28; WDI data are from World Bank 1998b: Table 6.8 and 1999: Table 6.7; and WEO data are from IMF 1999: Table 2.5. BOPSY net data exclude outward investment from Malaysia, and are therefore likely to be slightly overestimated.

Direct and Equity Investment in the Mexican Crisis

The greater distance in time means that the behaviour of direct and equity investment in the Mexican crisis is somewhat easier to assess. Based on IMF (1998a) data, portfolio equity investment amounted to $11 billion in 1993, equivalent to 3.2 per cent of GDP. In the first quarter of 1994, it was still higher at an annual rate of $13.9 billion (3.7 per cent of GDP). In the second and third quarters – well before the crisis hit in December – it fell back to just $2 billion per annum (0.5 per cent of GDP); and a net outflow equivalent to $1.5 billion per annum (0.4 per cent of GDP) was recorded in the final quarter. Net flows remained minimal in the first three quarters of 1995, at less than $0.2 billion per annum (0.1 per cent of GDP). As is expected in the East Asian case, the recovery in inflows was slow and partial: in 1997, net inflows were $3.2 billion (0.8 per cent of GDP), 70 per cent below the 1993 peak (IMF 1998c).

While direct investment remained well above the 1993 level, it too fell substantially during the course of 1994, from $12.6 billion per annum (3.7 per cent of GDP) in the first quarter to $6.9 billion per annum (2 per cent of GDP) in the fourth quarter – although the net foreign exchange effect of this reduction will have been limited by the associated purchases of capital goods. The dip was both shallower and shorter than for portfolio equity investment: inflows in 1995–6 were only 15–20 per cent below the 1993 peak, and more than double the level of previous years; and a new high was achieved in 1997 (IMF 1998c). However, it coincided with a doubling of FDI profits, from a steady rate of $2.3–2.5 billion per annum in 1990–3 to $4.8 billion (1.3 per cent of GDP) in 1994, declining only as far as $3.8 billion (0.9 per cent of GDP) in 1997.

Nonetheless, the combined effect of changes in direct and equity investment during 1994 represents a very substantial economic shock – a reduction of capital inflows equivalent to nearly 6 per cent of GDP in just nine months, with only a very limited recovery over the following year. However, it is important not to exaggerate the importance of this shock to the overall crisis: other financial and capital account transactions (excluding outward investment and lending by Mexican residents) amounted to a net inflow of $29.2 billion per annum (8.3 per cent of GDP) in the first quarter, but a net outflow of $38.1 billion (10.8 per cent of GDP) in the fourth quarter. This represents a shock more than three times as great as that attributable to changes in direct and equity investment, so that the change in direct and equity investment accounted for slightly less than a quarter of the overall shock.

Thus the volatility of equity flows (and the procyclical movement of direct investment) at least contributed to the financial shock which precipitated the financial crisis in Mexico: while it did not *initiate* the crisis, and was not the decisive factor, it almost certainly magnified the shock significantly.

Portfolio Equity Investment and Contagion

Portfolio equity investment has also been an increasingly important factor in the contagion of successive financial crises (prior to the Brazilian crisis, which had a much more limited impact on equity flows to other countries). The Asian crisis, in particular, demonstrated the potential fragility of the high rates of return available in 'emerging' markets, causing a general loss of confidence and a widespread exodus. The Russian crisis created, at least temporarily, a general sense of panic and a major 'flight to quality' in which large volumes of capital were moved out of all kinds of risk-bearing financial investments and into the lowest risk (and lowest return) instruments – developed country government bonds. On this occasion, even developed country stock markets were hit, although this effect proved to be relatively short-lived.

Some indication of the scale of this effect can be gleaned from *The Economist*'s quarterly 'portfolio poll', which provides information on the investment portfolios of a group of major international institutional investors. The proportion of the investments of these investors in two broadly 'emerging' market categories (Asia excluding Japan, and the Americas excluding the US) are shown in Table 14.3.

These figures suggest a very considerable reduction in institutional investors' holdings in 'emerging' markets between mid-1997 and the end of 1998, by 55.8 per cent in the case of Asia, and 81.4 per cent in the case of the Americas. This is partly a result of a reduction in the overall weight of equity in the portfolios, but the reduction in the proportion of equity investment in these markets is of substantially greater significance, especially in the case of the Americas.

These figures overstate the extent of disinvestment, because part of the reduction in the value of investments will be a result of the declining prices of shares held by the investors over this period. However, this does not explain the whole of the reduction, especially in the case of the Americas. As shown in Table 14.4, the fall in stock market indices in dollar terms between mid-1997 and end-1998 is significantly less for Asian markets, and much less for Latin American markets, than the portfolio reductions observed above. Only two stock markets in Asia (Indonesia and Malaysia), and none in Latin America, fell by more than the unweighted average reduction in institutional investors' portfolios. On the working assumption that the shares held

Table 14.3 • Exposure of Major International Institutional Investors to Emerging Equity Markets, mid-1997 and end-1998

	Equities (% of portfolio)		Non-Japan Asia (% of equities)		Non-Japan Asia equities (% of portfolio)		% change	Non-US Americas (% of equities)		Non-US Americas equities (% of portfolio)		% change
	Q2 1997	Q4 1998	Q2 1997	Q4 1998	Q2 1997	Q4 1998		Q2 1997	Q4 1998	Q2 1997	Q4 1998	
Commerz International	60	54	9	3	5.40	1.62	−72.0%	2	0	1.20	0.00	−100.0%
Crédit Suisse	50	47	4	0	2.00	0.00	−100.0%	5	4	2.50	1.88	−24.8%
Daiwa Europe	65	30	7	17	4.55	5.10	+12.1%	9	0	5.85	0.00	−100.0%
Julius Baer	50	50	12	1	6.00	0.50	−91.7%	2	0	1.00	0.00	−100.0%
Lehman Brothers	86	64	9	5	7.74	3.20	−59.9%	6	2	5.16	1.28	−75.0%
Robeco Group	47	40	3	4	1.41	1.60	+14.2%	3	0	1.41	0.00	−100.0%
Average (unweighted)					4.52	2.00	−55.8%			2.85	0.53	−81.4%

Notes: Figures for equity as a proportion of total portfolios and for the geographical distribution of equity are from 'Our Portfolio Poll' (*The Economist*, 19 July 1997: 79), and 'Our Quarterly Portfolio Poll' (*The Economist*, 16 January 1999: 86). Other figures in the table are calculated on the basis of these numbers. All investors for which data are provided for both periods are included in the table.

Table 14.4 • Changes in Stock Exchange Indices between mid-1997 and end-1998 (in US Dollar Terms)

Asia		Americas	
China	−2.4%	Argentina	−47.8%
Hong Kong	−33.4%	Brazil	−54.3%
India	−39.5%	Chile	−45.7%
Indonesia	−83.5%	Colombia	−34.7%
Korea	−46.5%	Mexico	−30.5%
Malaysia	−64.9%	Venezuela	−55.0%
Philippines	−52.0%		
Singapore	−39.0%		
Taiwan	−38.0%		
Thailand	−50.6%		
Average	−45.0%	*Average*	−44.7%

Notes: Figures are calculated on the basis of stock market indices and exchange rates for 2 July 1997 ('Emerging Market Indicators', *The Economist*, 5 July 1997: 130) and 30 December 1998 ('Emerging Market Indicators', *The Economist*, 2 January 1999: 98). Average changes cited are the unweighted averages of the percentage changes shown.

by institutional investors in each region performed in line with the unweighted averages for stock market performance, this would imply that they had sold around one-sixth of their initial holdings in Asia, and two-thirds in the Americas.[62]

However, the extent of selling in Asia may be seriously understated by these estimates, because three of the investors had started to increase their stakes in Asian markets in the latter part of 1998 – two of them on a very substantial scale.[63] If the proportion of equities in 'emerging' markets had remained at the troughs reached during the second half of 1998, the average share of the investors' overall portfolios in 'emerging' Asian equities at the end of 1998 would have been only 0.96 per cent – less than half the actual figure, and a reduction of 78.8 per cent since mid-1997. Again making the working assumption that institutional investors' portfolios performed in line with the unweighted average of stock market indices in dollar terms, this would imply the sale of more than three-fifths of the shares held in these markets in mid-1997.

Again, data are more readily available to assess the role of portfolio equity investment in the contagion process following the Mexican crisis of 1994 – although once again this is seriously complicated by discrepancies between IMF and World Bank data. The IMF data suggest that the crisis had a major effect on the flow of portfolio equity investment to Brazil (where it fell by 62 per cent, or 0.7 per cent of GDP), and to Chile (where the flow was reversed, with an impact of 2.3 per cent of GDP – substantially more than for Mexico). However, the World Bank figures suggest much smaller effects, the impact on Brazil becoming almost insignificant at 0.1 per cent of GDP, while that on Chile is reduced to 0.9 per cent. These data also show a moderate negative impact on Argentina (for which the IMF provides no data), equivalent to 0.4 per cent of GDP.

The Last Crisis and the Next

The after-effects of the Asian crisis, and of the financial and policy responses to it, are likely to accelerate the advent of the next crisis considerably. The crisis itself artificially depressed stock markets in emerging economies, as international investors fled for 'safe havens' such as developed country government bonds. As they return to the market, they are buying back their shares substantially more cheaply than they sold them.

Equally, the devastating effects of the crisis and of the consequent adjustment programmes on local economies have placed enormous financial pressures on local businesses, and given rise to widespread bankruptcies.

> In Thailand, Korea and Indonesia, the abrupt change in economic conditions has produced a systemic crisis. High interest rates and rising debts, plus capital losses associated with exchange rate depreciations, have pushed a large segment of their banks and corporations into insolvency simultaneously.... In Thailand, 47 percent of listed firms are estimated to have balance sheet losses greater than equity. As a result, non-performing loans are estimated to range from an estimated 20 to 35 per cent of total loan portfolios. In Indonesia, 78 per cent of listed large firms are bankrupt according to this criterion, and non-performing loans may reach as high as 50 per cent. In Korea, 71 per cent of corporations have exchange rate and interest rate losses greater than equity, and non-performing loans also range from 20 to 35 per cent.... Each month that passes worsens the situation because interest costs continue to mount. (World Bank 1998c, Ch. 7: 4)

It seems likely that locally owned companies will have been disproportionately affected: while the operations of transnational companies are by no means unaffected by the crisis, they are generally less integrated with the local economy, and are likely at least to be kept afloat by their parent companies. TNC operations selling primarily in the domestic market will be more severely affected, due to the reduction in demand associated with the crisis; but they are likely to benefit over the long term by the reduction in competition as local competitors face bankruptcy.

The result is that the locally owned companies hit by the crisis, and their productive assets, are available at exceptionally low prices; and few local investors have the resources to invest in them, leaving the field open to transnational companies. Some emerging market governments, especially in

Asia, actively sought foreign investors to 'rescue' such businesses in the aftermath of the crisis.

At the same time, IMF programmes in some countries (such as Indonesia) entailed an acceleration of privatisation programmes, at the very time when domestic investors were least able to participate, and foreign confidence was weakest. Other countries, such as Venezuela, continued with privatisation programmes through the Asian and Russian crises, despite a major reduction in the likely revenues.

Even the short-term foreign exchange benefits of such post-crisis investments are likely to be minimal in many cases. The main price paid by a foreign investor for taking over a bankrupt enterprise is in the form of taking on its debts. This means, not only that the initial foreign exchange inflow will be limited, but also that the new foreign affiliate will have to transfer additional foreign exchange out of the economy over the longer term to service the debts it has acquired. Moreover, since one of the main reasons for the wave of bankruptcies across Asia was the increase in the cost of servicing foreign debts as a result of devaluation, bankrupt companies are likely to include those with the largest debts to foreign creditors relative to their overall size.

The result is a virtual 'fire sale' of companies and production facilities, in which the prices paid are very low; the actual foreign exchange inflow associated with the investment is still lower, and may in some cases be negligible; and the ability to buy is largely limited to foreign investors. The fact that so many countries are in the same situation at the same time intensifies competition for direct investment funds, pushing the prices paid by foreign investors down still further. This process was slow to start following the Asian crisis, as potential investors waited for prices to reach rock-bottom, but is likely to prove substantial overall.

At the same time, there is likely to have been a large and sustained reduction in direct investment in new capacity. Few transnational companies would in any case be likely to invest in the construction of new capacity in the countries affected by the crisis in its immediate aftermath, because of the poor prospects for domestic markets, the increased uncertainty, and in some cases (notably Indonesia), the risk or reality of political instability. The availability of a large stock of existing productive capacity at artificially depressed prices will discourage new investment still further. There is also a risk, at least, that direct investment will be attracted away from other countries, including investment which would otherwise have created new capacity.

The result of such 'fire sale' investments may be to limit the reduction in direct investment to the countries affected by the crisis. However, this will occur at a high long-term cost.

- There will be a marked acceleration in the build-up of the stock of inward direct investment, and in the transfer of ownership of productive capacity from local to foreign investors.

- The amount of initial capital inflows will be artificially lowered relative to the increase in the stock of liabilities and the ultimate foreign exchange outflows.

- A major shift is almost inevitable, from investment which creates new capacity (which can have a positive balance of payments effect, at least in the export sector) to investment which takes over existing capacity (which almost inevitably has a negative impact).

- Investment may be attracted away from other countries, forcing them to offer still more favourable terms to prospective investment to avoid this and intensifying the competitive bidding away of its developmental benefits.

Conclusion

Foreign direct and equity investment almost certainly did not cause the Mexican and Asian financial crises. However, they did make a substantial contribution both to the underlying weakness of some of the affected economies, and to the economic shocks which precipitated the crisis – most conspicuously in Malaysia, but also to a lesser extent in Mexico, Thailand, Indonesia and the Philippines. Only in Korea do FDI and equity investment appear to have played no significant role in the crisis. Equity investment also played a major role in the process of contagion, spreading the effects of the crises far beyond their original roots.

However, the Asian crisis seems actually to have reinforced economists' unquestioning faith in direct investment. Non-crisis economies are presented as having either relatively small capital inflows or 'larger ones dominated by net direct investment' (Chote 1998: 7). Chote concludes that 'Inflows in the form of foreign direct investment should be encouraged.' Ito and Portes (1998) recommend wariness towards short-term capital inflows, but dismantling restrictions on foreign direct investment as a means of encouraging long-term capital inflows. The *Economist* warns against capital controls as 'deterring the long-term foreign direct investment that is essential for growth in developing countries' ('The World Economy: On the Edge', 5 September 1998: 23). In some cases, notably Korea, the financial 'rescue' packages which followed the crisis were conditional on further liberalisation of FDI régimes.

It is perhaps not surprising that such potentially misleading conclusions have been drawn, in view of the shortcomings of the official data (as discussed in chapters 5 and 6) and the general predilection of economists and policy makers for FDI; but it is none the less dangerous. Moreover, the dangers can be expected to increase progressively over time, as stocks build up – particularly if the shift towards mergers and acquisitions and investment in service sectors continues.

If the potential costs of direct investment are not taken into account in the design of mechanisms to anticipate and deal with financial crises, this will greatly accelerate the process, as foreign investors take advantage of 'fire sales' and depressed stock markets to buy up existing productive capacity at artificially low prices. There is a real danger that the inappropriate response to recent financial crises by the international financial system has laid the foundations for the next one.

Future financial crises can be expected to have broadly similar effects, unless ways are found to avoid them, or to deal with them more effectively. As well as the short-term vicious circles, whereby the effects of crises – undermining investor confidence, depressing export prices and triggering competitive devaluations – intensify the crisis itself, we may be entering into a longer-term vicious circle, whereby each crisis creates the conditions which will ultimately generate the next crisis. Direct and equity investment could play a central role in this process.

15

Conclusions and Policy Implications

Summary: an Accident Waiting to Happen?

This book has presented an alternative to the very optimistic view of equity investment, and especially foreign direct investment, in developing countries which currently prevails among mainstream economists. This alternative view suggests the following conclusions.

- Stocks of direct and equity investment – especially the former – are very substantial in a number of developing countries, and both are growing very rapidly in many cases.

- The rates of return on direct and equity investment are very high, both in absolute terms and relative to other types of capital flow, and are highest in the poorest countries.

- High rates of return mean that host countries can avoid outward net transfers over the long term only by allowing a very rapid exponential build-up of the stock of inward investment, profit remittances and investment inflows. The rate of increase is greatest where the rate of return is highest – that is, in the poorest countries.

- There are serious questions about the sustainability of direct and equity investment flows at recent levels, due to their dependence on a number of temporary phenomena: privatisation processes, the return of flight capital, the one-time shift associated with asset diversification by Northern financial institutions, and low real interest rates in developed countries. As these processes are completed, and circumstances change, inward net resource transfers will become still more difficult to sustain.

- Net transfers on direct investment, and especially portfolio equity investment, are strongly procyclical in nature, and are therefore likely to compound the impact of economic or political crises.

- Equity investment is also subject to strong contagion effects, which may spread the effects of a crisis in one country to its neighbours or other countries with which investors (however irrationally) associate it.

Net resource transfers represent only part of the picture with respect to the balance of payments effects of direct investment, in that they also have an effect on exports and imports. However, the optimistic view of direct investment in this regard is again questionable.

- Partly as a result of high rates of return, the net foreign exchange effects of direct and equity investment on the host country may be much less favourable over the long term than is generally assumed.

- For equity investment and some types of direct investment (especially the purchase of existing productive capacity and new investment in non-tradeable sectors), the net foreign exchange effect will be substantially negative.

- The net foreign exchange effect of investment in new capacity in the export sector will be less positive from the perspective of developing countries as a whole than for the host country, and is likely to be substantially negative in many cases, because of the effect of increased export production on prices in the world market.

As a result, only direct investment which creates new capacity for the production of non-price-sensitive exports will generate clear foreign exchange benefits over the long term. This suggests a serious risk that over-reliance on equity investment and on FDI (particularly FDI through mergers and acquisitions, and in non-tradeable sectors) could create the underlying conditions in which foreign exchange crises could occur. Given the volatility of equity investment and the procyclical nature of net transfers on direct investment, they could also give rise to the shocks needed to precipitate such crises. They appear to have contributed significantly to, or at the very least exacerbated, the recent Mexican and Asian financial crises.

These problems are not adequately recognised by economists and policy makers, who still have an idealised view of direct investment, which appears to have been reinforced rather than weakened by the Asian financial crisis. This very positive view rests partly on preconceptions, and partly on the commercial interests of transnational companies and their political strength in developed countries; and it is able to persist without serious criticism because the data on direct and equity investment – particularly on stocks of inward investment, but also on capital flows and profits – provide at best an unreliable picture, and in some countries a seriously misleading one.

Various other positive effects have been attributed to direct investment, particularly in terms of technology transfer and employment, but again these may be exaggerated.

- While direct investment in new capacity is likely to create some jobs, this is likely to be off-set by a reduction in employment in locally owned enterprises, at least in the case of non-tradeable sectors.

- In most cases, technology transfer is unlikely to extend beyond foreign affiliates, where the benefit accrues to parent companies rather than to the host country.

- Developing countries have competed away much of the benefit of direct and equity investment through tax, regulatory and other concessions.

- In some cases (such as investment in the telecommunications sector), direct investment which has a negative direct effect on the balance of payments may have sufficient positive spill-over effects on the rest of the (locally owned) economy to be beneficial overall. However, such cases are likely to be relatively few; and their scope will be reduced further as the balance of ownership within the economy as a whole (and thus the potential benefits of such investments) shifts further towards foreign investors.

Recent and prospective developments in international rules and norms (notably the Uruguay Round agreements and the prospective Multilateral Agreement on Investment) seem likely to accentuate these problems, as they are strongly oriented towards the interests of multinational companies rather than those of host countries. They have the effect of locking in the concessions made to foreign investors by developing countries at the time when their need for foreign investment was greatest and the competition for inflows most intense.

Finally, the existence of substantial stocks of direct and equity investment may constrain and/or influence policy both through economic necessity, as host countries need to attract ever-increasing inflows to avoid an outward net resource transfer; and through political pressures, as the role of transnational corporations in the economy increases. This undermines sovereignty and democracy, and is likely to reduce the welfare of the population.

The Next Crisis and the 1980s Debt Crisis

As discussed in Chapter 2, there are some close parallels between the current build-up of direct and equity investment liabilities and the build-up of foreign debts in the 1970s, which culminated in the 1980s debt crisis.

- There is a 'no-risk' myth. In the 1980s case, this arose from the view, so memorably expressed by Walter Wriston of Citibank, that 'countries can't go bankrupt'. The new version might be expressed, from the investor's perspective, as 'direct and equity investment can't make a country bankrupt'; and, from the host country's perspective, as 'direct and equity investment are good for you'.

- Equity investment in 'emerging markets' in the 1990s, like syndicated lending in the 1970s, was largely a matter of fashion, accentuated by the herd-like behaviour of the providers of capital. Like many smaller banks in the 1970s, many institutional investors were sucked into markets they did not fully understand by high rates of return and the 'no-risk' myth, and the need to be seen not to be falling behind their competitors.

- As in the 1970s, the 1990s financial flows have been welcomed by the developed countries and international institutions. In the 1970s, the 'recycling' of OPEC oil surpluses was seen as a means of easing the burden of adjustment to higher oil prices (and latterly to falling export prices and increasing interest rates). In the 1990s, FDI and portfolio investment were seen as signalling a welcome restoration of (some) developing countries' access to international capital flows following the 1980s crisis.

- As in the 1970s, it is implicitly assumed that sufficient new inflows can be attracted into recipient countries over the long term to avoid substantial outward net resource transfers; but no serious consideration has been given to the implications of the resulting exponential growth of liabilities.

- As in the 1970s, data systems are inadequate to measure the build-up of liabilities; and insufficient efforts have been made to improve them because of the underestimation of the risks entailed.

- As in the 1970s, insufficient attention is given to the uses of the capital which is provided. In the 1970s, this was a question of failure to differentiate between investment and consumption, and between economically viable investment, for example in infrastructure, and 'white elephant' projects. In the 1990s, the comparison was between the construction of new productive capacity and the purchase of existing capacity, and between tradeable and non-tradeable sectors.

- As in the 1980s, when developing countries were pressured into pursuing export promotion strategies in response to debt problems despite their counterproductive effects on commodity markets and export prices, little or no account was taken of the effects of FDI on export production in one country on the international economic environment facing other developing countries. The result is a serious positive bias in assessments of the overall effect on developing countries as a whole of development strategies based on the promotion of export-oriented FDI.

Despite these parallels, there are clearly some important differences between the financial flows of the 1990s and those of the 1970s. However, in some respects, at least, these tend to increase rather than reduce the risk of a financial crisis.

First, both the myth of direct and equity investment, and the official encouragement given to them, operate on the demand side rather than the supply side. In the 1970s, banks were reassured that there was no risk, and were at least tacitly encouraged to lend, while there was some (muted) urging towards restraint on the part of developing country borrowers. The result was to increase supply and reduce demand, limiting the cost to borrowers. In retrospect, it seems clear that the risk premiums charged on loans (generally up to about 2 per cent per annum on loans to governments) undervalued the actual risk entailed rather than exaggerating it.

In contrast, the myth of direct and equity investment operates primarily on the demand side. Developing countries are assured that these forms of financing are beneficial from a development perspective; they are actively encouraged, through adjustment programmes, to make policy concessions to attract such flows; and they are urged to sign up to agreements, such as those encompassed in the Uruguay Round, NAFTA and bilateral investment treaties, to lock in the concessions that they have made. There is no equivalent pressure on direct investors.

The result is to increase developing countries' demand for direct investment, without producing a corresponding increase in supply; and to intensify competition among developing countries for the available resources. This in turn increases the return to investors at the expense of developmental benefits to host countries. Thus where the 1970s myth lowered the cost of lending, and thus reduced (but clearly did not eliminate) the risk of crisis, the 1990s version increased the cost of direct and equity investment and thus makes a crisis all the more likely.

The situation is somewhat different – though not much better – in the case of equity investment. Here, the myth of high, risk-free rates of return does generate an artificially large supply of capital. However, while this reduces the cost of equity capital to companies, it also pushes up share prices, generating large capital gains to investors – and equally large potential costs to the capital account of the balance of payments.

Second, while syndicated lending was countercyclical (until 1982, when lenders lost faith in the system), net transfers on direct and especially portfolio equity investment are markedly procyclical. When developing countries faced the 1973 oil price shock and the multiple external shocks of 1979, they could ease the pace of adjustment by borrowing more (although in retrospect they did so too much in the latter case). By contrast, when other circumstances turn against a country, direct and equity investment decline, adding to their need for adjustment rather than helping to limit it. By compounding the effects of other economic shocks, this again increases the likelihood of a crisis.

Third, the liabilities associated with direct and equity investment are incurred by the private rather than the public sector. In the 1970s, liabilities arose from government decisions to borrow, and were thus at least partly within the control of governments (although their policy making in this regard was constrained by external developments and domestic constraints, and their judgments may, in retrospect, have been questionable). At the present time, liabilities arise mainly from decisions by private companies (except in the case of privatisation); and, while they may be influenced by macroeconomic policies, the scope for governments to maintain any level of control over the build-up of liabilities is very limited – and reduced further by the progressive removal of capital controls. Again, this adds to the risk of crisis.

This problem is compounded by a fourth difference between the 1970s and today: the different nature of the liabilities being created. In the 1970s, the liabilities took the form of loans, which are repayable according to a fixed schedule of principal and interest payments. The cost of floating-rate debts may be increased by higher interest rates; but the extent of this effect in any particular year is limited relative to the overall scale of the liability. Direct, equity and other portfolio investment, by contrast, are not subject to such limits: investors can pull out whenever they wish (although they may face capital losses, or lose part of their capital gains, as a result). This greatly increases the volatility of overall capital flows, particularly in the case of equity investment.

This aspect of direct and equity investment also seriously complicates the financial response to crises when they arise, at least within the current framework of international finance. The traditional response to a financial crisis, which has been retained in the Mexican, Asian and Russian crises, is to provide new loans to governments, phased over time, with each disbursement conditional on macroeconomic targets and specific policy changes. Subject to caveats about the legitimacy of conditionality and the appropriateness and mutual consistency of the targets and policy conditions (Woodward 1992: Vol. I, Ch. 2), this broad approach was at least coherent, in the sense that it had the *potential* to work in the 1980s crisis: governments had to make debt-service payments which were phased over time; so it made sense to lend money to governments phased in accordance with their financial commitments.

In the current-style crises, it is no longer governments' financial commitments which give rise to balance of payments problems (at least until they are forced to take over the liabilities of private companies); and the potential outflow of capital is not phased over time, but occurs all at once, as investors rush for the exit when the crisis strikes. Moreover, confidence is crucial: the need is primarily to reassure investors that it is safe to leave their investments in place; and subjecting each disbursement of a 'rescue' package to conditionality makes it uncertain that it will actually be made, which seriously undermines any effect the package might otherwise have had in strengthening confidence (Woodward 1999).

Financial responses to crises in the 1990s were further weakened by a fifth contrast with the financial flows of the 1970s. Syndicated loans came from a clearly identifiable set of lenders – the commercial banks – who were tied together in groups (syndicates) for the provision of each individual loan. There was considerable overlap between the membership of the syndicates for different loans, particularly among the larger banks; and the individual loans were tied together through cross-default clauses and sharing provisions. This gave rise to a reasonable degree of common interest, and a basis for collaboration between banks when crises occurred.

More importantly, the banks had an established mechanism for collective action (the so-called 'London Club') and the instruments to act collectively in response to crises (rescheduling and 'concerted' lending). The process was often problematic, but it generally worked eventually. Faced with a financial crisis, the banks could act in their own collective interests by deferring debt-service payments, so as to limit the adjustment required to a rate which would not jeopardise their ultimate repayment by seriously damaging the economy's long-term prospects. Ultimately they could agree to a (generally very limited) degree of debt reduction.[64]

Direct and portfolio investors, by contrast, represent a much more disparate group, with much less commonality of interest. Direct investors seldom share their investments with others and, where they do, typically only one or two other foreign investors are involved. In many cases, they compete directly with each other, either in the domestic market or for export markets. Portfolio equity investors buy shares as individual investors. There is no linkage between any two share purchases by different investors, even when they buy shares in the same company. In the event of a crisis, each investor's interest is only in selling the shares before others do. Bond purchasers share no more than the possession of bonds, even where the bonds came from the same issuer at the same time. Typically, neither equity investors nor bondholders even know who their fellow investors are. This seriously limits the scope for collective action.

Equally importantly, there are no mechanisms readily available to deal with these liabilities in a financial crisis, even if there were collective agreement among investors to do so. There is no moratorium option, as in a public sector debt crisis; and the reimposition of capital controls is complicated where the mechanisms for applying them have been dismantled – and, as Malaysia found following the 1997 crisis, is likely to be treated with official hostility and widespread vilification.

One could envisage a voluntary suspension of profit remittances on direct investment, of dividends on equity investment or of interest on bond issues; but without exchange controls there would be no means of ensuring that companies complied with them; and individual investors could repatriate their capital simply by selling their investments, unless they were prohibited from doing so. If they were sold to a local resident, this would represent a capital outflow.

In short, both the similarities and the differences between the 1970s and the 1990s should give rise to considerable cause for concern. The parallels suggest that the accumulation of external liabilities, and the complacency which surrounds it, may mean that we are heading towards a period of endemic financial crisis. The differences may not merely exacerbate this risk, but also largely invalidate the current means of dealing with such a crisis.

Where Are We Now? 2001 and 1979

With the Asian and Russian financial crises, we may have reached the equivalent point to 1979 in the build-up to the 1980s crisis. In 1979, the second oil price shock occurred, compounded by a sharp rise in interest rates, falling commodity prices and a slow-down in demand for exports. Extrapolating from the experience of the first oil price shock in 1973, lenders and borrowers alike concluded that the resulting financial gap for the developing countries could be met by more of the same type of borrowing – that is, primarily, syndicated loans from commercial banks.

In retrospect, they were clearly wrong. The changed international economic environment meant that this strategy was no longer viable: a combination of rapidly increasing liabilities (due to much higher real interest rates) and collapsing debt-servicing capacity (due to weak export markets and falling commodity prices) led directly to the 1982 crisis.

Much the same may be happening again now with regard to direct and equity investment. The Asian and Russian financial crises further strengthened the positive attitude to direct investment; and efforts to promote it have, if anything, also been strengthened – as witness the inclusion of measures to liberalise direct investment in the IMF programme for Korea, as well as the continued efforts to negotiate the Multilateral Agreement on Investment. At the same time, the attitude of the leaders of the international financial system towards capital account liberalisation has barely changed: while sympathy for the use of capital controls in crisis situations has increased somewhat among the smaller developed country governments, the major players still appear to regard this as at best a desperate last resort.

However, quite apart from questions about the appropriateness of direct and equity investment before the crisis, and their role in its genesis, the international economic environment is now much less favourable for these forms of investment. The crisis has had three effects.

- It has made investors much more risk-averse, so that they are likely to demand a still higher rate of return to compensate them for a given level of risk.

- Its devastating economic effects, social impact and political repercussions on 'emerging' markets make investment there much riskier, which is likely to reduce the price investors are willing to pay for a particular investment, so as to increase the expected rate of return.

- The wave of corporate bankruptcies and near-bankruptcies in the affected countries, coupled with massive devaluations and the virtual collapse of stock markets, means that the market is being flooded with companies and productive facilities at 'fire sale' prices; and privatisation programmes are, if anything, being accelerated (in Indonesia, for example), further adding to the glut, and thus further depressing prices.

As in 1979, if efforts to attract foreign capital back in the form of direct and equity investment are successful, the result will be to accelerate the build-up of liabilities without a commensurate effect on the now seriously limited capacity of national economies to bear them. Again, there is a close parallel with 1979–81, when the use of syndicated loans to sustain government current spending rather than productive investment, meant a rapid growth of debt-servicing obligations with little effect on debt-servicing capacity.

There is a real risk that the end of the 1990s will, with hindsight, prove to have been the turning-point on the road to crisis – as the end of the 1970s were for the 1980s debt crisis. This suggests an urgent need to reconsider where we are and where we are heading – to find ways to avoid the impending crisis, and to deal with it should it nonetheless occur. This has major implications for various current policy debates: on the Multilateral Agreement on Investment; on the proposal to extend the IMF's mandate to cover capital account liberalisation; and on how to reform the international financial architecture to deal with 'Asian-style' financial crises.

The Multilateral Agreement on Investment[65]

Reducing the risk of a future crisis arising from direct and equity investment means primarily changing the nature of the market for these forms of investment. In the case of direct investment, the primary objective is to ensure a positive developmental impact at a sustainable foreign exchange cost. This in turn requires a more controlled process of competition for FDI flows than operates at present; and a more selective approach to FDI flows at the national level.

As discussed in Chapter 10, the proposed Multilateral Agreement on Investment (MAI), as it is currently envisaged, is likely to have exactly the opposite effect. In effect, it will institutionalise the current process of mutually destructive competition between developing countries for direct investment inflows at precisely the time when it is most intense. This will increase the cost of direct investment and reduce its benefits to host countries as a whole; and it is likely to preclude any significant degree of selectivity in policies towards FDI. This is more likely to contribute to future financial crises than to make a major contribution to sustainable development.

This suggests a need to reverse the logic of the MAI. Rather than seeking to promote the interests of investors, and thereby institutionalising the competition for FDI among host countries, the MAI should seek to discourage mutually destructive competition so as to maximise the developmental benefits of FDI to host countries. This means, for example, limiting the tax incentives and subsidies which can be offered to direct investors; imposing minimum standards on technology transfer into the wider economy; establishing appropriate environmental policies (such as the 'polluter pays' principle); and applying general rules in such areas as profit remittances, the repatriation of capital and local ownership. It might also be possible to incorporate standards relating to working conditions (governing health and safety, working hours, the use of child labour and other matters), and on the local content of production (the proportion of inputs purchased locally), although these elements would require a considerable degree of flexibility, reflecting differences between the circumstances of individual countries.

This would limit the benefits which countries could bid away, and set a floor to the developmental price they could offer to prospective investors.

The result would be to avoid, or at least to control, the 'race to the bottom' inherent in the current competition for direct investment flows; and thus to allow developing countries (and host countries more generally) to secure a greater share of the potential economic gains from direct investment.

Such a 'reverse logic' MAI could also legitimise a more selective approach to direct investment at the national level, so that the rejection or restriction of particular types of investment which are least beneficial or most costly (retailing and fast-food outlets, for example), or differentiation between investment which entails the creation of new productive capacity and that which entails only the transfer of ownership, need not imply a hostile attitude to FDI in general. In view of the very limited developmental benefits and very high foreign exchange costs of some types of FDI, this is a key component of any strategy for avoiding FDI-led financial crises.

A 'reverse logic' MAI could be highly beneficial, in terms both of limiting the long-term foreign exchange costs of direct investment, and of enhancing its contribution to sustainable economic development. However, it would be of limited effect if it were not backed up by a more general change in attitudes and policies towards direct investment. In particular, it is essential to avoid including policies of universal FDI liberalisation in future IMF and World Bank policy programmes; and to change the nature of bilateral investment treaties (and trade agreements with similar elements) correspondingly. Changes would also be required in the World Trade Organisation (WTO) and the relevant Uruguay Round agreements (those on Trade-Related Investment Measures, Trade in Services and, possibly, Trade-Related Intellectual Property Rights).

The IMF and Capital Account Liberalisation

A similar reversal of logic is required in the case of equity investment and other short-term commercial capital flows. Whereas the current proposal is to establish a ratchet mechanism for capital account liberalisation under the auspices of the IMF, recent experience would seem to suggest a strong case for a greater degree of coordination and control of capital movements, to ensure that developing countries do not incur unsustainable burdens of external liabilities, or become over-dependent or vulnerable to abrupt reversals of capital flows.

The experience of the Mexican and Asian crises appears to suggest that capital controls have had some effect in limiting the impact on countries which have retained or reimposed them. The World Bank (1997b: 172) found that capital controls 'were effective in the short run in reducing the

overall magnitude of capital inflows as well as influencing their composition'
in the first half of the 1990s. Moreover, while they did not protect Mexico,
they appear to have been successful at least in limiting contagion following
the Mexican crisis. Based on World Bank (1997b) analysis,

> Five of the six countries (Chile, Columbia [sic], Indonesia, Malaysia and Thailand)
> categorised as less affected by the Mexican crisis were among those which imposed
> or reimposed capital controls, while the sixth (Korea) already had a relatively
> restrictive capital account regime. Apart from Mexico itself, only Brazil was
> among the seven countries classified as more affected by the crisis despite tight-
> ening capital controls. (Woodward 1998a: 50, end note 18)

A similar pattern may also apply to the impact of the Asian crisis, at least
in terms of its effects on growth among the low- and middle-income
countries of the region (although this may be affected by subsequent changes
in economic projections). Among the low- and lower-middle-income
countries of East and South East Asia,

> The slowest projected growth rates for 1997–9 are in Thailand and Indonesia
> which have gone furthest in liberalising their capital accounts; the fastest is for
> China, which has throughout maintained the least open régime. Malaysia (which
> reversed its initial liberalisation more substantially, to regain control over its
> monetary policy) and the Philippines (which opened its capital account more
> recently than Indonesia and Thailand) fall between the two. (Woodward 1998a:
> 25–6)

This casts serious doubt on the advisability of seeking to extend and
entrench capital account liberalisation. The most limited approach would be
simply to avoid the extension of the IMF's mandate and to exclude provisions limiting restrictions on capital account transactions from future IMF
programmes, at least until the current crisis is resolved. This would leave
entirely at the discretion of each individual country both restrictions on outflows at times of crisis or acute speculative pressure on exchange rates, and
controls on inflows (to limit disruption from volatile capital flows, the risk of
later outflows and the transfer of ownership of productive capacity).

Alternatively, as in the case of the MAI, the proposal could be reversed: a
mandate for capital account restrictions could be written into the IMF's
Articles of Agreement, but with a view to approving restrictions imposed by
member countries, and thus giving them greater legitimacy and legal
weight.[66] However, it is not clear that this is necessary at present, as capital
account restrictions have not generally been subject to legal challenge.
Neither would it seem feasible without giving the Fund discretion over the
approval of restrictions, which (as the Fund currently operates) would almost
certainly be used to promote the capital account liberalisation agenda.

Within the policy space created (or maintained) by this approach, various models can be envisaged for limiting short-term financial inflows at the country level. One widely cited case is the very successful Chilean experiment. This requires investors to make an interest-free deposit at the Central Bank equivalent to a certain proportion[67] of their investment for a fixed period of twelve months. This effectively acts as a tax on foreign capital inflows; and, since the absolute cost is unaffected by the duration of or the return on the investment, it is much greater for investments which seek small speculative gains over a short period than for longer-term investments. This has the effect of limiting the volatility of financial flows, without entirely disconnecting the financial system from the global economy. It also has the benefit of providing the Central Bank with additional foreign exchange reserves in proportion to the increase in liabilities arising from capital inflows; and the interest earned on the deposit reduces the public sector deficit.

Dealing with Crises: Lessons from the Asian Experience[68]

As discussed earlier, the Asian crisis has demonstrated serious shortcomings in the mechanisms currently available for dealing with balance of payments crises in the international financial system as it now operates. The instruments used in the past are now seriously counterproductive, in that they cause serious damage to the financial interests of creditors and investors as well as to development and welfare in the countries affected.

In effect, the international financial community has to wait until a crisis happens, then gathers contributors to a 'rescue' package and negotiates an adjustment programme, before lending money to the government, phased over time, with each payment conditional on specified policy changes. Every element of this process is problematic in the context of recent crises. It means that the financing arrives only some time after the crisis starts; that the total amount available is limited by the willingness of donors to contribute; that the crucial initial payment, made when foreign exchange is most needed, is further reduced by the need to hold back resources as a means of enforcing policy conditionality; and that any effect on confidence is limited, both by uncertainty while the package is being put together, and by the uncertainty about whether the conditions attached to later disbursements will be met. The counterproductivity of conditionality is increased still further by its use, particularly in the Asian case, to apply inappropriate economic policies which are widely seen as having made the situation worse rather than better.

The delays and uncertainties both compound the crisis and add to the contagion effect. Because confidence is not restored, capital flows out still faster as the crisis progresses, leading to exchange rate overshooting: the reversal of the herd instinct means that the initial devaluation is far greater than is justified by the economic fundamentals prior to the crisis, and the exchange rate switches very quickly from being overvalued to being seriously undervalued. This is immensely damaging, not least to companies with large foreign debts, causing widespread bankruptcies and disrupting production.

Thus the exchange rate overshooting is largely self-justifying: the massive devaluation, coupled with the effects of the continued flight of foreign capital and misconceived adjustment programmes, devastates the real economy; and this seriously limits the scope for the exchange rate to recover to what would previously have been a realistic level. The result is that the exchange rate remains much lower for much longer than would have been justified by the economic fundamentals prior to the crisis.

This also intensifies the contagion effect, by compounding the problem of competitive devaluation. When the country's exchange rate falls, its exports become cheaper, and its competitors in export markets are less able to compete. Their export prices decline as they try to maintain their market share; and their export volumes fall as they fail to do so. The resulting deterioration in their balance of payments adds to pressure for devaluation, even as the initial crisis reduces capital inflows. When the devaluation occurs, overshooting is again almost inevitable; and the knock-on effects on the second country's competitors add a further twist to the vicious circle of competitive devaluation.

Even the *form* of financial support – loans from governments and international financial institutions to the affected governments – is inappropriate, because the foreign exchange outflows are from the private sector. The effect of this type of 'rescue' package is thus to socialise private sector risks and liabilities. The crisis arises from profit-motivated commercial transactions between private sector companies; but the cost, both of financing the rescue and of servicing the loans which are made, are borne by governments and ultimately taxpayers.

Moreover, while 'rescues' are largely ineffectual, or even counterproductive, from the perspective of crisis-affected countries, they operate to limit the losses which creditors and investors would otherwise incur as a result of their mistaken individual decisions and of a crisis precipitated by their collective actions. This raises the spectre of 'moral hazard' – by protecting them from the effects of their own actions, 'rescues' strengthen the incentive for them to act similarly in the future, and thereby to create further financial crises.

The Asian and Russian crises clearly demonstrate the inadequacy, ineffectiveness and inappropriateness of the current international financial arrangements to resolve or even contain – let alone to prevent – the 'new' financial crises. If, as has been argued in this book, such crises are indeed likely to become increasingly common, it is essential to introduce new and more effective mechanisms to deal with them, if we are to avoid a prolonged period of endemic and potentially global financial crisis.

Woodward (1999) proposes a means of doing this. Essentially, it is based on a global intervention fund financed by a very small tax (of perhaps 0.25 per cent) on all foreign exchange transactions (the Tobin tax). In the event of speculative pressure on the exchange rate of a member country's currency[69] this fund would automatically intervene to support the exchange rate, conditional only on a predetermined acceleration of the rate of depreciation, if necessary, within a crawling-peg exchange rate system.[70]

Tobin tax

This relatively simple proposal would have considerable advantages over the current arrangements.

- The financial response would be immediate and automatic, acting to prevent crises before they happen rather than seeking to contain the situation only after irreparable economic damage has been done.

- There would be no policy conditionality (except on the exchange rate) to make future support uncertain, which would help to bolster confidence. (Support for structural economic reforms would continue separately where needed – although the nature of the reforms to be supported also requires fundamental reconsideration.)

- The incentives for speculative attacks would be massively reduced, as the resources available to protect currencies would be much greater, reducing the probability of such attacks being successful, while the limitation of exchange rate changes to variations in the pace of progressive devaluations (rather than on step devaluations) would considerably reduce the potential benefits from successful speculation. Speculators would have little chance of success, and their gains would be very small if they did, making the gamble unattractive. Since speculators would be frustrated rather than protected, the problem of moral hazard (or at least this dimension of it) would be avoided.

- The gradualist approach to exchange rate adjustment would avoid overshooting, allow the real economy time to adapt to lower exchange rates (limiting the economic and social impact of crises), and greatly reduce contagion through competitive devaluation.

- There would be no loans to or from governments, so that private sector liabilities would not be socialised.

In short, this approach would greatly reduce the likelihood of financial crises, limit their contagion between countries, and greatly reduce their impact, both on developing countries and on international investors. It would also considerably reduce the direct costs to the international financial institutions and the developed country governments.

Conclusion

At the end of the twentieth century developing countries faced a series of serious financial crises which differed markedly from those which had occurred previously. This reflected a radical change in the nature of financial flows to developing countries. The initial effect was to raise serious questions in academic and policy-making circles about the nature of the international financial architecture, and the direction in which international financial markets were heading. However, complacency was quickly restored; institutional reforms at the global level were watered down, almost to the point of non-existence; and the earlier direction of international policy – towards the promotion of private sector flows – is progressively being restored (albeit with a slightly greater degree of caution). Implicitly, the 1990s financial crises were seen as a problem of transition rather than a new paradigm.

The arguments put forward in this book also suggest that the 1990s were a transitional phase – but that they represent a transition to what could be a prolonged period of endemic financial crisis, at least for middle-income developing countries. If this view is justified, the longer-term policy responses have been at best ineffective and in some respects perverse, raising the risk of serious economic and human consequences.

This chapter has proposed changes in the international economic system to limit the risk of such a period of crisis – although the distance we have already travelled towards this scenario means that it would at best take many years before the risk could come close to being eliminated. The further we move in the present direction, the longer the process will take to reverse, and the greater the risk of renewed financial crisis in the meantime.

In practice, however, while the change of climate following the events in Seattle in late 1999 may slow down the process at least temporarily, it seems unlikely that the present direction of policies will change fundamentally in the near future. This will require two underlying changes.

First, it requires a change in attitudes to private sector capital flows, and particularly foreign direct investment. The present positive view is potentially seriously misleading and, perversely, has been reinforced rather than weakened by the experience of the Asian financial crisis. Only when a more realistic attitude prevails, and the downside of direct investment is seriously addressed, will the climate be right for the policy changes which are urgently needed.

The second change which is required is political. The international financial system at present is heavily dominated by the major developed country governments, through both formal and informal structures, in a political structure which is a travesty of the model of 'good governance' which these governments, and the international institutions they dominate, seek to promote in the developing countries. The major developed countries' relationships with direct and portfolio investors are fundamentally different from those of developing countries: outward investment is generally at least as important as inward investment; inward investment is generally much smaller (relative to the size of the economy) and cheaper; and the balance of payments constraint is a much less dominant policy concern.

The problem is compounded by the direct political influence of transnational companies at the national level in many of the countries concerned, through their personal connections with politicians, their importance in the economy as a whole, their well-resourced lobbying, and in many cases their role as major financiers of political parties. Only when governments represent the interests of their populations and not their business communities, and have political influence proportional to the populations they represent, can we realistically expect to achieve an international financial and economic system which will genuinely serve the interests of people, and not of transnational companies.

Data Discrepancies and the Balance of Payments Effects of Direct Investment in Thailand

Data deficiencies make Thailand a particularly difficult country in which to assess the impact of FDI. There are two major problems with the IMF data for FDI flows to Thailand: the exclusion of reinvested profits from both recorded investment and recorded profits; and the misclassification of an unspecified amount of FDI as banking flows over an unspecified period (which suggests that some FDI profits may also be misclassified as banking income). To make a valid assessment of the potential role of FDI in Thailand's balance of payments, it is clearly essential to consider the potential effects of these factors.

The published data would appear to confirm that these problems are significant. While Thailand is generally seen as having been exceptionally successful in attracting FDI in the 1990s (prior to the 1997 crisis), it is almost unique among non-African developing countries in having sustained a more or less continuous decline (by nearly half in dollar terms) in reported FDI inflows in 1990–94. FDI flows to the rest of the East Asian and Pacific region increased by about 450 per cent over the same period. In addition, the apparent rate of return on FDI (even based on the UNCTAD stock figures, which will be underestimated to the extent that inflows are underrecorded) is an implausibly low 3 per cent per annum, compared with the World Bank's estimate for developing countries as a whole of 16–18 per cent.

Table AI.1 illustrates the possible effects of correcting these data problems. It is based on three assumptions.

- 25 per cent of the financial account discrepancy noted in Chapter 6 is assumed to be attributable to the misclassification of FDI flows.

- Profits in each year are assumed to be 12 per cent of the stock of FDI at the end of the previous year (based on the UNCTAD estimate for the end of 1989, plus cumulative flows in subsequent years).

Table AI.1 • Estimated Balance of Payments Effects of FDI in Thailand, 1990–96 ($bn)

(a) Official data	1990	1991	1992	1993	1994	1995	1996
Imports of capital goods	1.2	1.0	1.1	0.9	0.7	1.0	1.2
Profits	0.3	0.1	0.3	0.4	0.5	0.5	0.5
FDI-related current account	−1.5	−1.1	−1.4	−1.3	−1.1	−1.5	−1.7
(% of GDP)	−1.9	−1.1	−1.3	−1.1	−0.8	−0.9	−0.9
Total current account	−7.3	−7.6	−6.3	−6.4	−8.1	−13.6	−14.7
(% of GDP)	−8.9	−8.1	−5.7	−5.1	−5.6	−8.1	−7.9
Non-FDI current account	−5.7	−6.5	−4.9	−5.0	−6.9	−12.0	−13.0
(% of GDP)	−7.0	−7.0	−4.4	−4.0	−4.8	−7.2	−7.0
Net inflow of FDI	2.4	2.0	2.1	1.8	1.4	2.1	2.3
FDI-related overall balance	0.9	1.0	0.6	0.4	0.2	0.3	0.4
Stock of inward FDI	8.0					17.2	19.6
(b) Revised estimates	1990	1991	1992	1993	1994	1995	1996
Imports of capital goods	1.4	1.5	1.8	2.4	3.4	3.9	3.2
Profits	0.6	1.0	1.3	1.8	2.3	3.1	4.1
FDI-related current account	−2.0	−2.4	−3.1	−4.1	−5.7	−7.1	−7.3
(% of GDP)	−2.5	−2.6	−2.6	−3.3	−4.0	−4.2	−3.9
Total current account	−7.6	−8.5	−7.3	−7.7	−9.9	−16.2	−18.3
(% of GDP)	−9.3	−9.1	−6.6	−6.2	−6.9	−9.7	−9.9
Non-FDI current account	−5.6	−6.1	−4.2	−3.6	−4.2	−9.1	−11.0
(% of GDP)	−6.8	−6.5	−4.0	−2.9	−2.9	−5.5	−6.0
Net inflow of FDI	2.8	2.9	3.5	4.8	6.7	7.9	6.4
FDI-related overall balance	0.7	0.5	0.4	0.6	1.0	0.8	−0.9
(% of GDP)	0.9	0.5	0.4	0.5	0.7	0.5	−0.5
Stock of inward FDI	8.3	11.2	14.8	19.6	26.3	34.2	40.6

Notes: Data used are from IMF (1998c), except those for profit remittances, which are from World Bank (1998a), and those for the stock of inward FDI, which are from UNCTAD (1997b). Imports of capital goods are assumed to be 50% of FDI inflows. Other assumptions for the revised estimates are as outlined in the text.

- It is assumed that profits on the stock of investment arising from mis-classification of flows are also misclassified, and these are therefore treated separately. The profit figures given in World Bank (1998a) are assumed to represent remitted profits on the stock of investment arising from recorded FDI inflows and the (unrecorded) reinvested profits on this investment; and an equal proportion of the profits generated by misclassified FDI are assumed to be remitted. All non-remitted profits are assumed to be reinvested.

These assumptions imply an increase in FDI inflows from about $2.8 billion in 1990 to a peak of about $7.9 billion in 1995, falling back to $6.4 billion in 1996. As shown in Table AI.2, this growth path lies broadly between those of Malaysia and the Philippines (the most comparable regional economies), and well below those of Indonesia, China and the rest of the East Asia/Pacific region. This suggests that the assumptions may if anything tend to err on the conservative side.

Table AI.2 • Indices of FDI Flows, East Asia, 1990–96 (1990 = 100)

	1990	1991	1992	1993	1994	1995	1996
(Official)	100.0	82.4	86.5	73.8	55.9	84.6	95.6
Thailand (revised est.)	100.0	105.8	127.2	170.2	235.2	263.0	196.8
Malaysia	100.0	171.4	222.2	214.6	186.1	177.1	192.9
Philippines	100.0	102.6	43.0	233.6	300.2	278.9	265.7
Indonesia	100.0	135.6	162.6	183.3	193.0	397.8	728.5
China	100.0	125.2	319.9	789.1	968.9	1028.1	1152.3
Other East Asia/Pacific	100.0	157.6	227.8	196.7	235.4	509.3	499.3

Notes: The revised estimates for Thailand are based on the figures in Table AI.1, using the assumptions outlined in the text. Other figures are estimated on the basis of data from World Bank (1998a).

The picture produced by these assumptions is nonetheless striking. FDI inflows are increased throughout the period, the underestimation peaking at $5.8 billion in 1995; the stock of FDI at the end of 1996 is more than doubled from the UNCTAD estimate ($40.6 billion compared with $19.6 billion); and profits are increased both by the larger stock of investment and by the inclusion of reinvested profits, again by an increasing margin, and by a factor of eight in 1996 (from the World Bank estimate of $510 million to $4.1 billion).

The resulting effect on the FDI-related component of the current account deficit is considerable. Based on the official figures, assuming that

$100 of inward FDI gives rise to imports of capital goods of $50, the effect would decline from just under 2 per cent of GDP in 1990 to less than 1 per cent in 1994–6. The effect implied by the revised estimates increases from 2.5 per cent of GDP in 1990–92 to around 4 per cent of GDP in 1994–6. This would be more than sufficient to push the deficit from being sustainable to being clearly unsustainable.

The effect on the overall balance, including capital flows, is much more limited, because reinvested profits are excluded from the capital account as well as the current account, while misclassified flows are included in the official data for the capital account. Nonetheless, the effect is significant in 1996, when the revised estimates imply a negative effect (−0.5 per cent of GDP), compared with +0.4 per cent of GDP based on the official data.

It should be noted that the revised estimates also imply a larger total current account deficit than in the official data, as unrecorded profits on FDI by definition are not included in the latter. The result is to increase the deficit in 1996 from nearly 8 per cent of GDP to nearly 10 per cent. Since investors' perception of the deficit, and therefore its psychological effect on capital flows, is likely to be based primarily on the published data, it is only the effect of the additional imports of capital goods which is relevant in this context. This amounts to around $2 billion or 1.1 per cent of GDP.

Overall, these estimates suggest that FDI may have had a major impact on Thailand's current account deficit in 1994–6, notwithstanding the much smaller effect implied by the official data. Together with the small negative impact on the overall balance in 1996, this could have contributed significantly to the financial crisis the following year. However, most of the effect would not have appeared in the *reported* current account deficit, limiting its psychological impact on investors, and reducing the likelihood that it brought about the reversal of capital flows. This prompts the ironic conclusion that if FDI did not contribute to the crisis, this is only because the shortcomings in the official data gave investors a false sense of security.

Clearly, the estimates which have been presented in this Appendix can be regarded as no more than indicative, as the assumptions are largely arbitrary, and the conclusions should therefore be treated with some caution. However, the assumptions are by no means extravagant − a rate of return well below the average for developing countries, and a growth of FDI broadly in line with the two most comparable countries, and substantially slower than other major countries, in the region. While the magnitude of the effect of FDI may be open to question, it seems clear that it was substantially greater than is implied by the official data, and likely that it was on a sufficient scale to cast serious doubt on the very favourable conclusions that have been drawn on the desirability of FDI following the Asian crisis.

▶ Appendix II

Balance of Payments Effects of Direct Investment in Malaysia
Data Limitations and Sensitivity to Assumptions

The estimates of the balance of payments effects of direct investment in Malaysia presented in Chapter 13 are subject to two possible problems. First, some of the assumptions on which they are based are essentially arbitrary (in particular, that 50 per cent of direct investment flows are spent on imported capital goods, and the application of the 1990–94 growth rates for affiliates' exports and other imports relative to the total figures in 1995–6); and, second, the nature of the data mean that no account is taken of import substitution. Accordingly, this Appendix discusses the effects of varying the assumptions, and of taking import substitution into account. The results are summarised in Table AII.1.

Clearly, the proportion of new inflows of FDI spent on imports of capital equipment is dependent in part on the division of inward FDI between the construction of new capacity and the purchase of existing capacity,[71] and the import intensity of the investment in the latter case. FDI through purchase appears to be relatively low in Malaysia: a comparison of UNCTAD (1997b: Annex Table B.7) with data from IMF (1998c) suggests that total mergers and acquisitions were of the order of 20 per cent of total FDI in 1990–95, but increased abruptly to 88 per cent in 1996 – although the compatibility of these two sources is questionable. Since a substantial proportion of FDI was also in the electronics industries, which typically require a substantial amount of imported equipment, the proportion of FDI inflows allocated to imports of capital goods is likely to be relatively high.

In fact, the results have limited sensitivity to variations in the proportion of new FDI flows spent on imports of capital goods, as this has two contradictory effects: while a higher proportion implies larger imports of capital goods, it also slows the growth rate of other imports, reducing their level in 1996. The effect of reducing the proportion to 25 per cent is to increase the effect of FDI on the current account deficit by 0.4 per cent of GDP in 1995,

Table AII.1 • Sensitivity of Estimated FDI-Related Current Account Balance to Changes in Assumptions (% of GDP)

	1990	1991	1992	1993	1994	1995	1996
Baseline current account deficit	3.1	8.1	5.0	5.7	9.0	10.0	8.1
Impact on deficit of							
Capital goods imports/FDI = 25%	n/a	n/a	n/a	n/a	n/a	+0.4	+0.1
Capital goods imports/FDI = 75%	n/a	n/a	n/a	n/a	n/a	−0.4	−0.1
Relative growth of exports 1% pa faster	n/a	n/a	n/a	n/a	n/a	−0.5	−1.0
Relative growth of exports 1% pa slower	n/a	n/a	n/a	n/a	n/a	+0.5	+1.0
Relative growth of non-capital imports 1% pa faster	n/a	n/a	n/a	n/a	n/a	+0.6	+1.0
Relative growth of non-capital imports 1% pa slower	n/a	n/a	n/a	n/a	n/a	−0.5	−1.0
Export/non-capital import growth at 1990–94 average	n/a	n/a	n/a	n/a	n/a	−0.7	+2.9
Export/non-capital imports at 1994 share of total	n/a	n/a	n/a	n/a	n/a	−1.0	+1.6
Import substitution = 5% of exports	−1.8	−2.0	−2.0	−2.1	−2.4	−2.6	−2.5

and by 0.1 per cent of GDP in 1996, while increasing the proportion to 75 per cent has the opposite effect.

A slightly greater effect could arise if the ratio were to change during the course of the period, for example because of an increase in direct investment through purchase. If this occurred between 1990 and 1994, it would imply a faster growth in non-capital imports, and thus a somewhat greater deterioration in 1995–6. However, if it occurred only in 1995–6, it would imply some improvement: a reduction in the ratio from a constant 50 per cent in 1990–94 to 25 per cent in 1995–6 would reduce the deficit by 1.2 per cent and 1.3 per cent of GDP respectively. However, the significance of this reduction is limited, in that the overall effect on the deficit would remain in the order of 7–9 per cent of GDP.

The projections are more sensitive to the assumptions made about the growth rates of affiliates' exports and imports in 1995–6. The effect of reducing (increasing) the relative growth rate of exports by one percentage point is to increase (reduce) the deficit by 0.5 per cent of GDP in 1995 and by 1.0 per cent in 1996, with an almost identical effect in the opposite direction in the case of imports.

Two alternative approaches could also be envisaged.

- If the absolute growth rate of affiliates' exports and non-capital imports in 1990–94 were extrapolated to 1996, the deficit would be reduced by 0.7 per cent in 1995, but increased by 2.9 per cent in 1996.

- If foreign affiliates' share of total exports and imports (excluding their imports of capital goods) remained at the 1994 level in 1995–6, the effect on the deficit would be reduced by 1.0 per cent in 1995, but increased in 1996 by 1.6 per cent.

More important than the specific assumptions of the projections, however, is the coverage of the data. The above discussion takes account only of transactions conducted by transnational companies and their affiliates, and therefore excludes import substitution, the diversion of production by locally owned companies from export markets to foreign-owned affiliates, and indirect effects of TNC operations on the import share of consumption, for example through advertising. It should be noted that incorporating these effects would affect the results for 1990–94 as well as the projections for 1995–6.

The import-substitution effect is limited by the strong orientation of direct investment in Malaysia towards export sectors (and service sectors such as retailing, where FDI is the main *means* of importing); but it is almost certain that some of the output of foreign affiliates, for example in the consumer electronics sector, was purchased locally; and that this will have substituted primarily for imports rather than directly or indirectly[72] for production by locally owned enterprises or for savings. It also seems likely (though less certain) that this will have outweighed other indirect effects on the trade balance. If, for example, foreign affiliates sold $1 of goods locally for every $10 they exported (and this substituted entirely for imports), and half of this effect was off-set by substitution for local production and savings and export diversion, this would reduce the effect of FDI on the current account deficit by an average of 2 per cent of GDP in 1990–3 and 2.5 per cent of GDP in 1994–6.

In summary, the projections for 1995–6 do not appear to be critically sensitive to variations in the assumptions made with respect to exports and imports, particularly in terms of the average effect over the two years. The magnitude of the changes arising from changes in the assumptions are limited relative to the baseline estimates; the effects of changing the relative growth rate assumptions are broadly symmetrical between exports and imports; and the alternative approaches have opposite impacts in 1995 and 1996, increasing the current account deficit only slightly overall.

The impact of the data coverage problems is both greater and more systematic, implying that the estimated impact of FDI on the current account deficit is biased substantially upwards throughout the period, and slightly more so in 1994–6 than in 1990–93. It is possible that this effect could be sufficient to eliminate the estimated negative impact on the overall balance in 1994–6; but it seems likely that the estimate of a current account deficit of foreign affiliates (at least after 1993), increasing to an economically significant level in 1994–6, would remain if these problems were corrected.

Notes

1 'Capital Controversies', *The Economist* (UK edition), 23 May 1998: 112.
2 More recently, the definition of capital in this context has been broadened beyond financial capital and physical capital (buildings, productive facilities, equipment, etc.) to include human capital (education) and especially technology (particularly productive technologies). However, productive technology generally needs to be embodied in physical capital, so that narrowing the technological gap between developed and developing countries also requires an increase in the supply of capital for investment.
3 On the impact of adjustment programmes in response to balance of payments crises, see Woodward (1992).
4 The East Asian crisis is discussed in greater detail in chapters 13 and 14.
5 However, in most statistical sources profit remittances in principle refer to total profits, including amounts retained or reinvested by the enterprise.
6 In the case of 'in-kind' investment, as discussed earlier, the investor may provide free access to 'intellectual property rights': in effect, the royalties are paid in advance, and the proceeds are used to finance the investment, reducing the capital inflow associated with the investment. Implicitly, this treats access to intellectual property rights as a form of capital, which also suggests that the associated income (that is, royalties) might legitimately be regarded as comparable with income on capital.
7 All data in this paragraph are from World Bank (1998a), Vol. II. Annual interest paid on private non-guaranteed debts averaged 6.5 per cent of the amount outstanding in 1991–6 for both middle-income and low-income countries. However, this excludes any amounts not paid for reasons such as rescheduling or renegotiation of debts, accumulation of arrears or bankruptcy of debtors, and is therefore likely to understate significantly the rate of interest *due* on loans.
8 This pattern appears to have become somewhat less pronounced since 1993, but nonetheless persists to a significant degree.
9 These countries are not named, but are presumably dominated by the larger economies in East and South East Asia and Latin America.
10 Sub-Saharan Africa excludes South Africa (which is classified by UNCTAD as a developed country) and Sudan (which is included in North Africa).
11 Equity investment flows to South Africa are available only from 1993, although substantial equity investment took place before that date. Since the aggregate figures for all developing countries from this date correspond almost exactly with the total of the figures for indi-

vidual countries, it seems likely that the discrepancy in the earlier years is accounted for by the inclusion of estimates for South Africa in the aggregate figures. Using the difference between the two series as an estimate of equity investment flows to South Africa, and applying an annual rate of return of 20 per cent, suggests a stock at end-1996 of around 20 per cent of GDP. Based only on the figures from 1993, the figure is around 6–7 per cent of GDP.

12 These figures are very approximate, being based on figures for FDI from the US, assuming the same relationship between investment and output for FDI from other sources.

13 'Suharto's Family Values', *The Economist* (UK edition), 14 March 1998: 79.

14 'Top of the Class?', *The Economist*, (UK edition), 21 March 1998: 108.

15 Reported in 'South Korea's Meltdown', *The Economist*, 13 December 1997.

16 As discussed later, there are major differences between the IMF's *Balance of Payments Statistics Yearbook* and the World Bank's *Global Development Finance* in their data on portfolio investment flows, in terms both of their country coverage and of the actual numbers where they overlap. World Bank (1998a) provides figures for portfolio equity investment in China and Malaysia throughout the 1990s; in Côte d'Ivoire, Estonia and Myanmar from 1994; and in Slovenia in 1996. However, no data are recorded for Senegal or Togo, despite their inclusion in IMF (1998c). Korea is no longer included in *Global Development Finance*, but data were provided for 1990–4 when it last appeared in the *World Debt Tables* (World Bank, 1996).

17 That is, for example, giving twice the weight to a country where the data cover four years to that given to a country where the data cover two years.

18 The term 'developing countries' is used loosely here, to include all countries which are classified as developing by either UNCTAD or the World Bank. Of the countries mentioned, South Africa is categorised as developing by the World Bank but not by UNCTAD, while the reverse is the case for Korea and Singapore.

19 In the case of a joint venture, the undervaluation is the amount of the loan multiplied by the foreign-owned share of the enterprise.

20 'Rough Trade', *The Economist* (UK edition), 8 August 1998: 65.

21 Except where assets are purchased from existing foreign investors.

22 Official FDI flow data in this paragraph and the next are taken from World Bank (1998a), except for North Korea, where the figure used is from World Bank (1997c): Table 5.2.

23 The average adjustment required is 17 per cent if the discrepancy is divided between developed and developing countries, and 97 per cent if it is all attributed to the latter.

24 In addition, the coverage of the data for Spain and Portugal is very limited.

25 The average adjustment required is 42 per cent if the discrepancy is divided between developed and developing countries, and 145 per cent if it is all attributed to the latter.

26 By definition, none of these countries provides data on reinvestment.

27 It should be noted that these figures are for foreign affiliates worldwide, not only in developing countries.

28 These figures are discussed in greater detail in Chapter 13.

29 Trade data may also be distorted by the effects of transfer price manipulation, as discussed in the previous section. However, for the purposes of assessing the short-term balance of payments effects of FDI, this should not be important, as the impact on the trade balance will merely counteract the effect on reported profits.

30 It should be noted that the question of whether privatisation *as such* is beneficial is beyond the scope of this book. The question in the present context is how privatisation with foreign participation compares with privatisation without foreign participation from the perspective of the host country's foreign-exchange position.

31 Under the Highly-Indebted Poor Countries (HIPC) Initiative, external debt is to be reduced (eventually) to a level deemed by the IMF and World Bank to be sustainable. Since this level is fixed, and no account is taken of FDI or equity liabilities, using privatisation proceeds to pay off part of the external debt will merely reduce the amount which would otherwise have been cancelled, leaving the total external liabilities higher than they would otherwise have been after the completion of the process. The implications of the exclusion of FDI and equity liabilities from the sustainability calculations in the HIPC Initiative are discussed in greater detail in Woodward (1998b).

32 This is actually a simplification, as the *company's* receipts and spending in local currency do not take account of the indirect foreign exchange costs of wage payments, the foreign exchange content of local inputs, or the foreign exchange savings from import substitution. However, if the classification of receipts and expenditure between local currency and foreign exchange is made as before, this approach remains valid.

33 It is, of course, important to avoid double counting. This means that taxes on wages and other inputs should be included *either* as part of wages and input costs *or* as part of taxation; and that taxes on locally sold produce should be excluded if figures for local sales revenues are net of consumption taxes.

34 Foreign investors might, for example, achieve an above-average rate of return if particular stocks were fashionable among foreign investors at a time when portfolio investment inflows were high (as the associated demand would push up their prices disproportionately); if domestic investors followed the lead of foreign investors, increasing the demand for (and thus the prices of) their shares; or if foreign investors followed more sophisticated (and successful) investment strategies than their local counterparts. Conversely, greater familiarity with local conditions could allow domestic investors to make higher rates of return.

35 Labour use may also be reduced by introducing labour-saving equipment. However, this constitutes new investment, and is therefore considered later.

36 The countries are Malaysia (average of 1980, 1985 and 1986), Thailand (1981–3), Philippines (1983–5), India (1978–82), South Korea, Colombia, Ecuador, Peru, Uruguay, Venezuela, Cameroon and Tunisia (all 1980–84), Côte d'Ivoire (1974–8) and Turkey (1977–81).

37 This is actually more complicated than is presented here, as any local production of non-tradeable goods for which the additional sales substitute is likely to have some foreign exchange cost, in the form of imported inputs and profits of other TNCs. In principle, this can be taken into account by adjusting the import substitution figure to include these foreign-exchange savings. The 40 per cent figure used here allows, for example, for 20 per cent substitution for imports, and 80 per cent substitution for non-tradeable goods with an average import content of 25 per cent.

38 This assumes that such investment takes the form of portfolio equity investment rather than FDI; and that the rate of return on outward investment is somewhat lower than that on inward investment. The latter is based on the assumption that most of the outward investment is likely to be in developed rather than developing countries (where the average rate of return is typically lower, because of the lower perceived risk).

39 Since the data source used provides data only on a quarterly basis, the pre-crisis period used is the twelve months to September 1994, so as to avoid distortion arising from the major capital outflow in December 1994. This is the peak period for net inflows of direct and equity investment.

40 This discussion is based on the corresponding section of Woodward (1998c).

41 There are some exceptions to this, such as the investment in Chile's CODELCO copper

project in the late 1980s, where production increased the world supply significantly. Even here, however, most of the effect was felt by other producing countries.

42 If production capacity in developing countries is owned by transnational corporations, much of the effect will be absorbed by the impact on profit remittances. There may nonetheless be some negative foreign exchange impact, to the extent that the foreign affiliates concerned reduce their local currency expenditure; but this will almost certainly be substantially less than the reduction in their total revenues.

43 While Dean *et al.* (1994) arguably overstate the weakness of trade reform in sub-Saharan Africa somewhat, the general point remains valid. The fiscal constraint is critical: 25 of 42 countries in sub-Saharan Africa rely on trade taxes for at least 30 per cent of total government revenues, and five for at least 50 per cent. Moreover, reliance on trade taxes is generally most acute in countries where overall government revenues are lowest (Woodward 1996: 55).

44 Most land-locked developing countries are also low-income countries.

45 Article VIII, Section 2(a) of the Fund's Articles of Agreement states that 'no member shall, without the approval of the Fund, impose restrictions on the making of payments and transfers for current international transactions'. This is modified by Article XIV, Section 2 to allow a member to 'maintain and adapt to changing circumstances the restrictions … that were in effect on the date on which it became a member', subject to a requirement that 'members shall withdraw restrictions maintained under this Section as soon as they are satisfied that they will be able, in the absence of such restrictions, to settle their balance of payments in a manner which will not unduly encumber their access to the general resources of the Fund'. In principle, the retention of restrictions contrary to these requirements may ultimately be penalised by expulsion from the Fund.

46 These figures exclude the case with the highest total and per-job cost ($483.5 million and $245,451 respectively), which occurred between the two periods (in 1991).

47 This assumes dividend payments totalling 1–2 per cent of the value of the shares each year.

48 This Box is reproduced from Woodward (1998a).

49 This discussion, and a slightly different version of Tables 11.1 and 11.2, first appeared in a paper for the Bretton Woods Project (Woodward 1998a); I am grateful to the Project for permission to reproduce it here.

50 'Into the Spotlight: a Survey of Mexico' (*The Economist*, 13 February 1993: 7) observed that 'The current-account deficit … is … large enough to raise the threat of devaluation among foreign investors'. 'Gone Tomorrow?' (*The Economist*, 29 May 1993: 105–8) reported Rogelio Ramirez de la O, a prominent Mexican economist, as warning of 'a big peso devaluation (of perhaps 15 per cent) … four months off', and MIT professor Rudiger Dornbusch as having warned 'a few months' previously that a devaluation was inevitable.

51 It should be noted that this figure includes some privatisation-related direct investment.

52 Unfortunately, consistent time series data are not readily available for Latin America for 1981–5. Profits increased by about 80 per cent over this period in Brazil and Chile, and from zero to $14 million in Uruguay; but they fell by about 30–40 per cent in Argentina and Mexico, and by 70 per cent in Venezuela. The overall effect on the change in net transfers is minimal – about –$170million in aggregate, compared with a change in the level of investment of $5.5 billion over the same period.

53 This situation may be compounded if governments undertake substantial privatisation during the crisis period – as part of the structural adjustment programmes on which financial 'rescues' are conditional, for example, as occurred during the Latin American debt crisis and the Asian financial crisis (Indonesia is a case in point). The result will be to increase the supply of companies and productive facilities, further depressing their market

prices. This is likely to imply a loss of potential revenue to the government (compared with selling at a later stage in the cycle) as well as worsening the long-term balance of payments effects of FDI.

54 Inflows of direct and equity investment may also have increased the current account deficit indirectly, through their effects on the real exchange rate. This is discussed in Chapter 14.

55 While only profit remittances represent an actual outflow of foreign exchange, it is total profit (including reinvestment) that is relevant to the current account balance. Since it is the current account deficit rather than the actual flow of foreign exchange which primarily affects perceptions of exchange rate over-valuation, the following discussion therefore focuses on total profits rather than profit remittances.

56 Note that part of the proceeds of direct investment through purchase are also likely to leak out of the economy, either to pay for imports or in the form of foreign investments by the seller (as discussed in Chapter 7). Such imports have an equivalent effect to that of imports of capital goods resulting from FDI in construction. In the case of investment outside the country, there would be a shift of the negative effect from the current account to the capital account, leaving the effect on the overall balance unchanged in the short term. However, the effect on both the current and overall balances would become somewhat more favourable over the long term, to the extent that the profits on the investment were returned to the country concerned.

57 The data used are from IMF (1998c), except profit data for Thailand (which are not provided in this source), and profit data for Indonesia in Figure 13.3 (which are seriously inconsistent with this source). The latter are from World Bank (1998a).

58 However, only about a quarter of this effect would have appeared in the published data for the current account deficit, limiting the potential psychological effect on investors.

59 UNCTAD (1997b: Table II.9) suggests a substantially greater increase in profit remittances from 1992, to $5,350 million in 1995 (see notes to Table 13.1).

60 One 'push' factor is also cited, namely the intensified competition from China in export markets for labour-intensive goods.

61 In principle, the discrepancy could arise from outward investment from Malaysia, which is not provided by IMF (1998c). However, while this seems plausible for 1997, it would require net outward investment of $1.5 billion from Malaysia in 1996, which seems improbably high.

62 It should be noted that the changes in exposure estimated here represent the percentage change in the *percentage share* of the portfolio in a particular group of markets. This will overestimate the percentage reduction in the absolute value of investments, to the extent that the value of the overall portfolio increased over the period concerned. For example, if total portfolio values increased by 10 per cent per annum over the 18-month period considered here, the reduction in exposure to non-Japan Asia would be 48.8 per cent, and that to the non-US Americas would be 78.6 per cent. Against this, one would expect the portfolios of major institutional investors in these markets to out-perform a random selection of shares. To the extent that they did, this would have an off-setting effect on the estimated sales.

63 Robeco Group increased its proportion of equities in non-Japan Asia from 1 per cent in the third quarter of 1998 to 4 per cent in the fourth quarter, and Commerz International from 2 per cent to 3 per cent, although the latter may be a result of increases in the value of shares rather than purchases ('Our Quarterly Portfolio Poll', *The Economist*, 10 October 1998: 121). Daiwa Europe was not included in the results for the third quarter, but held only 2 per cent of its equities in non-Japan Asia in the second quarter, compared with 17 per cent in the fourth quarter ('Our Quarterly Portfolio Poll', *The Economist*, 11 July 1998: 99).

64   See EURODAD (1995: 38–40) for an assessment of the true impact of the early Brady deals, which were the sole form of debt reduction for the major middle-income debtors.

65   This section and the next also appeared (with minor editorial differences) in Woodward (1999). As noted there (footnote 11), the dichotomy between the two proposals is much less clear-cut than is presented here. Proposals for the Multilateral Agreement on Investment (MAI) include matters which extend beyond direct investment into the realm of purely financial transactions. The capital account liberalisation (CAL) proposal is widely seen as potentially extending into areas of direct investment well beyond its purely financial effects on the balance of payments capital account. The MAI/CAL distinction used here is thus a simplification, focusing on the primary dimensions of each proposal.

66   A similar approach – IMF approval of the accumulation of interest arrears on foreign debts, thus rendering the associated contractual obligations legally unenforceable – has been proposed in the context of both the 1980s debt crisis (Woodward 1992: Vol. I, Ch. 4) and the 1994 Mexican crisis (Eichengreen and Portes 1995).

67   Following the 1998 Russian crisis, this proportion was reduced to zero, as no further discouragement to capital inflows was seen as necessary. However, the mechanism remains in place, and the proportion can be increased again if and when this is seen as necessary.

68   This section is based on the more detailed presentation in Woodward (1999).

69   Realistically, membership would probably need to be limited to countries with convertible currencies.

70   Crawling-peg exchange-rate systems have been widely used by developing countries since the 1980s. They entail the government setting the exchange rate, but allowing it to fall by a small, pre-announced amount at regular intervals (by 0.1 per cent every week, for example). The rate of depreciation (or 'slippage') may be varied when the need arises.

71   However, it should be noted that some of the capital inflow of FDI through purchase will also leak out of the economy, either to pay for imports or in the form of investments outside the country. This would have a similar short-term effect on the overall balance to imports of capital goods, but outward investment would shift the effect from the current account to the capital account, and any remittance of profits would lead to a positive effect on the current account in the longer term.

72   That is, either by substituting directly for consumption of equivalent locally produced goods, or by switching expenditure away from other locally produced goods.

Bibliography

Agénor, P.-R. and Montiel, P. (1996) *Development Macroeconomics*. Princeton, NJ: Princeton University Press.

Agosin, M. (ed., 1995) *Foreign Direct Investment in Latin America*. Washington D.C.: Inter-American Development Bank.

Bachmann, H. and Kwaku, K. (1994) *MIGA Roundtable on Foreign Direct Investment Policies in Africa: Proceedings and Lessons*. Washington D.C.: World Bank, MIGA Policy and Advisory Services Research Paper.

Bergsman, J. and Shen, X. (1995) 'Foreign Direct Investment in Developing Countries: Progress and Problems'. *Finance and Development* 32(4): 6–8, December.

Brandt, W. and Giddy, I. (1977) 'Profitability and Concentration of Foreign and Domestic Firms in Brazil'. Paper presented at the Academy of International Business Annual Meeting, Orlando.

Caves, R. (1996) *Multinational Enterprise and Economic Analysis*. Cambridge Surveys of Economic Literature, Second Edition. Cambridge: Cambridge University Press.

Chote, R. (1998) 'Financial Crises: the Lessons of Asia'. In CEPR, *Financial Crises and Asia*. London: Centre for Economic Policy Research.

Crotty, J., Epstein, G. and Kelly, P. (1997) 'Multinational Corporations and Technological Change: Global Stagnation, Inequality and Unemployment'. Third draft.

Dean, J., Desai, S. and Riedel, J. (1994) *Trade Policy Reform in Developing Countries since 1995: a Review of the Evidence*. Washington D.C.: World Bank, Discussion Paper No. 267.

Dunning, J. (1993) *Multinational Enterprises and the Global Economy*. Harlow: Addison-Wesley.

EURODAD (1995) *World Credit Tables, 1994–5: Creditor-Debtor Relations from Another Perspective*. Brussels: European Network on Debt and Development.

Goldsbrough, D., Coorey, S., Dicks-Mireaux, L., Horvath, B., Kochhar, K., Mecagni, M., Offerdal, E. and Zhou, J. (1996) *Reinvigorating Growth in Developing Countries: Lessons from Adjustment Policies in Eight Developing Economies*. Washington D.C.: International Monetary Fund, Occasional Paper No. 139.

Halpern, L. (1998) 'Assessing Current Account Sustainability in Transition Economies'. *Europa* (Centre for Economic Policy Research), No. 6, May.

Husain, I. (1996) 'Globalization and Liberalization: an Opportunity to Reduce Poverty'. In UNCTAD: *Globalization and Liberalization: Effects of International Economic Relations on Poverty*. New York/Geneva: United Nations.

IFC/FIAS (1997) *Foreign Direct Investment*. Washington D.C.: International Finance

Corporation/Foreign Investment Advisory Service, Lessons of Experience, No. 5.

IMF (1992) *Balance of Payments Statistics Yearbook, 1992.* Washington D.C.: International Monetary Fund.

IMF (1993) *Balance of Payments Manual.* Fifth Edition. Washington D.C.: International Monetary Fund.

IMF (1997a) *Balance of Payments Statistics Yearbook, 1997.* Washington D.C.: International Monetary Fund.

IMF (1997b) *International Financial Statistics, April 1997.* Washington D.C.: International Monetary Fund.

IMF (1998a) *International Financial Statistics, April 1998.* Washington D.C.: International Monetary Fund.

IMF (1998b) *World Economic Outlook and International Capital Markets: Interim Assessment, December 1998.* Washington D.C.: International Monetary Fund.

IMF (1998c) *Balance of Payments Statistics Yearbook, 1998.* Washington D.C.: International Monetary Fund.

IMF (1999) *World Economic Outlook, May 1999.* Washington D.C.: International Monetary Fund.

IMF/World Bank (1997) 'Uganda: Preliminary Document on the Initiative for Heavily Indebted Poor Countries (HIPC)'. Document IDA/SecM97-41, International Monetary Fund/World Bank, 14 February.

Ito, T. and Portes, R. (1998). 'Dealing with the Asian Financial Crisis', *European Economic Perspectives*, Centre for Economic Policy Research.

James, H. (1996) *International Monetary Cooperation since Bretton Woods.* Washington D.C.: International Monetary Fund/Oxford University Press.

Jansen, K. (1995) 'The Macroeconomic Effects of Direct Foreign Investment: the Case of Thailand'. *World Development*, 23(2): 193–210.

Lall, S. and Streeten, P. (1977) *Foreign Investment, Transnationals and Developing Countries.* Basingstoke: Macmillan.

Monopolies Commission (1973) *Report on the Supply of Chlordiazepoxide and Diazepam.* London: HMSO.

ODI (1997) 'Foreign Direct Investment Flows to Low-Income Countries: a Review of the Evidence'. Briefing Paper No. 1997(3), Overseas Development Institute, London.

Plasschaert, S. (1996) 'Transfer Pricing and Taxation'. In UNCTAD Division on Transnational Corporations and Investment: *Transnational Corporations and World Development.* London/Boston: International Thomson Business Press.

Rao, J. M. (1997) 'Development in the Time of Globalization'. Paper for Workshop on Globalization, Uneven Development and Poverty, UNDP, New York, 24–25 October.

Sader, F. (1995) *Privatizing Public Enterprises and Foreign Investment in Developing Countries, 1988–93.* Washington D.C.: World Bank, Foreign Investment Advisory Service Occasional Paper No. 5.

Soros, G. (1998) *The Crisis of Global Capitalism: Open Society Endangered.* London: Little, Brown and Company.

Tang, R. (1979) *Transfer Pricing Practices in the United States and Japan.* New York: Praeger.

Tang, R. (1981) *Multinational Transfer Pricing: Canadian and British Perspectives.* London: Butterworth.

UNCTAD (1996) *World Investment Report, 1996.* New York/Geneva: United Nations.

UNCTAD (1997a) *Trade and Development Report, 1997.* New York/Geneva: United Nations.

UNCTAD (1997b) *World Investment Report, 1997.* New York/Geneva: United Nations.

UNCTC (1981) *Transnational Corporations in the Bauxite/Aluminium Industry.* ST/CTC/20

United Nations Centre on Transnational Corporations. New York: United Nations.

Woodward, D. (1992) *Debt, Adjustment and Poverty in Developing Countries*. London: Pinter Publishers/Save the Children (UK).

Woodward, D. (1996) 'Effects of Globalization and Liberalization on Poverty: Concepts and Issues'. In UNCTAD: *Globalization and Liberalization: Effects of International Economic Relations on Poverty*. New York/ Geneva: United Nations.

Woodward, D. (1998a) *Drowning by Numbers: the IMF, the World Bank and North-South Financial Flows*. London: Bretton Woods Project.

Woodward, D. (1998b) 'The HIPC Initiative: Beyond the Basics'. In EURODAD, *World Credit Tables, 1998*. Brussels: European Network on Debt and Development.

Woodward, D. (1998c) *Globalization, Uneven Development and Poverty: Recent Trends and Implications*. Working Paper, United Nations Development Programme, New York.

Woodward, D. (1999) *Time to Change the Prescription: a Policy Response to the Asian Financial Crisis*. Briefing, Catholic Institute for International Relations, London.

World Bank (1993) *Global Economic Prospects and the Developing Countries, 1993*. Washington D.C.: World Bank.

World Bank (1994) *East Asia's Trade and Investment: Regional and Global Gains from Liberalization*. Washington D.C.: World Bank, Development in Practice Series.

World Bank (1995) *Financial Flows and Developing Countries, February 1995*. Washington D.C.: World Bank.

World Bank (1996) *World Debt Tables, 1996*. Washington D.C.: World Bank.

World Bank (1997a) *Global Development Finance, 1997*. Washington D.C.: World Bank.

World Bank (1997b) *Private Capital Flows to Developing Countries; the Road to Financial Integration*. Policy Research Report. Washington D.C.: World Bank.

World Bank (1997c) *World Development Indicators, 1997*. Washington D.C.: World Bank.

World Bank (1997d) *World Development Report, 1997: the State in a Changing World*. New York World Bank/Oxford University Press.

World Bank (1997e) *African Development Indicators, 1997*. Washington D.C.: World Bank.

World Bank (1998a) *Global Development Finance, 1998*. Washington D.C.: World Bank.

World Bank (1998b) *World Development Indicators, 1998*. Washington D.C.: World Bank.

World Bank (1998c) *East Asia: the Road to Recovery*. Document SecM98-706, World Bank.

World Bank (1999) *World Development Indicators, 1999*. Washington D.C.: World Bank.

Index

advertising 103, 132, 174, 222

Africa 9, 46, 169; North 188; sub-Saharan 7, 31, 40-1, 54, 60, 94, 115, 134, 146, 150, 152-3, 225n, 227n

agriculture 16-17, 39, 78, 115, 129

aid, cost of investment compared with 31, 48; decline of 134; and dependence 36; economic rationale for 5-6; and financial flows to developing countries 27, 29-31, 131, 134; and low-income countries 36-7

American region 192-4

Angola 42-5

Antigua 41

Argentina 12, 43-4, 58-9, 94, 164-5, 194-5, 228n

Asia 46-7, 138, 164, 169, 192-4, 200, 204, 209-10; East 1, 9, 40-1, 60-1, 77, 159, 172-97, 210, 216, 218; newly industrialising 115; South 40-1; South East 159, 174, 210

Austria 69, 72

Azerbaijan 42-3, 67

balance of payments 2, 5-14, 20, 22-3, 25, 61, 63, 69-71, 76, 81-2, 90, 119, 132, 143, 162, 164, 170, 173-86, 197, 200-3, 205, 211-12, 215, 217-19, 228n, 229n, 230n

bankruptcy 195-6, 207, 212

banks Central 119, 211; commercial 6, 9-10, 13-14, 27, 29-31, 36, 53, 55, 120, 131, 202-3, 205-6; development 6; internationalisation of 39; local 83, 161, 195; 'London Club' of 205; records of 53; and speculative bubbles 187

Belgium 69, 72

bilateral investment treaties 136, 138, 203, 209

Bolivia 44-5, 59

bonds 6, 8, 11, 15, 27, 36, 119, 131, 157, 192, 195, 205-6

boom–bust cycle 187

Botswana 45, 55-8

Brady Initiative/Plan 122, 157, 230n

Brandt, W. 76

Brazil 17, 33, 43-4, 47, 59, 76, 115, 164-5, 192, 194-5, 210, 228n

British Monopolies Commission 76

Bulgaria 43

Cambodia 55-7

Canada 73

capital, controls 197, 204, 206-11, *see also* capital account liberalisation; gains, *see* profit; repatriation 7-8, 112, 131-2, 143-6, 206, 208; efficiency 25, 80, 95, 98-107, 114; equipment 58, 65, 83, 180; flight 157-8, 163, 192, 199, 212; formation 121-2; goods 110, 174-84, 191, 229n, 230n

capital account liberalisation (CAL) 137-8, 141-2, 183, 203, 207-10, 227-8n, 230n

Caribbean region 40-1, 47

Carlyle, Thomas 2

Central America 17

Central American Common Market 17

Centre for Economic Policy Research (CEPR) 173

China 17, 32-3, 43-4, 47, 54, 65, 71-2, 76, 187, 194, 210, 218, 229n

Chile 42-4, 55, 59, 165-6, 194-5, 210-11, 227n, 228n

233

p6. Sources of capital flows.
p13. Idiotic assumptions – due diligence?
25-26. Agreements for FDI
27. Shift in lending.
30. Tax regimes + availability of finance.
39. FDI as trade in non-tradeable services
47. Foreign affiliate exports / China
72. Transfer Pricing
95. Increased efficiency or foreign exchange cost ⇒ repatriate profits.
114. FDI foreign exchange impacts generally negative ⇒ summary
117. What happens to capital raised by selling shares in local companies.
124. Technology transfer + FDI?
126. FDI + policy
131. Competition for FDI

133. VI.P. What alternatives to TNCs or not invest.
186. High saving in South (curious. (S.E. Asia) North Afr.
208. Reone (?)
211. Chile + "tax on foreign capital inflows"

Zed Titles on Globalization

The ongoing headlong rush towards an economically much more integrated world – which is usually referred to as globalization – is intimately connected to the changing nature of capitalism, and to one strand of economic theory and policy which is currently dominant – neoliberalism. Zed Books has published an extensive and growing list of titles which explore these processes and changes from a variety of perspectives.

Capitalism In The Age of Globalization:
The Management of Contemporary Society
Samir Amin

Women, Population and Global Crisis: A Political-Economic Analysis
Asoka Bandarage

The New Imperialism: Crisis and Contradictions in North–South Relations
Robert Biel

Cooling Down Hot Money: How to Regulate Financial Markets
Walden Bello, Nicola Bullard, Kamal Malhotra (eds)

The Globalisation of Poverty: Impacts of IMF and World Bank Reforms
Michel Chossudovsky

Impasses of Market Society
Christian Comeliau

Intellectual Property Rights, the WTO and Developing Countries:
The TRIPS Agreement and Policy Options
Carlos M Correa

Capital Accumulation and Women's Labour in Asian Economies
Peter Custers

An Introduction To The WTO Agreements
Bhagirath Lal Das

The WTO Agreements:
Deficiencies, Imbalances and Required Changes
Bhagirath Lal Das

The World Trade Organization:
A Guide to the New Framework for International Trade
Bhagirath Lal Das

Structural Adjustment, Global Trade and the New
Political Economy of Development
Diplab Dasgupta

The Limits of Capitalism:
An Approach to a Globalization Without Neoliberalism
Wim Dierckxsens

The Free Trade Adventure:
The WTO, the Uruguay Round and Globalism: A Critique
Graham Dunkley

The Age of Transition:
Trajectory of the World-System, 1945–2025
Terence Hopkins and Immanuel Wallerstein et al.

The Other Davos
The Globalization of Resistance to the World Economic System
François Houtart and François Polet (eds)

Neo-Liberalism or Democracy?
Economic Strategy, Markets, and Alternatives for the 21st Century
Arthur MacEwan

The Global Trap:
Globalization and the Assault on Prosperity and Democracy
Hans-Peter Martin and Harald Schumann

Global Futures: Shaping Globalization
Jan Nederveen Pieterse (ed.)

Eco-Socialism or Eco-Capitalism?
A Critical Analysis of Humanity's Fundamental Choices
Saral Sarkar

The Trouble with Capitalism:
An Enquiry into the Causes of Global Economic Failure
Harry Shutt

The Globalisation of Finance:
A Citizen's Guide
Kavaljit Singh

Taming Global Financial Flows:
Challenges and Alternatives in the Era of Financial Globalisation
Kavaljit Singh

Naming the Enemy:
Anti-Corporate Social Movements Confront Globalization
Amory Starr

100 Ways of Seeing an Unequal World
Bob Sutcliffe

The False Dilemma:
Globalisation – Opportunity or Threat?
Oscar Ugarteche

For full details of this list and Zed's other subject and general catalogues, please write to:
The Marketing Department, Zed Books, 7 Cynthia Street, London N1 9JF
or email Sales@zedbooks.demon.co.uk
Visit our website at: http:/www.zedbooks.demon.co.uk